WE CAME,
WE SAW,
WE LEFT

ALSO BY CHARLES WHEELAN

The Rationing: A Novel

Naked Money: A Revealing Look at Our Financial System

The Centrist Manifesto

Naked Statistics: Stripping the Dread from the Data

10 ½ Things No Commencement Speaker Has Ever Said

Revealing Chicago: An Aerial Portrait (with Terry Evans)

Naked Economics: Undressing the Dismal Science

WE CAME,
WE SAW,
WE LEFT

A FAMILY GAP YEAR

Charles Wheelan

W. W. NORTON & COMPANY

Independent Publishers Since 1923

Copyright © 2021 by Charles Wheelan

For information about permission to reproduce selections from this book,
write to Permissions, W. W. Norton & Company, Inc., 500 Fifth Avenue,
New York, NY 10110

For information about special discounts for bulk purchases, please contact
W. W. Norton Special Sales at specialsales@wwnorton.com or 800-233-4830

Manufacturing by Lake Book Manufacturing
Production manager: Julia Druskin

Library of Congress Cataloging-in-Publication Data

Names: Wheelan, Charles J., author.
Title: We came, we saw, we left : a family gap year / Charles Wheelan.
Description: First edition. | New York : W. W. Norton & Company, [2021]
Identifiers: LCCN 2020035520 | ISBN 9780393633955 (hardcover) |
    ISBN 9780393633962 (epub)
Subjects: LCSH: Wheelan, Charles J.—Travel. | Parent and teenager. |
    Voyages and travels.
Classification: LCC G465 .W465 2021 | DDC 910.4—dc23
LC record available at https://lccn.loc.gov/2020035520

W. W. Norton & Company, Inc., 500 Fifth Avenue, New York, N. Y. 10110
www.wwnorton.com

W. W. Norton & Company Ltd., 15 Carlisle Street, London W1D 3BS

1 2 3 4 5 6 7 8 9 0

For Team Wheelan:
We did it, and it was great.

History will be kind to me, for I intend to write it.

—*WINSTON CHURCHILL*

CONTENTS

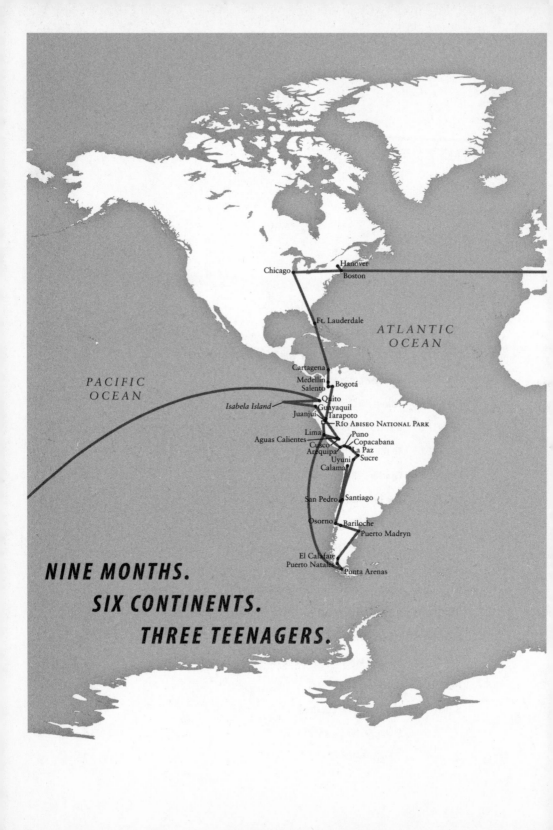

NINE MONTHS.
SIX CONTINENTS.
THREE TEENAGERS.

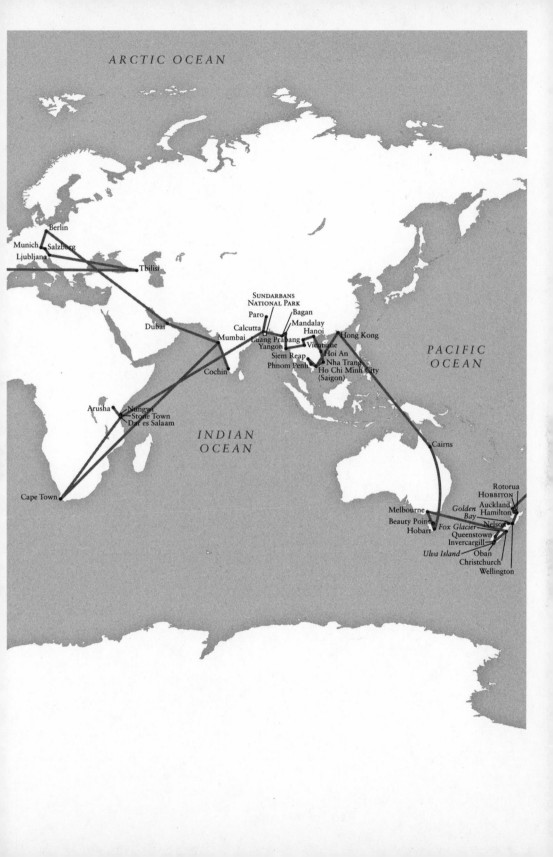

WE CAME,
WE SAW,
WE LEFT

Chapter 1

Lost in Medellín

Could Katrina and CJ have been grabbed off a crowded metro train at rush hour?
If so, how would I explain that to my mother?

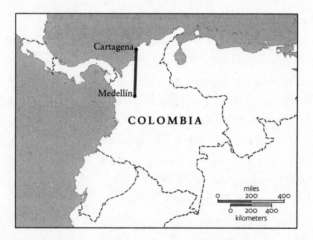

TWO OF MY CHILDREN WERE MISSING. I was standing on a train platform in Medellín, barely ten days into a trip that would, in theory, take
our family around the world. It had been over an hour since Katrina,
eighteen, and CJ, thirteen, had disappeared into the rush-hour may-
hem. Yes, Medellín, Colombia, the former seat of Pablo Escobar's drug
empire, one of the most violent places on the planet in the 1980s and
'90s. During that period, Colombia was a country where drug kingpins
bribed compliant police officers and politicians and assassinated those
who could not be bought.

It was a country where the narcos corrupted the state from within
while guerrilla groups fought to overthrow the government—a simmering civil war that was funded by extortion, drug trafficking, and
kidnapping.

Where children from wealthy families were snatched off school buses, taken deep into the jungle, and sometimes held for months until their families could scrape together the huge ransom.

Where so many people were kidnapped during the height of the violence that Colombia's biggest radio station developed a program explicitly designed for kidnap victims and their families. Beginning at midnight on Saturdays, the show offered Colombians an opportunity to call in and broadcast messages to kidnapped relatives.

Yes, that Medellín.

Of course, by the time I found myself on a train platform in the fall of 2016, Colombia had transformed itself. The government and the left-wing FARC rebels, the biggest guerrilla group, had negotiated a peace deal that would soon be put to a public referendum. Pablo Escobar was dead. Violent crime had plummeted. *But still: Where were my children?* We had been separated at rush hour when we could not all squeeze on the same train. That was now feeling like a long time ago. Why were Katrina and CJ not texting me? What could go wrong for two American kids wandering lost in Medellín?

The rational part of my brain was saying: Not much. I work with data. I wrote a book on statistics. The real dangers in life for young people, in Medellín or New Hampshire, are motor vehicles and smoking and suicide and sun exposure. Getting kidnapped in Medellín in 2016 was more like a shark attack—a relatively improbable event that captures an undue amount of public attention. But I watch "Shark Week." I've read about people who were struck by lightning twice. Unlikely events are unlikely—but they are also events, which means that they happen. As an hour drifted toward ninety minutes and Katrina and CJ had not turned up or texted, the rational part of my brain was losing out to the more imaginative side. I began thinking of the lottery slogan, "Someone's gotta win, might as well be you," only it was being twisted into, "Some people still get kidnapped, maybe it was them?" I was running out of alternative explanations for why two reasonably intelligent teens had not found a place with Wi-Fi from which they could contact my wife, Leah, or me.

As I waited idly and ineffectually on a train platform, making sure not to lose my own Wi-Fi connection, various scenarios began worming their way into my mind. Could Katrina and CJ have been grabbed off a crowded metro train at rush hour?

If so, how would I explain that to my mother?

◈ ◈ ◈

Just a few weeks earlier, the Wheelans had set out on a "family gap year." In fact, we would only be traveling for nine months, but why mess with a good slogan? The first stop on our adventure was Colombia. We had plans to continue traveling for another eight and a half months. My wife, Leah, and I had recently turned fifty. This was a midlife adventure, arguably more constructive than buying a sports car or having an affair. Thirty years earlier, after we had both graduated from college, we had set out on a similar adventure, traveling around the world from the fall of 1988 through the summer of 1989. That backpacking trip, which cost us each less than a Honda Civic, was the defining experience of our young adulthood. Now, having spent two decades living in Chicago and then a handful of years in New Hampshire, we were seeking to replicate our around-the-world experience, albeit with our teenage children.

So who are we? I am a professor of public policy at Dartmouth College in Hanover, New Hampshire. Leah is also an educator; she was teaching math at a nearby high school. Katrina, our oldest daughter, was eighteen when we departed. She had graduated from high school the previous spring and had been accepted to Williams College. She deferred her admission, giving her a year during which she would be unencumbered by any formal responsibilities—a true gap year. Katrina is arguably the most intellectual member of our family. She once remarked *in middle school*, "I don't know why anyone bothers to memorize the quadratic formula when it's so easy to derive." I nodded in bemused acknowledgment since I have no idea how to derive the quadratic formula.

For Katrina's eighteenth birthday, Leah and I did not buy her a car, or a new phone, or Taylor Swift tickets. Rather, we arranged for her to have lunch with Esther Duflo, a famous MIT economist who has since won the Nobel Prize. Esther, as Katrina referred to her around the house, is a development economist, meaning that she works on issues related to global poverty. For a high school project, Katrina had studied one of Esther's academic papers that explained how information flows through an Indian village. Katrina then "improved upon the model" (her words) to explain how gossip spreads through Hanover High School. I sent a random e-mail to Esther Duflo offering her a free meal in Cambridge if she would share a birthday lunch with a brainy eighteen-year-old. Esther was gracious enough to accept, and a month later Katrina and I met her at a French restaurant. Katrina and Esther talked about math, India, and development economics while I enjoyed pappardelle with asparagus and fresh peas.

The gap year adventure would give Katrina nine months to read extensively and pursue whatever interests captured her attention. We had no doubt that she would make the most of the time. For her part, Katrina was eager to explore the world, though not necessarily to spend 24/7 with the parental units. She would never use a phrase like "parental units." Rather, it's the kind of thing I would say, which would cause her to roll her eyes and walk away dismissively. Katrina's plan was to leave us periodically to meet up with friends in different parts of the world. Roughly ten percent of the students in her graduating class were taking a gap year; many were planning to travel internationally.

Our son and youngest, CJ, was a rising eighth-grader. CJ had embraced the international trip enthusiastically, provided that he could still enter high school with his classmates. To make that happen, we would have to teach CJ the essentials of eighth grade during our travels: geometry, science, American history, and English, including one substantial research paper. The state of New Hampshire ("Live Free or Die") is relatively permissive with regard to homeschooling. We would have to work with CJ regularly on the road, but it was not going to require a Herculean effort to get him promoted to high school.

CJ is an "exuberant child," which is the euphemism one of his elementary school teachers came up with during parent-teacher conferences to describe the fact that he talks a lot. CJ talks so much that his friends in fourth grade began calling him "Wally." Why did they call him Wally? Because when his teacher separated him from the class (for talking) and seated him facing a wall, his friends allege that he named the wall and began talking to it. CJ's exuberance is bundled with the two most important attributes for any kind of adventure: a sense of wonder and a willingness to engage with anyone who happens to come along. At the beginning of the trip, I asked CJ to write down what he hoped to get out of our adventure. He wrote that he was looking forward to "experiencing diverse and incredible nature." He mentioned the Great Barrier Reef in particular. In that same journal entry, CJ wrote, "There is really only one thing I'm concerned about. Myself. And, by that I mean controlling myself and trying to be less annoying. We are going to be spending nine months together."

Our daughter Sophie, sixteen, was not with us in Colombia. This was not some kind of *Home Alone*–type accident in which we forgot her on the way to the airport. Sophie would be joining us later in the trip. She was the one member of the family who was not a huge fan of the family gap year. In general, Sophie likes good Wi-Fi, strong water pressure, and a dependable flush toilet. If she has to travel, she prefers the luxurious variety: grand hotels, fluffy bathrobes, mints on the pillows, that kind of thing. Sophie was also reluctant to miss her junior year of high school—not because it is the most important academic year for a college-bound student, but because she is a social child who likes to spend time with her friends. Also, as a varsity volleyball player, she did not want to miss the fall volleyball season. None of this was unreasonable. Of the five members of the immediate family, Sophie would sacrifice the most by being away for a long stretch, a cost that was compounded by the fact that she was the least excited about the adventure.

We had negotiated a deal in which Sophie would stay behind with my in-laws for two months—until the end of volleyball season—at which point she would meet us in Lima, Peru. Sophie is a good negotiator, in large part because she is the most stubborn member of the family. A defining moment of her childhood was an incident the family now refers to as "Bananagate." Sophie was not a good eater as a child. In particular, Leah and I were constantly cajoling her to eat a healthier breakfast, or any breakfast at all. On one particular morning when Sophie was seven, I was walking her to school and I asked her what she had eaten for breakfast. "A banana," Sophie answered too quickly. I was immediately skeptical. There were no bananas in the house, and I told Sophie as much.

Unfortunately, Sophie is not one to stop digging when she finds herself in a hole. Instead, she typically drives a backhoe into the small hole and works hard to make it deeper. Faced with an apparent lack of bananas in the house, Sophie explained with conviction that my mother had brought bananas on a recent visit. I knew this was implausible for all kinds of reasons, so I asked Sophie what she had done with the peel after she ate her banana. Sophie—now excavating with furious resolve—replied confidently, "I put it in the trash."

After school drop-off, I returned home and checked the trash can. There was no banana peel. Obviously this conflict was no longer just about eating a healthy breakfast. When Sophie arrived home from school and I raised my banana-related suspicions, she urged me to check the garbage can again. There, resting atop the trash, was a banana peel. As we learned from Watergate, the cover-up is often worse than the crime, and Leah and I were nearly certain that a massive cover-up was under way. *But we were not absolutely positive.* Could I have missed the banana peel on my first search? Sophie was sticking by her story. We tried the good-cop approach, patiently explaining the virtues of telling the truth. Then we tried the bad-cop approach, describing the horrible things that happen to people who lie. Sophie did not budge. Worse, she explained tearfully how tormenting it was for her to tell the truth and not have her parents believe her. *"What if you never believe me in my whole life!"* the seven-year-old Sophie wailed.

Hours later, with the conflict still unresolved, I was lying on a couch in the living room reading a magazine. Sophie was sitting silently on the couch opposite me. Apropos of nothing, Sophie burst into tears and yelled, *"I didn't eat a banana!"* She subsequently confessed to the cover-up as well. She had acquired a banana peel in the school lunchroom, carried it home, and laid it atop the trash.

Sophie's relationship with the truth has improved steadily over the years. The underlying stubbornness has not changed much.

Meanwhile, we had picked up an additional child for the first several weeks of the trip: our niece Tess. When we first floated the gap year plan, my wife's sister asked if Tess, thirteen, could travel with us for part of the South America leg. Tess was studying at a Spanish immersion school in Boulder, Colorado. What better way to immerse oneself in the Spanish language than to travel across South America? For Leah and me, taking along Tess required serious deliberation. We had to consider the dynamics of traveling with someone outside the immediate family and the responsibility of doing so. In the end, Tess joined our travel ensemble.

Thankfully Tess was standing next to me on the Medellín metro platform. That was the good news: At least I had not lost someone else's child. *I was really thinking that.*

❖ ❖ ❖

Our first week in Colombia had been wonderful. According to plan, we met Tess in Fort Lauderdale and flew to Cartagena, another city etched into my mind because of its role in the drug wars. Cartagena, just a two-hour flight from Florida, is where South America meets the Caribbean: impressive Spanish architecture; a hot, humid climate interrupted periodically by afternoon showers; and an absorbing history, including three centuries as one of the continent's most active slave ports. We booked an affordable Airbnb apartment in the Getsemani neighborhood, a fun and vibrant area not far outside the walls of the old city.

We had a rigid daily budget for the trip. Cartagena was the first place it would be put to the test. Would our housing allowance be sufficient for us to stay someplace convenient, comfortable, and safe? We strongly preferred to be in a central location where we could walk or use public transit to get wherever we needed to go. We would endure hardship as necessary—that is part of having adventures in interesting places—but none of us was eager to be uncomfortable for nine months. Sophie was not the only member of the family with a preference for a decent shower and a working toilet.

The Cartagena apartment was encouraging on this front. Our budget allowed us a comfortable space with two bedrooms and air-conditioning that worked mercifully well. We immediately set out wandering the colorful, narrow streets, where moss and flowers were crowding every available space, including the wrought-iron balconies hanging off the centuries-old buildings. The city was fun and beautiful and easy—but still, it was Cartagena, Colombia. My paranoia was inflamed on the second day when we arrived back at our apartment and my camera was gone. We were only days into the trip and already one of the most valuable things we had brought along was missing! I had a horrible feeling of disappointment and violation. Leah, stoic in most situations, was saddened as well. Our impression of Colombia had been so different than what we had expected. We were enjoying strolling the streets unmolested and without fearing for our safety. And now this.

Theft is a reality everywhere. In fact, I had been so afraid of having my camera stolen in Cartagena that—now this was just a hazy memory—hadn't I hidden the camera before we went out of the apartment? If that were true—yes, I definitely hid the camera—where exactly would I have put it so an intruder would not find it? Evidently a very good hiding place, because I was having trouble finding it myself. The whole family was enlisted in the search. I re-created my mindset: What would be the best place to hide a camera bag so an intruder would not find it? Sure enough, there in the back of a cupboard in our bedroom, hidden from view by several extra pillows, was my camera bag.

❖ ❖ ❖

We are wanderers. We like museums and monuments, but they rarely make for a thrillingly memorable experience. We prefer to pick a destination or activity for the day—even something as mundane as buying an electrical adapter or mailing a letter—and then make that the adventure. Things happen along the way, especially food. Every street corner in Cartagena was packed with carts heaped with fruit, grilled meat, fried things, baked things, and grilled things with fried things on top. I was enamored of the orange juice vendors, who would load five or seven oranges into an ingeniously simple crushing machine (manual or electric). With a flick of the switch or a crank of the handle, the machine would smash the whole oranges and fresh juice would come dribbling out of a slot in the bottom. One of my first tasks each morning was to head out to buy fresh orange juice—even before I made coffee, which says a lot.

We soon discovered two street food favorites: the empanada lady and the avocado guy. Empanadas, little pockets of dough stuffed with cheese or meat and then fried, were for sale just about everywhere. CJ quickly pronounced that a woman with a stand several blocks from our apartment—a single chair and table—made the very best chicken empanadas in all of Cartagena. As we gained confidence in the city, and as CJ developed a serious but entirely affordable empanada habit, he implored us to let him go by himself to the empanada lady. We made him memorize the route through Cartagena's mazelike streets: turn right out of the apartment, then left, then right, and she should be sitting in her chair on the left side of the street. CJ appreciated the independence; the rest of us enjoyed the paper bag full of fresh empanadas that he returned with.

Early in our Cartagena stay, our goal for the afternoon was to find an ATM machine. These are the kinds of modest goals that are sufficient to set in motion a Wheelan family adventure. In our defense, finding an ATM in Cartagena is harder than one might think. One legacy of the decades of violence in Colombia is that the ATM machines tend to be tucked in the back of stores and banks, rather than exposed to the street. We found an ATM on the second floor of a grocery store. In the small plaza outside, there was a guy holding a large machete in front of a wooden cart piled high with enormous avocados. I gave him the equivalent of thirty cents, and, in a brilliantly choreographed series of movements, he grabbed an avocado from the pile, hacked it in half with his machete, pulled out the pit, and then asked in Spanish if I wanted lime and salt. *Yes and yes.* The rest of the family did the same, and we sat on a cement wall in the plaza eating chunks of avocado with plastic spoons—the tropical equivalent of ice cream.

We knew Rhonda would not be happy with us. One month earlier, the whole family had spent nearly five hours at the local travel clinic for our final medical prep, everything from tetanus boosters to prescriptions for malaria medicine and "just in case" antibiotics. A well-intentioned nurse named Rhonda gave us an earnest lecture on travel safety: don't swim in fresh water; don't pet stray animals; *and no street food.* When we bought our first empanada from a street vendor roughly twenty-five minutes into the trip, we paused to offer an apology to Rhonda. This would become a common refrain as we wandered the streets of Cartagena. "Sorry, Rhonda," one of us would say between delicious mouthfuls.

We spent our final evening in Cartagena in a small plaza near our apartment. During the day, we had barely noticed the place. It was a relatively small, nondescript patch of cement in front of a church where five narrow streets came together. Around sundown, as the heat of the day was dissipating, the food vendors opened their carts and the plaza began to fill: young couples, old couples, families, tourists, young boys doing gymnastics, and a few police officers keeping a casual eye on it all. Periodically the big doors of the church would open, casting a glow from inside onto the diverse groups of people assembled on the plaza. There was a ceremony going on in the church, perhaps a baptism or confirmation. At one point, a family came outside to pose for a photo, all of them dressed for the occasion, including a young daughter in a beautiful white dress.

We ate, and we sat, and we ate some more: grilled kebabs, grilled corn, arepas (corn disks wrapped around cheese or any combination of meats), and, of course, empanadas. A store on the corner sold very cold beer by the bottle for about a dollar, less some change for bringing back the empty bottle. On a hot night with delicious food, the beer tasted like I was in the bleachers at Wrigley Field on a July afternoon. The plaza exuded a wonderful sense of community. We felt welcome, or at least not out of place. Among the five of us, we had four people with a working knowledge of the language. When we spoke in Spanish, the answer typically came back in Spanish, unlike, say, in France, where even decent French tends to elicit a response in English. "Colombia has been all pleasant surprises," I wrote in my journal that night.

Medellín had started out the same way. We boarded the night bus from Cartagena to Medellín, a thirteen-hour ride. The other passengers climbed aboard wearing down jackets and carrying blankets, as if we were headed to an Arctic research station. Fortunately, we had been warned that the buses in Colombia are air-conditioned to near-freezing temperatures. Team Wheelan wore layers of clothing.

We also loaded ourselves with the maximum dosage of Dramamine. One of our defining characteristics as a family is a propensity for motion sickness. On previous trips, various members of our team had thrown up on boats, cars, and buses on five different continents, including a particularly unfortunate incident in Turkey when Katrina hit our tour guide with a projectile strike from the seat behind him. For all that, my niece Tess, who had proved to be an easy and delightful travel companion, took motion sickness to a new level. We quickly learned that she was at risk of getting sick on any mode of transit longer or rougher than an escalator.

The temperature on the bus dropped into the fifties; we spent most of the ride in a Dramamine-induced hibernation and woke up to morning in Medellín, a lovely city built on the side of a mountain. The ride was easy, comfortable, and uneventful. We had created a blog so that friends and family could follow our progress, and I offered up a post with a title suggesting far more adventure than we had experienced: "The Night Bus to Medellín!"

The Medellín bus station was an orderly, quiet place. We sat down to gather ourselves and immediately made an exciting discovery: *free Wi-Fi at the Dunkin' Donuts.* This constant need to stay connected was both a surprise and a modest disappointment. When Leah and I made our first global backpacking trip in 1988, part of the allure of the trip was disappearing into exotic places. We picked up our mail once a month at

American Express offices and called home rarely. For long stretches, no one knew where we were. The world is different now; that is the reality. The kids wanted to stay in touch with their friends through all the usual social media channels. Leah and I felt it would be unfair to haul them away from home for nine months and deny them that. Meanwhile, most of our travel logistics were accessed most easily online: maps; confirmations from our Airbnb hosts; TripAdvisor recommendations; and so on. Thus, it was a good start to our morning in Medellín when one of us discovered that we could get free Wi-Fi with no password by loitering just outside the Dunkin' Donuts in the bus station.

The day just got better from there. It was a Sunday, and Leah suggested that we walk to a park where there was a farmers' market every weekend. Leah has the brain of the Phi Beta Kappa computer science major that she is, coupled with the patience of a human resources director. Before making a mid-career switch to teaching, she worked in the software industry, eventually starting her own consulting firm. During the start-up phase, she and I tried to share a home office. On the third day of this arrangement, I was writing while she was holding a conference call with her team of consultants, forcing me to overhear half of the conversation. "How do you feel about that, Michael?" Leah asked. There was some blather I could not hear, and then Leah said, "Gerry, what do you propose we do with the territory?" And then, "How does everyone else feel about that?" This went on for another half an hour.

Eventually I exclaimed, "Oh my god! I can only hear half the conversation and it's completely obvious to me what has to happen! They need to split the territory and share the revenue!" Leah covered the receiver and whispered, "Of course that's what they need to do. But they need to come to that conclusion on their own." I moved my office to a different room in the house that afternoon.

Leah likes to balance the checkbook, whereas I assume that the bank will contact me if there is a problem. When something breaks around the house, I ignore the problem or bang on the object repeatedly. I once threw an undependable laser printer out the back door of our house, where it crashed into pieces on the patio. Our neighbor Jane was watering flowers in her backyard at the time; she never looked at me the same again. In contrast, Leah watches YouTube videos that explain things like "How to Replace a Range Top Burner Spark Igniter." Leah likes guidebooks and she loves maps.

Leah's love of planning solved one of the most stressful things about travel, particularly low-budget travel: the constant decisions—every meal, every night of lodging, every bus or plane ticket. We had learned in traveling with other families that sometimes group travel works beautifully, and sometimes it makes me wish I were having dental work done. The difference lies in whether there is a shared vision for the experience. Do you get up early or sleep in? Do you cook at home or go out? Do you spend the day wandering aimlessly or visiting eight museums? Are you doing all of this on fifty dollars a day or eight hundred? Each one of those is a decision, laden with even more pressure because everyone expects their travel experience to be awesome. We had learned while traveling as a family over the years—*it takes a lot of trips to throw up on five continents*—that we travel well together. To deal with the incessant decision making, we adopted the benevolent dictator model. That was Leah, with our acquiescence and appreciation. She was also the budget czar, which meant that the activities she suggested generally conformed to what we could afford to spend.

We left the Medellín bus station and walked uphill carrying our packs. The park was about a mile away; the uphill slog with all our stuff made it feel like ten miles. The weather was cool, but since Medellín is nearly a mile above sea level, we were soon struggling to catch our breath. I said nothing, for fear that Leah would hand me the *Lonely Planet* guide to Colombia and say, "Knock yourself out." I suspect the others were thinking the same thing. Eventually we arrived in a large city park, a green oasis in the heart of the city. The farmers' market was in full swing, with rows of stalls at which vendors offered fruit, honey, nuts, flowers, cheeses, arepas, and other enticing items.

The farmers' market was nice enough, and the park was lovely, but the most interesting thing was watching what Leah described as "Colombia's beautiful people" go about their weekend in a public park.

For the record, *Colombia's beautiful people are really beautiful*. We bought some fruit and cheese and bread, yes, but mostly we sat and observed other people buying fruit and cheese and bread: families, young couples pushing strollers, friends meeting over coffee. One feature of the park was a sprawling flower garden that had been designed as a butterfly sanctuary. I spent the better part of an hour taking butterfly photos. The image I had of Medellín before we arrived did not include a butterfly sanctuary or yuppies buying artisan honey.

We spent the next morning doing assorted tasks in our Airbnb apartment. The kids did schoolwork; I wrote in my journal and organized photos. Leah made a plan for the afternoon: We would walk to the central bus station to buy onward tickets and then take the metro to see a sculpture garden in central Medellín. The walk (downhill!) to the bus station went fine, including stops along the way to buy and eat assorted fried foods. We bought the bus tickets and then headed to the metro. The station was modern and orderly, but we arrived at rush hour and every train that pulled into the station was packed. At that point, just one week into our journey, we made one rookie travel mistake after another.

Though we'd had time together on the platform, Leah had not told us where we would be getting off the train. Nor, to be fair, had we asked. A crowded train pulled into the station. I could tell immediately that only one or two of us would be able to squeeze on. Leah was closest to the train door, and she was able to push her way on. Just as she boarded the train, CJ, who was standing near a map of the metro system, yelled, "San Pedro!"

I assumed this was our stop, so just as the doors were closing, I repeated loudly to Leah, "San Pedro." The train pulled away. My niece Tess and I squeezed onto the next train. Katrina and CJ pushed their way onto a car several trains later. The five of us were now on three different trains. We would all get off at San Pedro and regroup.

Or not.

As I looked over the heads of the other passengers at a metro map posted on the wall of our train car, I could not find the San Pedro stop. I searched more methodically, checking every stop on every route on the whole Medellín metro system. Eventually I realized what must have been dawning on the rest of the family at about the same time on the other two trains: *There is no San Pedro stop.*

Why did CJ yell, "San Pedro"? This question would be at the heart of the subsequent family investigation. For now, we were on three different trains with no idea where to get off. We all had devices that could be used to text via Wi-Fi, but only my phone had an international calling plan. That meant we could not communicate with each other unless we all had Internet access, which we did not have on our respective trains. Each of us responded to this situation in a way that made sense—though the collective response was problematic. Leah got off at the station nearest to where our overnight bus had arrived. Tess and I got off at San Antonio, which is a major hub for the system. Both Leah and I had the same idea: get off the train, find Wi-Fi, connect by text, and then designate a place to meet up. Unfortunately, CJ and Katrina—the ones who would go missing—had a different plan.

The San Antonio platform where Tess and I got off was a bustling but orderly place with a handful of retail shops. There was no public Wi-Fi, but I could see on my phone that there was a private network for the station officials. I did my best to explain to an attendant that I had been separated from my family and needed Wi-Fi to find them. My Spanish was evidently good enough to get the point across; he took my phone and nonchalantly typed in the password for the private network. Soon a text popped up from Leah. She would wait at her station in case the kids turned up there; if not, she would take a train to where Tess and I were waiting.

I waited for a similar text from Katrina and CJ. And I waited. Fifteen minutes became half an hour. What could the two of them possibly be doing? At first I was not even concerned, let alone alarmed. Medellín is a charming city. The metro system was clean and orderly. There were no nefarious characters lingering about our station. The fact that the trains were crowded with ordinary people going about their business was a good thing. How could someone kidnap two Americans from a crowded train? At one point, Tess sat down on the floor, resting against a wall. A security official hustled over and told her politely that sitting on the floor was not allowed. This made me feel better. Any place that takes security seriously enough to forbid sitting on the floor should be a safe place for two American teenagers.

But where the heck were they? I began to feel more anxious. After an hour, I approached a transit police officer. "Mis niños son perritos," I said. *My children are puppies.* The police officer quickly figured out that I was trying to say that my children were lost. He was kind but not overly concerned. I suspect he envisioned several unaccompanied toddlers riding the metro, perhaps a three- and a five-year-old, or maybe two infants left in their bassinets. "How old are they?" the officer asked. "The girl is eighteen," I said in Spanish. He gave me a look that I can best describe as a combination of bemusement, confusion, compassion, and a healthy dollop of pity.

"Can't you just call her?" the officer asked earnestly. I explained that I could not, while simultaneously recognizing that "losing" an able-bodied eighteen-year-old did not make much sense. Katrina was old enough to drive, to vote, to serve in the military, and even to have a child of her own. The officer said something I interpreted to mean, "She'll turn up." As a courtesy to me, and perhaps to punctuate his own boredom, he agreed to have Katrina paged across the entire Medellín metro system. At the peak of rush hour, the alert went out. What I could understand of it was: "*Spanish Spanish Spanish* KATRINA WHEE-LAN! *Spanish Spanish Spanish* KATRINA WHEELAN!"

Still nothing.

Leah arrived at our station and we waited some more. We said relatively little to one another, and that was probably a good thing—no finger-pointing about whose idea this trip was or anything like that. The police officer would ask periodically if we had heard anything. He did not seem particularly concerned about the missing Americans. Because a guy responsible for security on the Medellín metro was unconcerned, I felt better. But as we reached the ninety-minute mark, dark thoughts began creeping into my mind. *What could they possibly be doing?* It had taken Leah only fifteen minutes to find Wi-Fi and connect with me. Why were Katrina and CJ still missing after an hour and a half?

They were on their way to San Pedro, it turns out. No, there was not a San Pedro stop on the metro. There was, however, a San Pedro bus stop in a distant part of the city. Because of a youthful combination of teenage self-righteousness (Katrina) and idiocy (CJ), the two of them were determined to make it to San Pedro. I should pause here and answer the crucial question at the heart of this whole debacle: Why had CJ yelled San Pedro in the first place? What was he thinking?

Nothing, apparently. The subsequent official investigation—a family discussion over dinner during which Leah authorized extra spending on margaritas—revealed that CJ had yelled San Pedro for no particular reason. I had assumed he was standing near the metro map because Leah had sent him there to gather information. Wrong. In fact, Leah had sent him to look at the map because he was being bothersome and she thought it would occupy him. To recap, CJ was standing near the map for no real reason, and then he yelled, "San Pedro!" for no reason, and yet he and Katrina decided that was where they should go.

Which they did. They got off the metro at the station closest to San Pedro—which was not close—and then began walking. And walking. I presume the folly of their plan dawned on them when they reached the San Pedro bus stop and did not find us there. They had no money for a taxi, so they walked back, eventually finding a Starbucks with Wi-Fi where they sent us a text. *According to the pedometer on CJ's iPod, they had walked 9.5 miles.*

Over dinner, we reviewed our "rookie mistakes": taking the metro at rush hour; not making sure we all knew the stop; not having a plan if we were separated; not giving enough money to Katrina for a taxi; and so on. We were rusty. And we had missed all the major sites in Medellín. "We need to understand how Katrina and CJ got lost so it won't happen again," I explained.

"We weren't lost!" Katrina declared. "We knew exactly where we were the whole time!" She then expounded on the distinction between the words "lost" and "separated," a point I was willing to concede. CJ did not care how we described what had happened. He was talking effusively about how cool the pedometer app was on his iPod. "We walked ten miles," he said proudly.

❖ ❖ ❖

A couple of things were clear. First, we really, really liked Colombia. There was a sense that the people had wrestled their country away from the dark side and did not want to give it back. Second, we had an interesting day, all things considered. Everyone was in a strikingly good mood over dinner, Katrina's protestations over my choice of words notwithstanding. We had learned a lot about Medellín. We were pleasantly surprised by our encounters with law enforcement. We had confronted a small obstacle and pushed through. No one had panicked. Neither Leah nor I had said anything regrettable while the children were missing. And now we were discussing all this over a nice meal (with margaritas) in a vibrant part of the city.

Maybe we would be able to pull off this crazy adventure travel thing after all.

Chapter 2

What Were We Thinking?

The family gap year would be an experience that we would share forever—like one of those family road trips, only much longer and with more bugs.

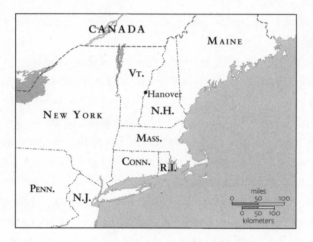

IF OUR FAMILY GAP YEAR were portrayed in a Hollywood film, I would hit my boss with a stapler, storm out of the office, take stock of my vapid life, and then head home, where I would tell my stunned wife and children: "Pack up. We're going around the world!"

Only the midlife part is correct. There was nothing impulsive about the trip, nor was there an eagerness to escape. For the record, my boss is a very kind man. In fact, one of the most appealing parts of the "gap year" plan was that we would be able to return to the life that we left. We were not looking for an escape, only a breather.

That notion of an extended family adventure had begun many years earlier as a half-baked idea, a kind of "what if?" I am the family brainstormer, the one who offers a fusillade of possibilities. Leah, the planner, curates the ideas with potential, steering them to a better place.

There was, for example, the time I proposed that we buy a house on an island in a lake in New Hampshire. We were still living in Chicago at the time; a friend told us about the property for sale, which was the only dwelling on the island. "How cool would it be to have our own island?" I declared.

"How would we get to the house?" Leah asked without judgment.

"By boat," I said.

"In the winter?"

"We could snowshoe across the ice—or maybe we'd have a snowmobile."

"What if one of us fell through the ice?" Leah asked.

"We would all wear survival suits, like the Alaska fishermen," I explained.

"Hmm," Leah said. "What if you just wanted to go out for coffee?"

Now I was stumped. I like to take short walks to get coffee when I need a break while working at home. As I pondered this dilemma, Leah offered a delicate redirect: "The house in New Hampshire sounds lovely. What if we bought something closer to town?" Three months later, we owned a small house (from which one can walk to several coffee shops) in the town of Hanover. We spent summers there for many years, renting the house out for the balance of the year. Eventually we moved to Hanover full-time. We do not own a boat or a snowmobile or survival suits. However, I feel compelled to point out our entire New Hampshire existence began with the house-on-the-island idea.

The family gap year evolved in a similar manner. Over the years, many ideas sank—moving to India for a year, buying a farm in Tuscany, raising goats in the backyard—while the notion of traveling the world with the family kept bobbing to the surface. Every once in a while, over a glass of wine or a Sunday breakfast, Leah and I would mull over the logistics. Could five people really step away from complicated lives for nine months? During these fanciful discussions, the "how" was always subservient to the "why." Before we loaned out the dogs, rented the house, and strapped on backpacks, we had to be committed to the journey. Why would two sane adults living comfortable lives want to travel for nine months in difficult places on a low budget, spending nearly twenty-four hours a day with three teenagers?

For a lot of reasons.

Because the world is an interesting place. I became "hooked on the world" in middle school. I was a suburban kid living in a nondescript subdivision in Northbrook, Illinois. You may have watched my adolescence in the movies. I attended the same high school as the late film director John Hughes: Glenbrook North. Many of my classmates were extras in *Sixteen Candles*. The school building was the setting for *Ferris Bueller's Day Off*. And I served one day of suspension in the Breakfast Club, albeit on a school day rather than on a Saturday.

Occasionally our family would go into "the city" (Chicago), which was foreign and exciting and mildly scary. My mother had been to Europe once; my father had never been outside of North America. In eighth grade, my Spanish teacher organized the ultimate learning adventure: a class trip to Cuernavaca, Mexico. In hindsight, I am amazed she had the audacity to take a group of middle school students to a developing country, but I am delighted that she did. We stayed with families and visited the usual tourist spots, such as the Aztec pyramids. What I remember most, however, was just walking around and experiencing a place that was radically different from everything I knew. The electricity would go out for long stretches; no one who lived in Cuernavaca seemed even mildly surprised by this. For me, the suburban middle school kid, the notion of regular power blackouts was mind-blowing, as was the food (not like Mexican food at home), the poverty, the vitality, and the sheer excitement of just walking around. I wanted more of it—"it" being the world.

In fact, I was so hooked on the idea of traveling the world that senior year in high school I floated the idea of taking a year off to travel before going to college. I formulated a serious plan before I went public with it: I would work after graduation, earn enough money to travel someplace interesting for a long stretch, and start college the following year. No one used the term "gap year" back then, but that is what I was trying to do. My parents thought this was an insane idea, as did my high school

principal and the college counselor. They were all risk-averse in a suburban kind of way. The powers that be were convinced that one year
of international travel would leave me with long hair, multiple body
piercings, and a permanent lack of interest in employment or college.

I buckled. My high school principal did give me one piece of mean-
ingful advice as he discouraged the gap year. "Travel after college," he
told me. "You'll get more out of it." He was right. On the other hand, if I
had traveled during a gap year, I would have arrived at college as a more
serious student. I applied to Dartmouth College because of its extensive
array of foreign study programs. My sophomore year I studied abroad
in France and lived with a local family. France was lovely; my French
family was charming. But what really rocked my world was the Eurail
Pass: a fixed-price ticket that allowed unlimited rail travel anywhere in
Europe for two months. *Any train, any time, any place.* I remember staring up at the departure board in the Austerlitz Station in Paris. That
was back when the signs were still mechanical, not digital, and every few
seconds there would be a whirring and clicking as some new destination
was posted: Madrid, Vienna, Rome, Copenhagen. I would think, *I can
get on any of those trains.*

During my junior year at Dartmouth, I arranged an internship at
an English-language newspaper in Kuwait. This was before the Iraqi
invasion and the first Gulf War. At the time, most Americans, including my parents, would struggle to find Kuwait on a map. (To be fair, it
is a very small country.) I called home to tell my parents that I would
be going to Kuwait for the summer. They were excited that I had a job,
and even more excited that I would be paying for my airline ticket by
selling the motorcycle I had inadvisably bought the previous summer.
Unfortunately, their enthusiasm waned dramatically when they hung
up the phone and opened the family atlas. Kuwait is a tiny country on
the Persian Gulf near the border between Iraq and Iran, two countries
that were at war at the time. The pay phone in the hallway of my dor-
mitory rang several hours later; someone roused me from my room to
let me know that my parents were on the line. "Do you know where
Kuwait is!" my mother exclaimed.

I did.

In 1987, Kuwait was as closed and conservative as Saudi Arabia. In many ways, the culture was alien: men in flowing white robes; a monotonous sandy landscape that was sometimes painted green to give the illusion of vegetation; the call to prayer that rang out five times a day; the Indian and Pakistani and Filipino men and women who would leave their families *for years at a time* to live in Kuwait while sending money home. When I went to the movies at the cinema near my apartment in Kuwait City, I was seated in the section designated for single men. I never spoke to a Kuwaiti woman during my ten weeks in the country. I met expatriate women who had come to Kuwait for various reasons but not one native Kuwaiti woman, married or single.

The Kuwaiti royal family ran the country with a firm hand. Autocracy was new to my American sensibilities. There was a government censor with an office in our building. One of my jobs was to show him photos for approval before we could run them in the newspaper. The censor was a friendly enough guy, though he spoke no English and I spoke no Arabic, so most of our interactions were done via pantomime. Every picture of a woman, for example, had to have her arms and legs covered. This presented a curious challenge when it came to women's fashion. Kuwaiti citizens (as opposed to the many foreigners imported to run the country) are rich and fashionable. What is a conservative newspaper to do when the fall fashion photos that come over the Reuters wire show bare legs, arms, shoulders, and backs? I was the solution. One of my jobs was to use a black felt-tip pen to lengthen skirts and add sleeves—*Christian Lacroix, as interpreted by Charles Wheelan with a Sharpie.*

Much like that middle school trip to Mexico, the Kuwait experience inflamed my interest in exploring the globe. After working a late shift at the newspaper, I would return home to my apartment and read into the morning hours, sometimes until sunrise, about other fascinating places: Nepal, Tibet, Burma, the South Pacific. One of my favorite books was a volume of Somerset Maugham short stories set in exotic locales at the height of the British Empire. *I wanted to go to those places.* I was learning that interesting travel does not sate the urge to explore; it feeds it. This is true even at age fifty.

Because Leah and I had done a global gap year once before, and we wanted to do it again. Leah and I met during freshman orientation at Dartmouth. We were assigned to do the "ice breaker" exercise with one another. This involved interviewing each other—two nervous students from different parts of the country—and then reporting back to the group. ("Leah is from Boulder, Colorado. She went to a public high school. She has two brothers and a sister . . .") The ice-breaking exercise went very well, though we did not begin formally dating until senior year. By then, we shared a vision for traveling after graduation. While I spent the summer in Kuwait, Leah had bicycled from Mexico to Canada, mostly along California Route 1.* She and her fellow riders made the eighteen-hundred-mile journey in about six weeks, camping along the way. *I had found a fellow adventurer.*

Leah and I recognized that the year after graduation presented a unique opportunity for a long spell of travel. Why not begin work a year later? We made a plan that would enable us to pay for the trip ourselves. I was lucky enough to graduate from college without debt. Leah had major student loans, so we constructed a budget in which she would prepay them for nine months. Our plan was to live at home or some other subsidized location after graduation, work multiple jobs, and then, when we had enough cash for a global adventure, fly west. Yet, as graduation approached, we were feeling the pressure that comes when one tries to run against the herd, just as I had when I tried to take a gap year after high school. Our friends were hustling to get corporate jobs. My parents were eager for me to become employed.

Curiously, many of our Dartmouth classmates openly discouraged our travel plan, in part because the campus was awash with groupthink regarding corporate recruiting. As graduation approached, even Leah

---

* This is one of the few times I'm aware of when Leah's planning skills were not top-notch. The prevailing winds in California blow from north to south, so a more sensible route would have been from Canada to Mexico.

began to waffle. She was offered a job by a prestigious consulting firm. She accepted the offer contingent on the firm deferring her start date for a year. This was a more modest request than it may appear. The firm hired a large batch of college graduates every year; there was no logical reason why she could not start work with the next cohort, just like deferring college admission. Alas, the firm felt otherwise and issued her an ultimatum: Start the job this year or there will be no job. I, on the other hand, had no employment offers. Much to my parents' horror, I had lofty plans to become a writer after our travels.*

Word got around campus that Leah was considering walking away from an attractive consulting job in order to backpack around the world with me. At one point during this stretch, a mutual friend walked up to her in a fraternity basement and said, "I heard you're being stupid." I could feel it happening again: risk aversion and conformity conspiring to foil my global travel plans. But this time there would be no buckling to convention. Leah turned down the job offer. Or, more accurately, she called the firm's bluff. Once she proved that she was willing to get on a plane rather than take the job, the company backed down and allowed her to start with the next year's hires. Not so stupid after all.

We worked jobs after graduation that allowed us to stockpile cash. Leah waitressed at a country club in Nantucket and lived rent-free in a bunkhouse on the grounds. I moved home with my parents. During the week, I worked at a law firm putting thousands of documents in chronological order. On the weekends, I caddied. At night (and sometimes during the day at work, admittedly), I studied the world atlas, planning our route. By October, we had saved enough cash for a nine-month global adventure. It would prove to be one of the most formative experiences of our lives.

After making our way west across the country, we tried to hitchhike from San Francisco to Los Angeles, where we would catch a flight to Tahiti. Our progress down the coast was slow—a series of short rides.

---

* Let the record reflect that I did become a writer. For example, I wrote this book.

Eventually we gave up and decided to take a bus the rest of the way to L.A. so we would not miss our flight. However, to take the bus, we needed to get one last ride from our hostel to the bus station. We went to the road and put our thumbs out. A kindly old man stopped and offered us a ride. He was at least seventy years old, smaller than both of us, and wearing a coat and tie. We told this elderly gentleman that we needed to go to the bus station. "Where are you going?" he asked.

"To the bus station," I repeated.

"Yes, but where are you going on the bus?" he insisted. He had a faint European accent that I could not place.

We explained that we had to get to the airport in Los Angeles by midnight in order to catch our flight. He looked at his watch and said, "I can take you to Los Angeles." And he did. We stopped for frozen yogurt, and later to see the Pacific Ocean. This kind man, Alex, drove us for five hours and dropped us off at LAX. Obviously at some point I felt compelled to ask him why he was so generous with his time. A little background is necessary to understand his answer. I was twenty-two at the time. I was tan and fit, with a crew cut for ease of travel. Alex pointed at me and explained, "I was liberated from a concentration camp by American GIs. When you were standing there by the side of the road with your pack, you reminded me of a soldier. I feel I owe a debt of gratitude to the country, and this is how I repay it."

That was our first week on the road. There were nine months of adventures. Some were simple and beautiful, like riding bicycles through rural Indonesia and seeing the brilliant green terraced rice paddies that I had studied in a class on monsoon Asia. Some were more unexpected and tumultuous. We arrived in Lhasa, Tibet, on the thirtieth anniversary of the Dalai Lama's flight to Dharamsala, India (where he still resides). Unbeknownst to us, the native Tibetans had seized on the occasion to launch a massive protest against China's occupation of Tibet. In response, the Chinese government cracked down ruthlessly. We watched from the lobby of our hotel as Chinese tanks rolled through the street. This was the spring of 1989. Several months later, the Chinese authorities would order soldiers to attack demonstrators in Tiananmen Square and we would realize that what we saw in Tibet was a warm-up act.

By then we were in Eastern Europe, where 1989 was also an extraordinary year. We arrived in Budapest just as the government lifted its ban on the books that had been illegal since the Communists took power forty years earlier. We could literally see freedom breaking out in the form makeshift tables the booksellers had stacked with previously illicit titles: *1984*, *Animal Farm*, and the like. I was left with a deeper, more visceral understanding of what life had been like behind the Iron Curtain, and also a great respect for the resiliency of the people now tossing those regimes aside.

Our world travels were a fifth year of college education, at a much lower cost than a year of tuition. We would be different people if we had not taken that trip. Now that we had our own family, it felt like it was time to do it again.

Because we needed/wanted a year to recharge and reflect. Leah and I had both been working very hard in different capacities for more than twenty-five years. We enjoyed our work, but we were tired. This was not retirement. If anything, it was the opposite: a chance to take a break so we would be reinvigorated to work for another twenty-five years. We are both privileged people in the sense that we do work that we find rewarding. Still, it is work. I had recently finished two books; those deadlines are always exhausting. I was also teaching classes and had launched a political organization, Unite America, designed to re-empower the political center. My to-do list never felt like it was getting any shorter.

In Chicago, Leah had founded the aforementioned technology consulting company. As the CEO, she did not have much time off, regardless of what the personnel handbook said. Later, after selling the business, she began her second career as a math teacher. Her intent was to teach in a high-poverty neighborhood. She completed an alternative certification program and was hired to teach third grade in a school adjacent to one of Chicago's notorious housing projects. The job arose suddenly because a third-grade teacher had quit three days into the school year. In the excitement of the moment, both Leah and I neglected to ask a crucial question: *Why does an experienced teacher quit after three days?*

We would soon have the answer. Teaching is hard anywhere. On the South Side of Chicago, there are layers of additional challenges. Most of Leah's students were living in tough environments. This often manifested in students' behavioral outbursts. Leah had a "panic button" in her classroom that she could push to summon a security guard if she felt that a situation was getting out of hand. It would be December—three months into the school year—before she finished a single school day without pushing the panic button.

When we moved to New Hampshire, Leah began teaching in a school district affected by rural poverty and the opioid epidemic. The racial makeup of the student body was different, but the challenges in the classroom and the broader community were similar. The job was exhausting, both physically and emotionally. The teaching experiences have made Leah, who was unflappable to begin with, even more so. They have also given her a sense of perspective with regard to the true nature of hardship and crisis, particularly for young children. When a well-meaning parent in our Hanover bubble recounts some educational snafu ("Mr. B—— hasn't returned any of the labs in Honors Biology and the students have no idea how they're doing, even though the midterm is Friday!"), her honest answer is, "I'm sure it will be fine."

There was one more thing. For me, this would also be time to learn: long days during which I could read, listen to podcasts, or do whatever else captured my intellectual fancy. The first time we traveled, I read books that I previously had not had time for (*War and Peace*) and reread some favorites (*The Razor's Edge*). At age fifty, I wanted to do that again: read, listen, think, stare out the window.

Because taking time off can be a great career move. My gap year after Dartmouth did not leave me facedown in a gutter, my parents' concerns notwithstanding. Ironically, it launched my writing career. Before we left on our post-college trip, I managed to finagle a job writing freelance articles for the *Valley News*, a small newspaper in the Hanover,

New Hampshire, area. I was technically a traveling correspondent, for which I would be paid fifty dollars for every story that made it into print. This was before e-mail and digital photos, so I had to write the stories longhand on airmail paper, shoot a roll of photos to accompany the piece, and then mail the story and the undeveloped black-and-white film back to White River Junction, Vermont. The mail could take up to two weeks, so I had to find stories that would be interesting to readers back home but not time-sensitive.

I interviewed Americans serving life sentences in a Bangkok prison for drug offenses. I stumbled across a Kentucky Fried Chicken in Bali and wrote a piece on how incongruous it was to find an American fast-food restaurant in a relatively rural part of Indonesia. I visited and photographed "needle park" in the center of Zurich, where there was a needle exchange for intravenous drug users set up by the Swiss government to curb one of the highest rates of HIV infection in Europe. There I interviewed a guy my age who told me politely, "Please stop talking for a minute," after which he tied a tourniquet around his arm and injected himself with heroin. He asked me not to use his name because his father was a prominent banker.

I discovered that I have a good "story sense," meaning that I can wander into a place and spot a story that is likely to be of interest to some distant audience. My gig with the *Valley News* meant that I finished the trip with "clips," a compilation of published stories that proved I was capable of reporting and writing. The best way to become a writer is by writing, and that is what the gap year had allowed me to do.

Because global travel would be an invaluable part of our children's education. Like many Americans, we live in a bubble. Hanover is unrepresentative of New Hampshire, let alone the United States or the world. It is smaller and whiter and richer and more rural than most of America. For many years we lived in Chicago, which is more urban and diverse than New Hampshire but still radically different from Ho Chi Minh City or Dar es Salaam. One of our most important obligations as parents is to educate our children, and one of the easiest and most enjoyable ways to do that is by taking them to interesting places.

Along the way, we would do the required homeschooling, but the real education would happen in the Amazonian jungle and on the streets of Cape Town.

The trip would also be nine months of uninterrupted family time. We recognized, obviously, that not every moment with teenagers is laden with fun and joy. Still, family time is (for the most part) a good thing, especially since Katrina, our oldest daughter, was on the brink of leaving for college. Our role as her parents would soon change—from managers to consultants, as one of my friends once described it. Katrina's siblings were not far behind. We had one last shot to make a lasting impact on their lives. The family gap year would be an experience that we would share forever—like a family road trip, only longer and with more bugs.

Because I am a huge proponent of high school graduates taking a gap year. I teach college students. To put a finer point on it, I teach highly motivated college students who have been running fast and jumping through hoops since middle school, if not earlier. Some of those students are burned out by the time I see them. Many would have benefited from some time off after high school to mature, work, and/or reflect on why they are going to college, especially given the cost of higher education. In one of the classes I teach, I ask students to define education: What is it supposed to accomplish? Then I ask them to evaluate their own schooling against their definition of education.

I get some depressing essays. Many students write about the joy they experienced in elementary school: how happy they were to go to school; how they studied science by hatching chickens and making pin-hole cameras; *how they loved learning.* And then those same students too often go on to explain how their love of learning was beaten out of them by standardized tests and lack of sleep and pressure to get into the right college. Their eagerness to learn was replaced by a bizarre and erroneous notion that education is somehow a competition, not a process whereby a person becomes more capable and complete. There is even a term for the elite high school students most consumed by this phenomenon: "crispies"—because they have burned out.

On occasion I teach military veterans who have enrolled in college after their service. These vets are profoundly different than my other students, both in their intellectual curiosity and in their respect for the opportunity that a college education affords. Obviously a year of traveling is not the same as active duty in Afghanistan. And many high school graduates are perfectly ready for college. Still, a year of anything between high school and college is likely to reinvigorate one's love of learning. Most of my Dartmouth students would have benefited from working for a year as a waiter or waitress before matriculation, if only to earn some money to offset the ridiculous cost of college and to get a better sense of the world beyond the Ivy League. College should not be just one more hoop; it is an extraordinary privilege afforded to a tiny fraction of the world's young people.

Because it is much, much cheaper than you think. Some people ask how much the trip cost; most people just wonder. The reality is that traveling around the world for nine months is significantly cheaper than staying at home. For example, we rented out our house while we were gone. That revenue became our housing budget for the trip. We took the monthly rent and divided it by thirty; that was how much we had to spend on lodging each night. We spend less on food while traveling than we typically do at home, mostly because food tends to be cheaper in developing countries, especially street food. We would not be driving in most places—so no gas, and only enough insurance to protect against the garage collapsing on the relatively decrepit cars we left at home. Most of our other incidental expenses would go away, too: work clothes, costly hobbies (e.g., golf), fancy entertainment.

We were swapping all that for a much cheaper day-to-day existence, even including plane, train, and bus tickets. In fact, the primary expense associated with traveling around the world has nothing to do with traveling around the world: It is forgone income. We would not be working for nine months. Even then, about forty percent of our income normally goes to taxes. The good news is that you don't have to pay taxes on income you don't earn! So, the real cost of our proposed adventure was about sixty percent of nine months of income. That is not a small number, but it is a far cry from what most people envisioned when we told them that we planned to travel around the world.

We are privileged in many respects. Leah and I have saved aggressively over the years. We have jobs with sufficient flexibility that we could step away for a year. More important, we are employable enough that we could have quit those jobs, if necessary, and expected to find similar work when we returned. This is, of course, the leverage that allows you to get a year off. We are lucky—period. *But sixty percent of nine months of income?* That is not Mark Zuckerberg kind of money. Think of it this way: If you plan to retire at age sixty-five, then doing what we did would require retiring at sixty-six instead—hardly a life-changing sacrifice. The point is that one does not need a trust fund or a winning lottery ticket to make a trip like this happen.

And finally, why not? We love to travel. The world is an interesting place. We have a finite amount of time left, and even less time with our children. Why not spend nine months of it doing what we love? In some ways, our experience was the opposite of what happened to George Bailey (Jimmy Stewart's character in *It's a Wonderful Life*). George feels boxed in by his small-town existence and pines to explore the world. At every turn, his travel plans are thwarted. He never makes it out of Bellows Falls, but in being forced to stay, he comes to appreciate the wonder of his day-to-day life. *That was our starting point.* We began our adventure with a deep appreciation for our day-to-day life. At every point in the trip, we looked forward to getting back to that life. But we did make it out of Bellows Falls.

Chapter 3

The Long Farewell

We have possessions: a house, two cars, two dogs, and a fish.
We would have to deal with all of these things.

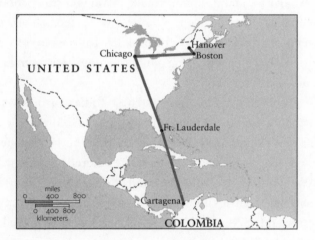

A FAMILY OF FIVE DOES NOT wake up in the morning and suddenly decide
to leave home for nine months. Because Leah and I had done such a
trip after college, we knew what is required in terms of planning. We
also knew what the conditions would be like if we were to travel on a
low budget in developing countries—and a low budget is the only thing
that would make a long trip possible. And we knew, or at least believed,
that our kids could manage rugged international travel reasonably well.
They had been doing it for years. At the University of Chicago, and later
at Dartmouth, I taught a course every fall that included an international
travel component: India, Turkey, Rwanda, Madagascar, Jordan. Each
year, the whole Wheelan family would tag along.

By the age of seven, Katrina had a better feel for travel in the developing world than some of my graduate students. On a trip to India,

one of my University of Chicago students developed some intestinal issues, as often happens in India. He was sitting in the back of the bus, bemoaning his illness and eating an ice-cream snack that he had just purchased at a roadside oasis. Katrina, barely in elementary school, sat down beside him. "Have you been brushing your teeth with tap water?" she asked solicitously. The grad student, who was in his mid-twenties, said that he had been. "You shouldn't do that," Katrina advised, shaking her head in surprise and disappointment. "And you really shouldn't be eating ice cream." Katrina eventually became so accustomed to travel in the developing world that when I took her to Washington, D.C., in middle school, she came scurrying out of the hotel bathroom and asked, "Can I drink the water here?"

Sophie was even younger on that first India trip. As we walked through a chaotic market in Bangalore, a hunched old woman who was barely four feet tall stepped in Sophie's path. The woman held out a cupped hand, jangling the coins she had gathered. Sophie reflexively took the coins out of the woman's hand. "Thank you," she said. The poor woman began shrieking like she had been physically struck. We quickly returned the coins, added a few more, and then had a long talk with Sophie about a hard subject.

As the family trip discussion evolved, the big question became "when," not "if." There were some natural parameters. We did not want any of the kids to miss their first or last year of high school. We assumed that once Katrina went off to college she would not be willing to leave school to travel with us. These constraints winnowed the possibilities down to one window: the year after Katrina graduated from high school. She could take a gap year. Sophie would miss her junior of high school—not ideal, but better than the alternatives—and CJ would miss eighth grade. *It was then or never.*

Leah and I did not want any professional obligations during the trip: no deadlines, no board obligations, no meetings, no conference calls. The trip was meant to be a gap year for the adults, too. Katrina would apply to college before the trip and with luck get accepted at a school she would be excited to attend. She would then defer for a year, which many colleges now encourage. As noted earlier, we would have to homeschool CJ and Sophie. Both Leah and I are educators; she is a certified teacher in New Hampshire.

We have possessions: a house, two cars, two dogs, and a fish. We would have to deal with all these things. The house was most important from a financial standpoint because we were counting on the rental income to subsidize our travel. Fortunately, we live in a college town with a robust rental market. We had a pretty good idea what the monthly rental income would be. The cars could sit idle in the garage for nine months with only minimal insurance. The dogs were the biggest emotional challenge. We would have to find foster families for them, either together or in separate homes. The fish did not require a great deal of advance planning.

Early polling showed that 66.7 percent of the children were in favor of the trip. Sophie was the holdout. She was the least excited about international travel, and she did not want to miss her junior year of high school. Sophie was perfectly capable of getting along in rugged places, but she had less interest in going to those places than the rest of us. We would have to manage the Sophie situation somehow. Neither of the two obvious solutions—forcing her to go or leaving her behind—was attractive.

The job. I have never liked the phrase "salary negotiation." It's too narrow. The correct phrase should be "contract negotiation." Salary is only one dimension on which a contract can be negotiated. You can also ask for a bigger office, a more competent assistant, a better coffee maker in the lounge—or time off. I am not a tenure-track academic. I work on three- or five-year contracts. Every time one of those contracts is negotiated, it is, as the verb would suggest, a negotiation. I enjoy my job and was eager to keep doing it. I just wanted an unpaid year off between contracts. In the end, I got nine months. I agreed to teach for two consecutive summers, leaving the intervening academic year free: September to June. That gave us nine months to travel, the same length as the original backpacking trip Leah and I had made.

Leah was teaching high school math. The district did not have a policy for unpaid leave that would guarantee a position when she returned. However, there is a huge shortage of math teachers in New Hampshire (and everywhere else). The district could not make any promises, but the powers that be indicated there would be a spot for her when she got back. If not, we knew from experience that half the schools in our area would be scrambling to hire math teachers during the summer of our return. So we had the job thing more or less worked out for both of us.

The extended family. My parents were healthy. Leah's mother was also in good shape. (Her father died when she was very young.) Still, our parents were not getting any younger. We recognized that an adverse health event, for any of our parents or for one of us, was one thing that might derail the trip. That was beyond our control. Right up until we flew out of the country, we always added a caveat when describing our plans: "Unless there is some reason we have to stay home." Life is about planning for what you can predict, and being realistic about what you cannot.

Obviously we did not need our parents' permission to take the trip, but for what it's worth, they were supportive. This was radically different than the first global adventure, when my parents were strenuously opposed. They feared that I would go full hippie on them. Instead, I kept my hair manageably short and proved over subsequent decades to be a respectable, taxpaying member of society. Once I even worked for a Republican. Meanwhile, my parents had begun to travel more and experience the joy of it. They also appreciated the educational impact that my international student trips were having on our children. Typically, we returned from those class trips in December. During the holidays, my parents would trot us all to the country club, where Katrina, dressed in some kind of velvet dress with a big bow, would casually tell my parents' friends about meeting the dictator of Madagascar (true), or climbing a volcano in Rwanda (true), or sleeping on a cement floor in a rural Indian village (also true).

Sophie may not be the most enthusiastic traveler, but she is the best storyteller, with a keen sense for what dazzles a country club audience. She would ask me for the benefit of her listeners, "What was the name of the woman we met in Jordan who is a direct descendent of Muhammad?" She served up adventure stories for the other children: "The monkey walked into our room and stole the bag of cashews. Then he climbed a tree and started throwing them at us!" As the adults clutched their plates in the buffet line, she might toss off a finale: "The villagers kept telling us, 'Make sure you don't step on a cobra!'"

My parents loved this.

The house. Renting out the house was a cornerstone of our plan, but it was not something we could do far in advance. The rental market does not work that way. However, our plan changed over Christmas while we were in Boulder, Colorado, with Leah's family. When we explained the trip to the extended family, my sister-in-law Noel mused, "Maybe we should shake things up for a year." A few minutes later she said, "We could move from Boulder to Hanover for the school year and rent your house." It was late in the evening, and we had gone through several bottles of wine, so none of us took the idea very seriously. The next morning, Noel and her husband Jeff (Leah's brother) peppered us with serious questions: How would their kids enroll in school? What would the rent be? How hard would it be to rent out their house?

I'll cut to the chase: Jeff and Noel decided to move to Hanover for the academic year with their three children and a dog. There were lots of good things about this development. We would have renters we trusted. We could be lazier about moving out our personal possessions. It also opened the door for a more substantial opportunity: Could Sophie stay behind with their family for a stretch and then join us in progress? By coincidence, Jeff and Noel's oldest daughter, Claire, was also a volleyball player. If Sophie remained in Hanover for the season, the two cousins would be playing together on the same high school team. At the end of the season, sometime in early November, Sophie could meet up with us in South America. Sophie said she would be genuinely excited for the trip if she could play volleyball and then join us en route. This became the working plan, which got us to one hundred percent approval among the children.

The pets. Jeff and Noel's family had a dog of their own; leaving them with two additional dogs was not a feasible option. (They would be able to take care of the fish.) We began asking everyone in our professional and social circles if they would be willing to look after a dog or two for nine months. Our informal networking eventually paid off. Lily, our ten-year-old semi-sedentary female Labrador retriever, went to friends who had an older Lab named Stella. The two old Labs became the "golden girls" of the neighborhood as they walked slowly around the block together.

We also had Caicos, a rambunctious three-year-old black Lab who had flunked out of a service animal training program after four months. (Frankly, we were shocked that he lasted in the program as long as he did.) A young couple on the Dartmouth faculty, Herschel and Julie, agreed to take Caicos. All evidence suggests that he was totally indulged for nine months. Herschel and Julie sent pictures periodically of Caicos lounging on the furniture surrounded by new toys.

The plan. We are now halfway through this chapter and there has been no mention of airline tickets or hotel reservations or anything related to traveling the world. *That is because most of the work is in the leaving.* Only after we firmed up things on the home front could we turn our attention to visiting other continents. Leah and I declared that every member of the expedition would be allowed a single pack that he or she would have to carry, plus a smaller backpack for a camera, books, a water bottle, and the like. The goal was to be totally mobile, meaning that each of us would be able to move through a crowded bus station carrying all of our stuff while having at least one hand free. This was not just about convenience; it was also to protect against getting pick-pocketed or having unattended bags stolen.

I subscribed to a number of high-end travel outfitters that regularly sent us glossy brochures for trips to every continent. We could not afford these exotic voyages, but we could re-create similar itinerar-ies more cheaply. There is no law against doing a *National Geographic* expedition to a cool place for one-tenth the price. I sat on our screened porch at night with a map of the world in front of me, trying to sketch out a route that made sense: minimizing long flights, arriving in places during the appropriate season, and so on. We had friends we wanted to visit in Mumbai, India, so that became a pin on the map. My brother suggested that he and his family meet us in the Galapagos for Thanksgiving. That became another pin in the map. Having a few of these firm destinations gave us some structure; otherwise the number of possible routes and destinations was infinite.

We allowed each of the children to pick one place they really wanted to experience. Sophie chose a safari in Africa. CJ selected scuba diving in Australia. Katrina demurred, opting instead to focus on ways to escape from us. She had high school classmates who would be traveling in Chile; she had another friend who would be studying in Germany and was keen to travel in Nepal and India. Katrina used her personal pick to make plans to meet up with these fellow travelers.

The route for the rest of the family evolved gradually, dictated in part by the seasons. We would begin in September in South America, where it would be spring. We would make our way south from Colombia toward the tip of Argentina and then double back to Ecuador for Thanksgiving with my brother. From there, we would cross the Pacific to New Zealand and Australia. We would head north through Southeast Asia during the winter (still very warm) and then visit our friends in India in the spring. At some point, we would detour to Africa, though the exact timing was ambiguous. Europe was not part of the original itinerary; it is an easy place for shorter vacations and we feared it would be too expensive for our budget.

For all the planning, there were only a few things that we needed to book in advance. One of them was space in the huts along the Routeburn Track in New Zealand. The bunks in the rustic cabins along this popular hiking trail are like campsites in America's national parks. They are not expensive, but the spaces fill up within hours of becoming available. Leah made a note of how far in advance we could book. On that day, while we were watching *Modern Family* in our living room, Leah went online and reserved five bunks in each hut along the trek. That gave us another pin in the map.

I booked free tickets for all of us from Fort Lauderdale to Cartagena, Colombia, using miles on JetBlue. Even then, we had not made any binding commitments. We could return our shiny new backpacks. We could cancel the New Zealand trekking reservations. We could tell our employers that we would be staying on the job and inform the in-laws that they could not rent our house. We could even get the miles back from JetBlue. It was all just an ambitious plan—until I booked the tickets from Ecuador to New Zealand.

On a warm June night, I went on Kayak and found cheap tickets from Quito to Auckland. *Nonrefundable tickets.* As I entered the payment information, I said to Leah, "We're going to do this, right?"

"We are," she answered confidently. I clicked the PURCHASE button. At that point, we had five seats—several thousand dollars' worth of nonrefundable tickets—on a Qantas flight across the Pacific Ocean.

The packing and the shots. Buying the backpacks was easy. The hard part was figuring out what to put in them. We all settled on some variation of the following: two pairs of long pants; one pair of shorts; two T-shirts; a long-sleeve shirt; a light sweater; a rain jacket; three or four pairs of socks and underwear; one set of sleeping clothes; a pair of hiking shoes; and a pair of flip flops. We carried a first-aid kit that had prosaic items like ibuprofen and tweezers; it also had sterile syringes in case one of us needed an injection in a place where there might not be a sterile needle. I added some personal things: my journal; backup glasses and sunglasses; a camera and telephoto lens; a Kindle; and my laptop.

The electronics were a source of debate. What did we really need? Each of us would have an iPhone or iPod that could double as a camera. Computers would be helpful for writing, schoolwork, travel planning, watching movies, and so on. Carrying more laptops would require less sharing, which would presumably minimize squabbling. On the other hand, the computers are heavy and would be an expensive loss if they were broken or stolen. We settled on two.

And then there were the books. I had a pile two feet high that I wanted to read on the trip. Yes, I have a Kindle, but I prefer reading the old-fashioned way. The challenge was that my books were as heavy as bricks and could have filled my whole backpack. With no plan for transporting this cargo, I left the books stacked on the floor—to be figured out later.

We made an appointment at the local travel clinic. In theory, each of us required a one-hour appointment. We persuaded the clinic to let us all come at once. This was the first trip-related activity we did as a group and it gave us a sense that the adventure was imminent. As we stepped up to the receptionist, I said loudly to CJ, "Don't tell them that you have gonorrhea." A woman sitting in the waiting area looked up from her magazine.

CJ exclaimed loudly, "I don't have gonorrhea." The receptionist looked up, as did two more people in the waiting area.

"Perfect," I said. "That's very convincing."

"Because I don't have gonorrhea!" CJ declared even louder.

"Totally believable. Just keep saying that," I said.

"How could I have gonorrhea?" CJ yelled. Everyone in the waiting area was now looking at him.

"Dad!" Katrina hissed. "You're acting like a nine-year-old." CJ chortled as he caught on. He was amused by a penis-related joke and the fact that we had successfully annoyed Katrina.

"I don't think most nine-year-olds would know what gonorrhea is," I told Katrina.

"That's true," Sophie added. CJ chortled some more. Katrina stared straight ahead, refusing to make eye contact with any of us.

"Just ignore them," Leah admonished.

"Why did you marry him?" Katrina asked accusingly, her nostrils flaring in frustration. *"Seriously."*

The five of us filed into a small examination room with Rhonda, our travel nurse. The normal protocol was for Rhonda to print a sheet listing the known diseases and other travel risks for each country that we would be visiting. By the time we got to our fourth country in South America—with places like India still to go—Rhonda was overwhelmed with stacks of paper. We decided it would be best to skip the balance of the paperwork and proceed to the shots. We had traveled in the developing world before and had therefore been immunized against most of the serious threats. One would think this would make the process shorter and easier.

In fact, our recordkeeping left something to be desired. Each of us brought a "yellow book" issued by the World Health Organization for keeping track of immunizations. Many of the records in our yellow books were unclear or illegible. "I have two yellow books," I reported to Rhonda, holding up one in each hand.

"You're only supposed to have one," she said.

"I had one, but I lost it," I explained. "I got another, but then I found the original. Now I use both."

"You're only supposed to have one," Rhonda repeated, as if that might make one of them disappear. She flipped through the pages in the two books. "You've been vaccinated three times for yellow fever," she said.

"That's good," I said proudly.

"One vaccination lasts a lifetime," she informed me.

"I guess I won't be getting yellow fever," I said.

Some of our immunizations needed boosters. For others, the recommended dosage or preferred drug had changed since we were first immunized. The hours rolled on as Rhonda dutifully administered shots. At one point I stepped out of the room to join a conference call. When I returned, the shots were still going on.

When the immunizations were done, Rhonda moved on to the information component of the appointment. "Here is what is most important," she advised. "Don't eat street food, don't play with stray dogs, and don't swim in fresh water." We nodded along. Rhonda wrote us a prescription for enough malaria pills to get us through the countries where the disease is endemic. "Good luck," she said earnestly as our family filed out.

We were now protected against illness, to the extent possible.

The in-laws arrive. I was sitting on the couch when Leah wandered into the room and said casually, "Jeff and Noel and their family will be here next week." It was mid-July. We were not leaving on our trip until September 1.

"Next week?" I asked in shock. What could possibly explain a six-week gap between their arrival and our departure? When my breathing returned to normal, Leah explained Jeff and Noel's plan. "They're not staying with us for six weeks," she assured me. "They're going camping and visiting friends on the East Coast. Our house is just a home base."

Rain derailed the first camping trip. The kids refused to go on the second one. Some of the visits with friends fell through, too. Then there was a family illness that precluded getting back into the minivan. To make a long story short, the five members of their family, plus the dog, moved into our basement for six weeks. Moments after they arrived, our dog, Lily, attacked their dog, Indy, meaning that the dogs could never be in the same place at the same time. Our house is small. Katrina and I are introverts. Ten people and three animals, not including the fish, were now living under one roof. It was like an evacuation after a natural disaster, only if there had been a flood or a wildfire, FEMA would have given us a trailer for Jeff and Noel's family to use.

[I promised Leah that I would let her read my description of this period before I submitted the manuscript to the publisher. What follows is my recollection of events, leaving it to Leah to expurgate things that might jeopardize family relations.]

If I'm being honest, ███████████████████████████████████████.
We soon learned that Esteban, Jeff and Noel's youngest son, likes to light things on fire. He proudly showed me his stash of fireworks in the garage. "The Fourth of July is over," I said.

"It's a holiday you can celebrate all summer," he said.

"I think it's just a one-day thing," I insisted.

Esteban nodded noncommittally. "Is that gasoline?" he asked, pointing to a red plastic container near the lawn mower.

I checked to make sure that our insurance premiums had been paid. Katrina moved all of her journals to a friend's house. I told Leah ██ ███████████████████████. Then, one afternoon while I was watching a golf tournament in the living room, I smelled smoke. At first, I thought I was imagining it. No, there was definitely smoke wafting in through the windows. I rushed out to the backyard, where all of the cousins had started a roaring bonfire. I put out the fire and issued stern instructions not to burn *anything* without permission. I told Esteban to focus on holidays other than the Fourth of July, maybe Halloween.

"It's cool when you put the candles in the pumpkins," he said.

"That's not what I had in mind," I said.

Sometime around then, Noel acquired a staph infection on her buttocks. This necessitated canceling another of the aforementioned trips. It also meant that Noel would have to treat the infection by soaking the affected area in a bathtub. The only bathtub in the house is in our bedroom. ███████████████████████████████ soaking her ass in our bathtub ███████████████████████████. This was not the only illness. Jeff and Noel's oldest daughter, Claire, came down with the flu. There was a vomiting incident, followed by an aggressive cleanup with assorted bleach products.

Katrina moved out of the house to stay with a friend.

Meanwhile, the dogs would eyeball each other warily anytime one of them would go in or out of the house. This created constant tension, as we were never more than three seconds from a dogfight. Jeff and Noel's dog spent a lot of time tethered outside on the driveway. This kept the dogs separated but caused Indy to bark and whine. The only spells of quiet came when Indy ran away, which was often. I could not enjoy that relative calm, however, because everyone in the house had to be mobilized to chase Indy around the neighborhood. I wrote in my journal: "███████████████████████████████████████ ██." Eventually I abandoned that plan because I couldn't find a shovel. Also, digging a hole in the backyard to dispose of the body seemed like a lot of work.

And then my mother-in-law arrived. ███████████████████ ██ ██ ██ ██ ██ ██

████████████████████████████
████████████████████████████
████████████████████████████
████████████████████████████
████████████████████████. Leah said to me, "It just looks bad when you drink scotch out of the bottle at dinner."

For all that, Jeff and Noel were doing us a huge favor—arguably making the trip possible—by taking Sophie for two months. Leah and I went out to lunch with them on the eve of our departure to discuss parenting strategies: rules, curfew, insurance information, and, of course, the travel logistics for Sophie to meet us in Lima, Peru. We were entrusting our teenager to someone else, and they were willing to take on that responsibility.

Around the same time, I figured out a solution to my pile-of-books problem: I mailed them to myself. There were three places I knew we would visit, no matter how much our itinerary evolved: Auckland, New Zealand; Hobart, Australia (where friends had offered us a home for a week); and Mumbai, India. I divided the books into three large padded envelopes and addressed each to a distant point on the globe. I walked into the post office on Main Street in Hanover and mailed the packages to addresses thousands of miles away. In theory, we would eventually show up to claim them.

Leah's family, part two. Sometime during the summer, we had the discussion with one of Leah's other siblings about whether Tess could join us for a portion of the trip in a Spanish-speaking country. As noted earlier, Tess was studying in a bilingual school and was eager to try adventure travel. We agreed to have her meet us in Fort Lauderdale and travel with us for three weeks in Colombia and Peru. Tess's parents drafted a series of legal documents so that we would be able, hopefully, to enter Colombia with a thirteen-year-old child who was not our own.

And then we left. The travel began with a Dartmouth Coach bus ride from downtown Hanover to Logan Airport in Boston. We posed for a group photo in front of the bus: Me, Leah, Katrina, and CJ. Sophie and the relatives were there to say goodbye. When the other bus passengers asked what was happening, we explained that we were headed around the world. They gave us skeptical looks—not unjustified given that we were only five minutes into the trip. We flew from Boston to Chicago to see my parents. They housed and fed us for a week, creating immediate budget savings.

And then on to Fort Lauderdale, where Tess met us without incident. The five us spent the night in a cramped airport hotel room that was both uncomfortable and unaffordable. It dawned on me, and perhaps on the others, that this was not a particularly pleasant way to travel. The accommodations would have to get bigger *and* cheaper once we were out of the country, or this adventure was not going to work. The next morning, we boarded the plane for the short flight to Cartagena. The humidity of the Caribbean belted us as soon as we climbed down the stairs of the plane onto the tarmac, as if we had walked into a bathroom where someone had just taken a long shower. The five of us walked inside to customs and immigration and joined the long line. Leah was carrying a folder of documents related to Tess: her birth certificate; an affidavit from her parents documenting that she was traveling with us; and myriad other signed, stamped, and notarized papers.

I made Tess rehearse answers to the questions the immigration officials were most likely to ask, as if I were briefing a witness for a deposition. "Don't say anything unless they ask you a question," I advised. "And then say as little as possible." We reached the front of the line and presented our five American passports. Tess stiffened up and stared forward. Leah clutched the folder of documents, prepared to offer up whatever legal paperwork might be necessary.

The immigration official gave us a cursory glance, stamped our passports, and waved us through. "Bienvenidos," he said as we shuffled by.

We were in Colombia.

Chapter 4

If You Want Peace, You Won't Get Justice

I took my camera out of my backpack and began shooting. Less than a minute later, an officer across the plaza pointed at me. I was well aware that soldiers and law enforcement types generally do not like to be photographed. The officer began walking briskly in my direction.

WE ARRIVED IN COLOMBIA in early September with no immediate onward plans. The idea was to make our way down the west side of South America to Patagonia before circling back north to Peru to meet Sophie. That left us two and a half months with no itinerary other than a general intent to move steadily south for four thousand miles. There were places we wanted to visit—Machu Picchu, the Amazon, the Bolivian salt flats—but there was not yet a plan for connecting them. We woke up on the first morning in Cartagena with ten unscheduled weeks ahead of us. Leah popped open her laptop to scout out potential adventures for the day. "Who wants to walk to the ocean?" she asked.

"Sure," CJ said without looking up from his book.

"Or we could go to the Slave Museum," Leah offered.

"Okay," I mumbled.

"Or the old part of the city?" Leah said.

"Yes," I said.

"Which one?" Leah asked.

"Yes," I repeated.

"How about if we impale ourselves on Spanish torture devices?" Leah asked.

"That could be fun," I answered while typing. (In my defense, I had heard the word "Spanish.")

Leah stopped asking questions. An hour later, she pronounced: "We will walk to the Slave Museum and then to the outdoor food market."

The walk took us through Cartagena's narrow streets with their pastel-colored buildings, wrought-iron balconies, and red-tile roofs. We passed a sixteenth century Spanish fort and a handful of churches, each with multicolored bell towers rising above the other buildings. There were flowers spilling over the balconies and creeping from every available space. The day was perfectly clear; the bright sun highlighted the colors of the city against the blue sky. All this colonial beauty made the Slave Museum feel like a slap in the face: a reminder that the lovely Spanish colonial architecture had a darker side. We spent an hour walking through exhibits documenting the scale of the slave trade and the cruelty of Spain's colonization of the Americas. I was pleased with this first dollop of homeschooling. "What did you think?" I asked CJ on the way out.

"The air-conditioning felt great," he answered. Obviously we still had work to do.

Leah led us on a scenic, meandering walk through the old city and along the ocean. Eventually the midday heat became punishing; there was no shade along on our route. We walked on. Leah paused occasionally to study the map in the guidebook. "Yes, this is Santa Maria Street," she said proudly. The walk was beginning to feel endless, but none of us dared complain openly lest we inherit the planning role. Instead, we resorted to passive-aggressive humor. "If I collapse and die, I want Katrina to curate my journals," I said.

"That would be so sad," CJ mused. "Dad's last journal entry would say, 'Looking forward to a long walk in Cartagena.'"

"But what if *I* don't make it?" Katrina asked.

"I really like Cartagena," Tess interjected. "This is a lovely walk, Leah. Thank you." As the cousin stowaway, Tess was duty-bound to be more polite than the rest of us. CJ pretended to vomit on the sidewalk.

"Do any of you know how to get home?" Leah asked.

"Are we still in Colombia?" I asked, prompting guffaws from the group.

Leah ignored me. "Anyone?" she challenged. We looked back at her blankly. "I didn't think so," she said. We ducked into a shady storefront for fresh orange juice, which cooled us down and raised our collective blood sugar.

The heat notwithstanding, Leah served up some early victories. Most important, we found a rhythm in Cartagena: one major adventure in the morning and then quiet time in the afternoon. Yes, the guidebook said there were ten "must-see" attractions in Cartagena, but squeezing ten things into three days would make us miserable. Leah offered us up the travel equivalent of a single delicious entrée each day instead of an all-you-can-eat buffet.

As noted earlier, Leah was the Budget Czar, also for lack of other applicants. She kept a spreadsheet with a record of every dollar spent. I learned how serious the accounting was going to be when I returned to the apartment after a pleasant morning stroll.

Leah: "What did you spend on breakfast?"
Me: "Two dollars on the empanadas."
Leah: "That's it?"
Me: "Yeah."
Leah: "Didn't you have coffee?"
Me: "Oh yes. That was a dollar."
Leah: "Any refills?"

Me: "Those were free." [Momentary relief on my part.]

Leah: "Did you buy the *Economist* on the way home?"

Me: "I did, yes." [Momentary relief now gone.]

Leah: "How much did that cost?"

Me: "I don't remember." [True.]

Leah: "Doesn't it say on the cover?" [Unfortunately, yes.]

Me: [Silent as Leah searches the small print on the cover of the
      Economist for the price in Colombian pesos.]

Leah: "Where did that pen come from?"

Me: "What pen?"

Leah: "In your left hand."

Me: "Okay, yes, I bought a pen with the *Economist*."

Leah: "Anything else?"

Me: "No, I think that's it."

Leah: "So you spent twelve dollars?" [The small print on the cover of
      the *Economist* indicated that it was very expensive in Colombia.]

CJ to Tess in the background: "He's so busted." [Teenage laughter.]

The budget numbers were somewhat arbitrary. When we divided
the monthly rent on our house in Hanover by thirty, it came to twenty
dollars a person per night. We allocated the same amount per day for
food and then twenty dollars per person for "other." All bus tickets,
entertainment, daily activities, and most flights would have to fit in
that "other" bucket. All in: sixty dollars per person per day. The budget
was essential to making the trip work. It is one thing to overspend on a
three-day vacation; it is another to go wildly off track for nine months.
We could not afford the latter. Leah and I agreed that if the budget left
us miserable or unsafe, we would raise our daily spending and shorten
the trip. Colombia suggested, happily, that we would not have to do that.

◈ ◈ ◈

With no onward tickets from Cartagena, we could go anywhere in
Colombia: the coast, a jungle trek, coffee country, the Amazon. Other

countries beckoned, too. Wouldn't it be cool to make it to the very tip of South America? Or Antarctica! To the east, Guyana and Suriname were tantalizingly untraveled. And Rio! What's not to like about Rio? Or Paraguay? I knew absolutely nothing about Paraguay, which made me want to go there. In the end, we decided to travel from Cartagena to Medellín, where, as described in the first chapter, *the children were not kidnapped*. After the excitement on the Medellín metro, we opted to explore a quieter, more rural part of Colombia: coffee country.

Emboldened by our first bus experience from Cartagena to Medellín, we booked tickets for a similarly long ride south from Medellín to Salento, a town nestled among the coffee estates in the Andes. Medellín is nearly a mile above sea level; Salento is higher still. The terrain grew greener and more densely forested as the bus carried us for seven hours along winding mountain roads. Just before sundown, we got off the bus in Salento's main square, a vibrant plaza surrounded by colorful one- and two-story buildings. Leah had booked rooms at a finca (farm) several kilometers out of town; we had no idea how to get there. The family mood gauge was flashing yellow as we stood with our bags in the picturesque central plaza. "Where is our hotel?" CJ asked.

"Let me get oriented," Leah said.

"We'll never find it," Katrina said. "Let's just check into a hotel in town."

"We've already paid for the finca," Leah said.

"What's a finca?" CJ asked. "That sounds terrible."

"Salento is beautiful," Tess added.

"No one threw up on the bus," I said, trying to sound upbeat.

"What if 'finca' means 'fleabag' in Spanish?" CJ asked.

"It means 'farm,'" Leah said sharply. "The pictures look lovely."

"Everything looks good on the Internet," Katrina said.

We opted to eat first and ask directions later. We carried our packs to a small open-air restaurant with a great view of the sun setting on the surrounding mountains. The cool air and plates of grilled meat, grilled fish, and french fries pushed the family's mood gauge to green.

As I paid the check, we asked our waiter how we might get to our finca. It was now dark and we had only vague directions—something about turning off the main road near a yellow bridge.

The waiter immediately summoned the owner of the restaurant, who declared on the spot that he would drive us there. Never mind that he had no better idea of where "there" was than we did. The owner rushed away from the table. Three minutes later, he drove a sedan into the dining area of the restaurant. I do not mean that he drove his car *near* the restaurant, or that he parked on the street just beyond the outdoor seating area. He drove his car into the dining area and parked next to our table. "Put the bags in the trunk," he instructed.

We squeezed six people, five packs, and assorted smaller backpacks into the restaurant owner's sedan. He drove us out of town on a dark, winding road. A dense fog had settled over the area. After several kilometers, we saw a structure that looked like it could be a yellow bridge. The restaurant owner turned his car onto a narrow dirt road. The headlights illuminated two dilapidated wooden buildings and an old swing set, all shrouded in the heavy mist. We could see nothing else, not even light in the distance. If this were a horror film, zombies would have appeared, walking stiffly out of the fog.

We got out of the car and used the flashlight function our phones to search for any clue of the finca. Eventually Tess spotted a small wooden sign for the Hotel Finca El Rancho[*] with an arrow pointing up a rutted path. We crowded back into the car and drove another kilometer to an inn at the top of a small hill. This turned out to be our finca, though it was hard to discern much about the place in the dark. We bade farewell to the restaurant owner, offering profuse thanks. We checked into three cozy but unheated rooms. The temperature was falling steadily; we climbed under layers of blankets, eager to see what daylight would bring.

"This place is awesome," CJ pronounced at breakfast the next morning. We were in a large open-air eating area with views in three direc-

---

[*] The curiously redundant name means, "Hotel Farm Ranch."

tions. By daylight, we could see that the finca overlooked a beautiful pasture with mountains beyond. The weather forecast was for seven consecutive days of rain; that first day, the forecast was proving sadly accurate. Even in a light rain—or perhaps because of it, with the tops of the mountains disappearing into the clouds—the views were impressive. Katrina made her way around the perimeter of the eating area snapping photos of the landscape.

The owner of our finca appeared at breakfast to take our dinner order and dispense travel tips. "Don't worry about a little rain," he admonished us in Spanish. "You should go to the national park." He told us how to catch the local bus into Salento by waiting on the side of the road near the yellow bridge. From there, we rode for twenty minutes in the back of a jeep with a handful of other international travelers into Los Nevados National Park, an area where the dense greenery of the coffee country abuts the mountains and volcanoes of the Andes, all frosted with layers of white and gray clouds.

"Whoa," CJ said as he climbed out of the jeep and stared up at the wax palm trees, the tallest palms in the world. The trees jut up as high as two hundred feet with a single, compact canopy of palm leaves at the top. The combination of these freakish trees, the steep green hills, and the overhanging mist created a Jurassic Park kind of beauty. We walked into a forest where a narrow trail led up a small mountain. The path followed a river, crossing back and forth along rickety bridges with signs warning in Spanish: CAUTION: ONE PERSON AT A TIME. We had no particular destination. Even if we made it to the top of the mountain, all we would be able to see was gray mist and our own colorful jackets. Instead, we hiked until we felt like turning around, admiring the dense, luscious vegetation and trying not to fall off the narrow bridges. We were so soaked that the rain stopped mattering. I had fun searching out the tiny flowers and colorful mushrooms hidden amid the dense greenery or in small crevices in tree trunks.

By the second morning, the weather had turned warm and sunny, proving the weather forecast blessedly wrong. "Te gusta montar a caballo?" the proprietor of the finca asked at breakfast.

"What did he say?" CJ asked.

"Something about mounting a cow," I said.

"Horse," Leah corrected me.

"He asked if we like horses," Tess said.

"For dinner?" CJ asked with concern.

"To ride, moron," Katrina said.

The finca owner suggested that we ride horses to a nearby coffee farm. No one will confuse the Wheelan family for cowboys, but horses are a really good way to explore—like hiking, only less work. Tess and CJ rode in the front, bantering to each other. I could see their mouths moving, but I was sufficiently adept with my horse that I could stay far enough behind not to hear them.

We rode for an hour to an organic coffee farm and then hiked through the steep fields, where avocado, plantain, and banana trees shaded the coffee plants. After the tour of the farm and a lesson in roasting beans, we drank coffee on the porch of the farmhouse. The owner of the farm pointed to a chicken strutting back and forth in the yard with an odd tuft of orange feathers on its head. "We call that the Trump chicken," he said, prompting laughter. I assured those sitting on the porch—the coffee farmer, his son, and some Australians who had toured the coffee farm with us—that there was no chance of Donald Trump being elected president of the United States. They seemed relieved by my expert political analysis.

In the evenings we relaxed in the covered open-air dining area that doubled as a communal gathering space. The Internet was intermittent at best, so we spent hours playing cards, reading, and writing in our journals. Our card game of choice was whist, a simplified version of bridge in which two-person teams compete against each other. I finished reading a biography of Nelson Rockefeller and began *It Can't Happen Here*, the 1935 Sinclair Lewis novel about a populist authoritarian leader who rises to power in America. When the temperature in the open-air common area became too frigid, we retired to our rooms and climbed into the comfortable beds. We slept especially well in Salento, both because of the cool nights at high altitude and because the only constraint on when we had to wake up was the risk of missing breakfast.

❖ ❖ ❖

We had arrived in Colombia at a historic inflection point. For half a century, the Colombian government had been fighting several rebel groups, the largest of which was the Revolutionary Armed Forces of Colombia (FARC). That armed conflict—the longest civil war in the hemisphere—was on the brink of resolution. Government officials and FARC representatives had been negotiating in Havana for several years. Right about the time we were leaving in Hanover, the two sides reached a tentative agreement under which the guerrillas would disarm and end their decades-long fight. In exchange, the Colombian government would grant FARC members some degree of amnesty, a guaranteed number of seats in the national legislature, and a monthly stipend to help them reintegrate to civilian life. We had known since before we arrived that the agreement would soon be put to Colombia's voters for approval in a national referendum.

Katrina had reached out to the *Valley News*, the newspaper I had written for on my first global adventure, and offered to write a series of columns during our travels. She pitched her editor a story on the Colombia peace agreement. The country was fatigued from decades of war. Polls were showing that the peace deal would be approved by a wide margin. It would be an uplifting story for readers back home: "Colombia Votes Overwhelmingly to Bring Fifty Years of Violence to an End."

As a cub journalist, Katrina was running into two problems. First, she did not like to interview people—not in English, and definitely not in Spanish. Second, every person she interviewed said they planned to vote "no" in the referendum, despite what the national polls were showing. In the evenings, she and I discussed why her interviewees might not be representative of the country. It was possible that she was going to places likely to attract "no" voters—the Colombian equivalent of asking members of the Nantucket Yacht Club if they are in favor of a wealth tax.

Katrina went back out and did more interviews in different places; again she encountered lots of people who planned to vote "no." The general theme she encountered among the "no" crowd was that the FARC were getting a better deal than they deserved. The guerrillas had terrorized the country for decades. Now, in exchange for giving up kidnapping, killing, and drug trafficking, they would get cash and seats in Congress rather than long prison sentences. The son of our finca owner spoke angrily about how the FARC had terrorized his family during the violence. He planned to vote "no," he told Katrina.

Katrina's reporting turned out to be more accurate than the national polls. Shortly after we left the country, Colombia's voters narrowly rejected the peace deal (50.2 percent "no" versus 49.8 percent "yes"). President Juan Manuel Santos resurrected the deal by renegotiating parts of it and then asking the Colombian Congress for approval, rather than the voters. Katrina had stumbled onto a larger lesson: The enticements necessary to get an armed group to put down its weapons will inevitably be repugnant to the population they have victimized. Who wants to put killers in Congress? But if violent groups don't get a better deal than they deserve, they won't give up the fight. No one voluntarily agrees to life in prison.

Some years earlier I had taught a class on the Northern Ireland peace process that ended up with a trip there. I remember a former member of the Irish Republican Army in Belfast telling me, "The bumper sticker is wrong. If you want peace, you don't work for justice."

Too many people have done too many terrible things to too many other people—and those other people have often struck back in ghastly ways. Justice is not consistent with reconciliation. Giving everyone what they deserve will likely prolong the conflict, not end it. Unfortunately, that does not make for a good bumper sticker: IF YOU WANT PEACE, HELP THE PEOPLE WHO KILLED YOUR FAMILY GET A FRESH START!

There was one other complication related to Katrina's reportorial work. Turns out she was not particularly keen on getting journalism tips from me, despite how helpful they were. Whenever someone would offer a pithy remark about the FARC or the upcoming referendum,

I would exclaim, "There's your quote! Write that down!" She would scowl ferociously in my direction. *Also, she really, really, really did not like it when I began calling her "Scoop."* Upon reflection, I should have stopped calling her Scoop when she told me to stop calling her Scoop.

Some of Scoop's friends were taking gap years, but most had gone off to college. This made Scoop highly sensitive to the fact that she was spending all of her time with her parents. She insisted on carrying her own passport. In the Fort Lauderdale airport, Leah and I stepped to the counter with CJ and Tess to check in. Scoop stood behind us and checked in separately. Once I instinctively told her to be careful while crossing a busy street. She roared, "I'm eighteen years old! I know how to cross the street!"

CJ and Tess, both thirteen, entertained each other. They looked like twins and most people we encountered assumed they were. They talked to each other incessantly. Tess was a wonderful traveler—pleasant and adaptable and interested in the places we were visiting. She spoke Spanish better than the rest of us. Only when Tess returned home a few weeks later (as planned) would we fully appreciate what an important companion she had been for CJ.

Leah and I had it easiest. Our travel regimen was just an extension of our everyday life. We had each other to talk to, and we were comfortable with our respective travel-related tasks. Leah planned the route and kept the budget; I took photos and managed the blog. Meanwhile, Sophie was still at home in Hanover, playing volleyball, taking classes like World Drumming, and using her free time to get started on her more substantive online classes. Or so we thought.

❖ ❖ ❖

For all the relaxing comfort of our finca, Bogotá beckoned. To get there, we would have to take another eight-hour bus ride eastward through winding mountain roads. The whole family loaded up on Dramamine, except for Katrina (the writer formerly known as Scoop), who opted against it, probably because Leah or I told her it would be a good idea. Katrina planned to use the bus ride to interview passengers for her

Valley News article on the peace referendum. Shortly after we pulled away from Salento, Katrina found a man eager to share his thoughts on the referendum. She settled into a seat across the aisle from him. The bus wound its way through the mountains, slowing down for the curves and then lurching uphill. "Excuse me," Katrina said as the man began talking about his family. She walked quickly to the bathroom in the back of the bus to throw up. She returned looking pale. "Sorry," she said to the man, who resumed his story. Five minutes later, Katrina stood up again and rushed back to the bathroom.

"Scoop, how is the interview going?" I asked as she passed me. For some reason this made her angry, even though I had suggested that she take Dramamine before we got on the bus. Katrina threw up six more times before our bus stopped at the Colombian version of a highway oasis: an open-air restaurant with long wooden tables. The stop turned out to be long and leisurely, allowing Katrina sufficient time to medicate and get beyond the motion sickness. After the meal, I walked out of the restaurant to admire the views. The moment has stayed with me—being on the side of the road in a tiny, picturesque, middle-of-nowhere mountain town.

The Bogotá bus station was bigger and more disorienting than the others we had encountered. We arrived after dark—tired, hungry, cranky, and mildly anxious about being in a new, chaotic place. I yelled at CJ for wandering away from me while I was in the bathroom. Leah got angry with me for yelling at CJ. I became frustrated with Leah when she transposed the numbers of the address for our Airbnb, causing us to spend a long time in a taxi looking for an address that did not exist. Eventually the taxi driver dropped us off on the street somewhere near where we thought the apartment ought to be. In the confusion, I made a currency calculation error and paid the driver ten times what I owed him—the equivalent of paying sixty dollars for a six-dollar ride. The driver expressed pleasant surprise and drove off. I was frustrated with myself for making the error, and then mad at the driver for not calling it out.

To recap: I was angry with CJ, Leah, the taxi driver, and myself.

Leah was angry with me. The others were generally cranky. Only the taxi driver emerged from this sequence of events in a good mood.

Things got better quickly. Our Bogotá apartment was in an elegant building in a residential area. The apartment was not big—two bedrooms, a small but functional kitchen, and a little common area with a table—but we immediately grew to love it because we were embedded in a charming neighborhood. A few blocks down the street, I found a bakery with a confounding array of freshly baked confections. The glass display case had four rows, each with six compartments of pastries: cheese; sugar; fruit; fruit and sugar; sugar and cheese. I asked about the prices but soon realized that I was overthinking the selection process. The items were so cheap that for two dollars I could fill a bag with everything that might possibly be good. Later in the day, Leah and I found a large supermarket and bought staples for our apartment: bottled water, cereal, milk, nuts, jam, Nescafé, dried fruit, beer. There was a doorman who greeted us effusively every time we went in or out. He told us how impressed he was that the gringos had figured out how to go grocery shopping.

Having been off-line in Salento, each of us seized on the apartment's strong Wi-Fi to catch up. Almost immediately the Wi-Fi became especially slow. "What's going on?" Katrina asked, looking suspiciously around the room.

"It was working fine until a minute ago," Leah said.

We stared at our devices waiting for the Internet to rebound, but it stayed frustratingly slow. CJ was the only one who had not complained. He was sitting on the couch with a guilty-looking grin, like he had just farted and was hoping no one would notice. Katrina rushed over and grabbed his iPod. "He's downloading a movie!" she yelled. CJ pleaded "no contest" and threw himself on the mercy of the family. Katrina canceled his download and we all went back to work.

We planned to be in Bogotá long enough that I bought fresh flowers for our apartment from a street vendor—and then we were forced to stay even longer. On our third afternoon, CJ rushed to the bathroom and threw up. This happened several more times. By evening, he was lying on the couch looking green. "I have never felt this bad in my life," he declared repeatedly. We bought him Gatorade to protect against dehydration as we tried to figure out what was going on. He had a modest fever but no other symptoms besides extreme nausea. Food poisoning? Something contagious?

"Katrina, can you look up the symptoms of Ebola?" I asked.

"That's not funny," CJ croaked.

"High fever," Katrina reported.

"Hmm," I said.

"Also, bleeding from every orifice," Katrina continued.

"Okay, we can cross Ebola off the list," I said.

"Please stop," CJ pleaded.

The next day Katrina came down with the same extreme nausea. The good news was that the pattern suggested something contagious like the flu rather than a more exotic travel-related illness. The bad news was that there were three more of us who might succumb. Katrina, who is not one to admit weakness, felt so bad that she could not sit up. When we played cards that night, we dragged her mattress into the living room so she could join the game while lying on the floor with her head propped on a pillow. The other players spread around her, using her mattress as a card table.

Our flexible schedule allowed us to shelter in place. We checked in with Sophie back home, who told us how much she was enjoying her junior year. She was taking courses like the aforementioned World Drumming with the understanding that she would use her extra time to make progress on her online classwork: precalculus, criminal justice, and chemistry. These classes were offered by the state of New Hampshire as part of the Virtual Learning Academy Charter School, or VLACS.

Leah decided to check the online VLACS portal to see how Sophie was doing in her three classes. "This cannot be right," Leah mumbled when she logged in. "Nada."

"What does that mean?" I asked.

"'Nada' means nothing in Spanish," Leah said impatiently.

"I know what 'nada' means," I said. "How could she have done no work in a month?"

"*Not one single assignment,*" Leah said (in English).

◈ ◈ ◈

Surprisingly, none of the rest of us fell sick. By Sunday, both CJ and Katrina were on the mend. Normally we were not particularly conscious of what day of the week it was, but in Bogotá, Sunday is ciclovia, a communal event in which a major avenue is closed to car traffic and opened up for bicyclists, Rollerbladers, runners, walkers, people with big dogs, people with small dogs, and anyone else who wants to enjoy a car-free stroll on a wide urban boulevard. We joined the throngs and walked all morning—nearly the entire length of the city. We admired the sites as we were swept along with thousands of people for whom Bogotá is home. We stopped for a while in a huge park where some kind of public exercise class had been organized. CJ enthusiastically performed aerobics along with the crowd.

On our final night in Bogotá we attended a "peace concert" in the main plaza to promote a "yes" vote on the referendum. We arrived early, expecting a large crowd. The security presence was impressive. The Bogotá police, the army, and all kinds of other uniformed officers were spread across the plaza. In fact, there seemed to be about five armed officers for every visitor. I decided to take some pictures. The plaza was picturesque under any circumstances; the police presence juxtaposed against the huge Spanish cathedral made for a great visual.

I took my camera out of my backpack and began shooting. Less than a minute later, an officer across the plaza pointed at me. I was well aware that soldiers and law enforcement types generally do not like to be photographed. The officer began walking briskly in my direction. I did my best "confused American" impression: I looked behind me and pretended that he must have been signaling to someone else. Despite a compelling dramatic performance on my part, the officer continued to stride with determination in my direction. When he was ten yards away, he raised his arm and made a small circle motion with his hand: the universal sign for, "Turn around." I obeyed and slowly turned my back to him. When he arrived at where I was standing, he pointed at my backpack. "Abierto," he said. Open.

I was genuinely confused. My backpack was already open; I had unzipped it when I took out my camera. As I stood there looking befuddled, the officer zipped the backpack closed. He wagged his finger and said in Spanish, "The plaza will be very crowded. Please be careful with your bag."

And off he walked.

Chapter 5

Into the Amazon

Our time at the lodge fell into a routine: during the stretches when I was not worried about dying, I felt deeply relaxed.

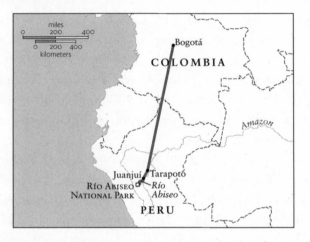

M<small>Y</small> <small>FIRST GLIMPSE OF THE</small> A<small>MAZON</small> was from a plane. We had left Colombia, taking off from Bogotá shortly before sunset, and I had drifted off to sleep. I woke up a short time later and looked out the window to see a river meandering through a dense expanse of green, as if someone had spilled a drink on a 1970s shag carpet. "That's the Amazon," Leah said. There was not a single building or sign of human habitation in sight, just the multiple shades of green that formed the canopy of the world's largest tropical rainforest: *roughly the size of the contiguous forty-eight United States.*

From thirty-five thousand feet, the enormous trees looked like florets on a head of broccoli, but I knew what was lurking in that dense tropical forest. I had begun reading *The Lost City of Z*, a book that details the remarkable and ultimately fatal adventures of British explorer Percy

Fawcett as he searched for an ancient Amazonian civilization. On his various expeditions, Fawcett and fellow explorers battled parasites, snakes, bugs, hostile natives, and impenetrable terrain. The book's central message is that the Amazon tends to win.

Our destination was the Abiseo Aventura Paradise, a small outpost owned by a married couple, Kevin Cleaver and Maria Nikolov, both of whom had spent their careers at the World Bank. A mutual friend had introduced us to them via e-mail. Their adventure lodge is located just outside the Abiseo National Park, an area that had been closed to visitors for decades. Even compared to other Amazon destinations, we would be heading deep into the wild. The flight from Bogotá took us to Tarapoto, a city in the interior of Peru. From there, we took a jeep ride for several hours to Kevin and Maria's home in the small town of Juanjuí. We would spend a day there before setting out for the adventure lodge by boat the next morning.

Kevin is American; Maria is Peruvian. Now retired, they split their time between Washington, D.C., and Peru, and would be traveling with us to their adventure lodge. Upon our arrival in Juanjuí, Kevin and Maria invited us to their home for an elaborate lunch outdoors, with bowls of fruit and myriad plates of other delicious local food. As we sat down to lunch, CJ was still heavily doped up on Dramamine from the long jeep ride. "Why are so many fruits round?" he asked in a loopy kind of way. "Fruits," he repeated. "That's a strange word. Fruits. *Fruits.*"

Leah and I ignored him. Kevin and Maria shared fascinating stories from their careers at the World Bank and asked about our travel plans. "Do humans really need ten fingers?" CJ interjected as he stared at his hand. Leah and I told Kevin and Maria about the places we planned to go to during the balance of the trip. This led to a discussion of our obligation to homeschool the children. CJ was still babbling semi-coherently. Kevin turned to me and said solicitously, "You're doing such great things with him. Every child learns in his own way."

We continued to swap stories with Kevin and Maria, marveling at the people we knew in common. "What if all the trees fell over at once?" CJ asked the table. Kevin nodded as he absorbed the question and then turned to me. "These days, people like CJ can lead very fulfilling lives. He seems so curious to learn." Leah and I exchanged a glance.

CJ added, "I suppose that's very unlikely—that all the trees would fall over at once. Unless maybe there was a hurricane or something like that."

"That's exactly right, CJ," Kevin answered.

"Do you like mangoes, CJ?" Maria asked, holding up a mango.

"I do like mangoes," CJ answered.

"Mangoes grow on trees," Maria said.

"Yes," CJ agreed. "Like apples."

"Exactly!" Maria said excitedly.

The Dramamine wore off as the lunch unfolded course by course. CJ continued to talk incessantly, with each statement making slightly more sense than the last, as if someone were slowly turning up the dial on his intellectual capacity. He and Kevin discovered a mutual interest in scuba diving. By dessert, they were discussing the impact of climate change on the world's coral reefs. "Even modest warming of the oceans can be devastating for the coral," CJ said.

"Wow," Kevin pronounced as we got up from the table. "CJ is quite a kid."

"Oh yes," Leah and I agreed heartily.

In the afternoon, Maria took us to visit her family's cacao farm, which was perched at the top of a hill. The cacao trees are short and broad, with pods the size of small footballs hanging from thick branches. None of us had ever seen a cacao tree or its fruit. She broke open a pod and showed us the milky white beans inside. "First you have to ferment the beans, then they get roasted," she explained.

Maria led us over to a squat bush with lime-green leaves. "What do you think that is?" she asked. We stared silently at the ugly plant. "It's a coca bush," she said. "That's where cocaine comes from." CJ's eyes widened as he imagined Kevin and Maria as cogs in a vast cocaine empire. "It's legal to have a few bushes," Maria explained eventually. "You can use the leaves to make tea, or you can chew on them. They're a mild stimulant, like coffee."

Kevin, who was walking along with us, described a USAID program that had induced Peruvian coca farmers to grow cacao instead. (What a difference one letter can make.) Both crops thrive in the region, but the world is presumably a better place when farmers supply chocolate makers instead of cocaine cartels. "But it has to make economic sense for the farmers," Kevin said. He explained that rising global demand for artisanal chocolate had driven up cacao prices, which gave the program a boost. "Every time you buy one of those fancy chocolate bars, it helps the cacao farmers," Kevin declared, giving Leah and I a new sense of pride in all the overpriced dark chocolate we had eaten over the years.

The crop substitution program became Scoop's second *Valley News* article. She eagerly snapped pictures of the trees and the cacao pods. At one point, while taking a photo of a bright yellow pod, she said, "This is cool." For Katrina, who tends to be parsimonious with outward displays of excitement, it was the equivalent of breaking into song and dance.

Maria walked us downhill and pointed to a band of dead cacao trees. "Global warming," she explained. Changing temperatures were slowly killing the trees at lower elevations. We headed back toward the center of town along a dirt road. "When I was little, these streets were running with blood," Maria said. During her childhood, the town had been terrorized by the leftist Shining Path guerrillas. In the 1980s and early 1990s, the Shining Path conducted bombings, assassinations, and mass killings, including attacks on civilians, aid workers, and tourists. "They killed anyone who didn't cooperate." The group's top leaders were eventually captured, and peace was restored to the parts of the country where the Shining Path had been active. Like Colombia, Peru was now a safer, more democratic place than it had been in decades.

That night at dinner, Kevin announced, "We're going to take a boat upriver to the lodge in the morning. Make sure everyone wears their life jacket." We nodded in agreement and said our farewells for the evening. As Maria gave us all hugs, Kevin mumbled, "The boat flipped over once, and a guy didn't come up." I thought maybe I had misheard him; the conversation moved quickly to something else.

When we got back to the hotel, Leah asked, "What did that mean—the guy didn't come up?"

"It seemed like a literal statement," I said.

"Which means what?"

"He drowned?" I said.

"On his way to the lodge?" she asked.

"It might have been on the way back from the lodge," I suggested.

"That's supposed to make me feel better?"

"We're going to be wearing life jackets," I assured her.

"Promise me we are not going to do anything crazy, especially with Tess," Leah implored.

"What do you mean by 'crazy'?" I asked.

Leah just stared at me.

"Okay," I promised.

✦ ✦ ✦

We traveled up the Huayabamba River on a long, narrow wooden boat about the width of a canoe, but four or five times longer. We sat on wooden planks, one or two to a row. "You can put any valuables into the dry bag," Kevin explained, holding up a waterproof bag about the size of a laundry sack with a top that screwed shut. "It floats," he added. I had planned to take photos as we traveled along the river to the lodge; now I wondered if I should put my camera in the dry bag instead.

"What about my camera?" I asked Leah.

"Your camera?" she answered. "If we tip over in the middle of the river, will the camera be your major concern?"

"I'll keep it with me and take pictures," I said. Hoping to reframe the discussion, I asked, "Should I get a shot of everyone in their life jackets?" No response. "I think they have a slimming effect," I added. Still nothing.

A half an hour after we launched, we reached a particularly fierce patch of rocky rapids. The boat driver, a local whom Kevin and Maria had hired to ferry us to the lodge, was steering the boat from the stern

using a single outboard motor that was now fighting the strong current
to a draw. Maria's brother Sander, who worked at the lodge, stood in the
bow looking for rocks and helping to plot a course. The engine whirred
away at full throttle but was not powerful enough to move the boat forward. After a few seconds, we began to drift backward.

The driver ordered us to move around in the boat, sending weight
to the front or the back in a way that would get the boat moving again.
He struggled to keep the boat pointed straight upriver. If we turned
sideways, the narrow boat might float downriver into a rock and flip
over. We switched seats compliantly; Sander barked orders to the driver
from the front. Eventually our little boat began moving forward again
and we passed safely through the rapids.

The banks rose steeply on both sides of the river. Huge patches of
land had been cleared or burned away. In some places, the vegetation
was still aflame or smoking. After an hour, we turned up the Abiseo
River, which was like leaving the main road for an uninhabited side
street. The riverbanks became steeper and more densely vegetated.
All signs of agriculture disappeared. The terrain felt more jungle-like,
though the temperature grew cooler as we gained altitude. Around midday we arrived at the lodge, which was perched on a bluff above the river.
We climbed out of the boat onto the rocky bank and walked up a steep
path with several switchbacks to a grass clearing surrounded by wooden
buildings. The main building had a series of simple but comfortable
bunk rooms that opened onto a large open-air porch.

Shortly after our arrival, two of the workers at the lodge persuaded
Katrina and Tess to come see their pet snail. I was unpacking my stuff
when Katrina returned. "Dad, you need to see the snail."

"I've seen a lot of snails," I said. "We get them all over the porch in
the summer."

"This one is huge," Katrina said.

"How big?" I asked.

"They keep it on a leash," she said.

I followed her to a spot behind one of the buildings where a snail the size of my hand was tethered to a tree. "Damn," I said after staring at the gigantic creature for a while. "We're not in Kansas anymore."

"Nope," Katrina agreed.

A short time later, we sat down to lunch at a long wooden table on the porch of the bunkhouse. The talented cook prepared wonderful meals, mostly from local ingredients: fish from the river, plantains, and other fruit. Maria revealed that she had brought a stash of special Peruvian beans with her in the boat and that the cook would be preparing them for us using a family recipe. "But you have to use the right beans," she said.

Special beans? I thought skeptically as my mind drifted to "Jack and the Beanstalk." And then the bean dish arrived at the table—rich and creamy with a hint of distinctive spice. They were bizarrely delicious. Kevin and Maria turned out to be "foodies": people, like ourselves, who take great pleasure in every part of every meal, whether it is grilled chicken on a stick in a Cartagena plaza, or a family recipe for beans. We lingered over the meal listening to the sounds of the forest while discussing everything from the World Bank to Peruvian politics to scuba diving.

After lunch, we returned to the boat and motored farther upriver into the national park. The river grew narrower; the banks became steeper, greener, and higher. The distant peaks were shrouded in fog. An eerie layer of mist floated just above the water. We stopped and hiked along a short rocky path to a giant waterfall with a swimming hole at its base. We swam in the brisk water (sorry, Rhonda) as the waterfall crashed down around us. "This is amazing," I told Kevin.

"Just wait," he said.

We returned to the boat and motored to a point where a narrow channel, barely ten yards across, diverged from the river. Kevin handed each of us a helmet with a headlamp strapped around it. He waded into the water, and we followed. The channel was shallow enough to walk, but the rocky bottom made it easier to swim. The trees formed a lush canopy overhead. We dog-paddled as the warm current carried us along.

Eventually we drifted into a cave, and the daylight disappeared. We turned on our headlamps, which cast rays of light in whatever direction we looked. The effect was like a light show on the smooth, damp walls of the cave. A dark object flitted into the light and then disappeared. Then another. "Bats," Kevin said, his voice echoing off the walls.

Eventually we turned around and began swimming toward the window of light in the distance. "Pretty cool, huh?" I asked Katrina as she paddled along beside me.

She nodded distractedly. After a moment she said, "How do you think Maria makes those beans?"

◇ ◇ ◇

The lodge was at a high enough altitude that there were no mosquitoes. To be clear, there were other insects: big ones, small ones, green ones, black ones, beautiful ones, scary ones. On two occasions, I focused my camera on a curious-looking bug only to have it attacked by another insect while I was taking the photo. After dark, we marveled at the amazing creatures hovering around the lights on the porch. Eventually we settled exhaustedly into our comfortable beds. There were lights in the rooms, but they were not bright enough to read by. I turned on my headlamp and opened *The Lost City of Z*.

I had read about three sentences when I heard a loud buzzing noise. I saw a blaze of movement as a creature the size of a ping-pong ball dive-bombed into my forehead. The bug hit me with such force that I fell out of bed, flinging my book against the wall. [There is some disagreement here: Leah maintains that it was my shrieking and panic that caused me to fall out of bed.] In any event, that was the last time I tried to read in bed with a headlamp in the Amazon.

The next morning, I was perched in a hammock strung between posts on the porch when several workers approached excitedly. "Come, come," they said in Spanish. I followed them for about twenty yards to an area where they had been clearing brush. "Venenoso," one of the men said as he pointed at the base of a green bush. I could see nothing other than wispy leaves. "Venenoso," he repeated. I had not learned that word in high school Spanish, but I had a pretty good idea what it meant. Eventually I made out a large green-gray snake coiled on the ground. It was a beautiful creature, camouflaged ominously amid the green leaves and brown soil. I crept close enough to get a photo, and then, upon returning to the lodge, advised the family to stop walking around in flip-flops. The Amazon basin has seventeen different kinds of poisonous snakes. There are antivenins for some of them, but we were too far from civilization for an antivenin to be administered in time.

For that afternoon, Kevin proposed a "short but steep hike." We returned to the river and took the boat to the trailhead. The hike was short, as promised. The trail led up a steep path through dense vegetation to the mouth of a cave. There was an old wooden sign posted near the cave entrance; whatever was written on the sign was covered entirely by moss. "Do you like caves?" Kevin asked. "This one has seven levels." He explained that we would climb down, level by level, until we reached an underground river, at which point we would swim. "Who wants to go?" he asked excitedly.

Tess and Katrina immediately opted in. CJ vacillated but eventually decided to go. "I'm fine waiting right here," Leah said. I have modest claustrophobia, but I joined the group to chaperone the kids. Also, it was a seven-level cave in the Amazon.

Once again, we put on the helmets with headlamps. Kevin declared that no individual could turn back once we entered. We turned on our headlamps and walked into the mouth of the cave. Almost immediately we encountered our first climb: a hole in the ground no bigger than a sewer grate. The walls and floor of the cave felt like wet clay. Every step required concentration. Each of us shimmied down feetfirst, carefully using clefts in the rock for hand- and footholds. Tess and Katrina made it look easy. Tess is a soccer player. Katrina is a cross-country runner. They are strong, slight, and nimble. I am a golfer, a skill that translates less directly to climbing through small holes in a cave.

CJ was the one I had to monitor closely, not because he couldn't do the climbing, but because he was the one most likely to panic. His general tendency is to think out loud, and it did not take long for him to begin processing the situation verbally. "What if we slip?" he asked. I instructed him that he was not allowed to speak—not a single word unless he had some urgent message concerning his immediate safety or the safety of the group.

"Okay, but what if—"

"*Stop talking*," I said with all the parental seriousness I could muster. He did. From that point on, CJ was a great climber. Our group fell into a rhythm, moving steadily down from level to level. Using hands and legs, we scampered through holes, across ledges, over slippery rocks. The cave was brightly illuminated by our headlamps. I found myself contemplating the likelihood that all of our headlamps would burn out at the same time, leaving us in the dark far belowground. With a group, the probability that all the headlamps would go out at the same time was infinitesimal. Or not, I reckoned. If all the batteries had been changed at the same time, they might also burn out at the same time. This is what people who write statistics books think about when they are deep underground in an Amazonian cave.

Down we went, through small holes and across narrow ledges, until we eventually reached the underground river. We paused on a beach of small pebbles that sloped gently down to the water. "We're going to swim, so leave any unnecessary clothing here," Kevin instructed. We stripped away shirts and pants and laid them on the bank. This moment threw one of CJ's personality quirks into sharp relief: he has an obsession with keeping his clothes clean. We had not known this before we left on the trip. Now we were seven levels underground—where one rockslide could trap us forever—and CJ asked me with great concern, "If I lay my pants on the rocks, will it leave a stain?" I do not recall my exact answer, but I suspect that I was not as patient and understanding as I might have been.

We waded into the cool water. Soon it became deep enough to swim, which was much easier than the climbing we had done on the way down. The subterranean river was more peaceful than eerie, with our voices echoing off the cave walls. We swam for ten minutes or so and reached a gently sloped beach similar to the one where we had entered the water.

"This is the end," Kevin said proudly. As we rested on the beach, he suggested that we turn off our lights. The cave went black; we listened to the gentle sounds of the river.

Then we did it all in reverse, reclaiming our clothes along the way. Climbing up the slippery tunnels was easier than climbing down. At one point, Kevin stopped and began looking around with his headlamp. "Are we lost?" CJ whispered. I did not reprimand him for speaking, since he had vocalized what I was thinking. My mind raced: How long would it take Leah to send for help? How quickly would a search party find us? How long can the human body go without food? Could we catch fish in that river?

We began moving again: walking and climbing steadily upward. Eventually Tess, who was near the front of the group, yelled, "I see light!" We walked into the daylight, where Leah was waiting for us. "How was it?" she asked casually.

"Awesome!" Tess and Katrina offered.

"I was only scared once," CJ said, now that he was free to talk.

We returned to the river and headed back toward the lodge. As the boat approached a tough patch of rapids, Kevin mused aloud, "We've never done this stretch going downriver." Steering downriver is even harder than steering upriver, as the boat moves faster and can more easily get turned sideways. Kevin explained that the driver usually takes the boat to shore and walks it along the bank past the rapids. I looked downriver at the surging rapids: frothing water leaping around large boulders.

"I think we're going to try it this time," Kevin said.

We were all in life jackets, and we knew to float downriver feetfirst if we were dumped out of the boat. "I bet we make it nineteen out of twenty times," Kevin pronounced. I'm not sure where his data came from, but my statistical brain calculated that nineteen out of twenty means a five percent chance of getting thrown into a surging river.

The boat drifted along until we were just above the rapids. "Feetfirst if you end up in the water!" Leah reminded everyone.

"We'll be fine," Kevin said. The driver gunned the motor and

plunged into the churning water. Speed and confidence are essential:
The driver must pick a line through the rocks and stick to it, like a skier
traversing a steep field of moguls. The front of the boat rose sharply
as we climbed a wave; I found myself looking up at Leah and Tess in
the bow. Almost immediately, the boat pitched forward and they were
below me. The driver stared stoically forward as we raced past rocks on
the right, then the left.

It was over in a matter of seconds, and again we were floating along
with the meandering current. "That was great, huh?" Kevin said.

◈ ◈ ◈

Our time at the lodge fell into a routine: during the stretches when I was
not worried about dying, I felt deeply relaxed. I spent afternoons lounging in the hammock. It turns out the sun sets more quickly near the
equator. There was a ball of orange above the trees around six o'clock
that fell quickly below the horizon. Over breakfast on our third day,
Kevin offered us a choice between "a relaxing walk around the lodge"
or "a more rigorous hike."

"A relaxing walk," Leah answered immediately.

I agreed. No rapids, no caves, no slippery rocks. Yes, there would
still be poisonous snakes, but they would scurry away if we talked loudly
and banged our walking sticks.

Our "relaxing" hike started out leisurely enough. We walked
from the lodge up a gentle path, observing the abundance of fascinating insects and flowers—colors and shapes I had never imagined.
We stopped to take a group photo at the base of a tree so large that all
seven of us could pose shoulder to shoulder in front of the trunk. This
was exactly what we had ordered: a nice, easy hike that would get us
back to the lodge in time for lunch and an afternoon of reading in the
hammock. So, why was Kevin carrying a machete?

At some point we lost the path, or we got on the wrong path, or
something else happened that presented us, according to Kevin, with
"an opportunity to combine two hikes into one." As best as I could tell,
this was a politic way of saying that we were lost. We had little hope

of finding the trail by thrashing through the jungle, Kevin's machete notwithstanding. The safest and most direct route back was along a creek that ran down to the Abiseo River. From there, we would be able to walk along the riverbank back to the lodge.

But this was a creek, not a path. In some places, we were able to walk beside it. In others, the vegetation was so dense that we had to get into the creek and step carefully from rock to rock. Where there were no rocks, we waded through the water. Every step required concentration. We made slow but steady progress as Kevin hacked away at the branches blocking our path.

Suddenly Kevin slipped on a rock and fell backward, flinging the machete twenty feet into the air. It happened so fast that none of us was able to react, in part because it was hard to do anything quickly on the slippery rocks. The huge blade spun end over end, like in a low-budget kung fu movie, before falling harmlessly into a bush. We retrieved the machete and plodded on. As we stepped over a rotting log that had fallen across the creek, CJ grabbed my shoulder and pointed. It took a moment for my eyes to recognize what he was pointing at. Perched upside down on the underside of the log was a spider with a body that looked like an avocado. "Holy ████!" I exclaimed, having never seen a spider that size, even in a book or a zoo. "Is it poisonous?" I asked Kevin.

"That's a good question," he replied, as if I'd asked him if the New England Patriots were going to have a solid defense this season.

At one point, Leah steadied herself by grabbing onto to a large rock. "Move your hand," I told her firmly. We have spent enough time together in all kinds of circumstances that she moved her hand before asking any questions. I pointed at a bullet ant scrambling across the rock. Kevin and Maria had been pointing out these ants—roughly an inch long—on rocks and tree stumps since we arrived. The good news is that the bullet ant sting is not deadly. The bad news is that it is considered to be the most painful bite or sting of any insect on the planet. They are called "bullet ants" because the sting feels like a bullet is ripping through your body. A reporter for *Esquire* described the bite this way: "There were huge waves and crescendos of burning pain—a tsunami of pain coming out of my finger. The tsunami would crash as they do on the beach, then recede a little bit, then crash again. It wasn't just two or three of these waves. It continued for around twelve hours. Crash. Recede. Crash. It was absolutely excruciating."[*]

Our "relaxing hike" was beginning to approximate the ill-fated adventures described in *The Lost City of Z*. Because we had been gone much longer than expected, workers back at the lodge had sent search parties out in two different directions to look for us. Meanwhile, as we slashed and sloshed our way through the creek, CJ lamented loudly: "My pants are getting really muddy."

"You have to be ▮▮▮▮▮ kidding me," I said. This caused tension with Leah, as we have radically different approaches to dealing with CJ's complaints. My strategy of forcing him to be quiet had worked in the cave. Leah was more indulgent, which, to my mind, merely encouraged him to whine. "You have to admit that this is definitely not 'a leisurely hike around the lodge,'" Leah pointed out.

"Fine," I conceded, "but complaining isn't going to get us back any faster." At some point, my prescription sunglasses were knocked off my hat by a branch. By the time I realized they were gone, I had no hope of finding them.

Neither of the search parties found us. Eventually we emerged on the broad, rocky banks of the Abiseo River. Butterflies of every shape and size—neon-blue, green, yellow, red—swarmed around the ground. Even the rocks were intriguing. I took photos of patterns and colors that looked as if they had been designed as a mosaic. As we walked leisurely toward the lodge, Maria pointed to a patch of ground without any rocks on it. "Quicksand," she warned. As I stared in disbelief, she told us the story of how her brother Sander had become stuck in quicksand while walking in this area. He was alone and sank all the way to his arm-

---

[*] Noah Davis, "What It's Like to Get Stung by the World's Most Painful Insect," *Esquire*, August 17, 2015.

pits. He saved himself by laying his walking stick across the quicksand, which stopped him from sinking long enough for someone from the lodge to find and rescue him.

◈ ◈ ◈

Over our final breakfast at the lodge, Kevin proposed one last adventure. "How about kayaking on the river?" he asked. Leah kicked me under the table. There was no need for prodding, however, because I was thinking, *Good god, no!* Tess's time with us was nearing its end. We had enjoyed a lovely three weeks with her; now was no time to put that at risk. The adventure lodge had been the experience of a lifetime. *Declare victory and retreat.*

Before departing downriver, we posed in front of the boat for a group photo with Kevin, Maria, and Sander (the one who had nearly disappeared in quicksand). They are kind, charming people with a deep respect for this unique part of the world. I felt sad to be leaving—even as I looked out at the river and thought, *I am so happy we are not kayaking.*

◈ ◈ ◈

We arrived in the Lima airport with bags stuffed full of wet, dirty clothes. Anytime I unzipped my pack, a jungle stench wafted out. We put Tess on a plane to Florida, where she would meet her mother. She had been a delightful traveler: adventurous, easy, and fun. The rest of us continued on to our Airbnb apartment, where the family immediately fell to squabbling over whose clothes deserved priority in the washing machine. (CJ's pants did get very dirty.) After a good shower, each of us tended to our various rashes and insect bites. CJ removed a tick from the webbing between two of his toes. I posted our stories from the Amazon on the blog, along with photos of the snakes, spiders, bullet ants, butterflies, exotic plants, and beautiful flowers.

As I settled into a comfortable bed on that first night in Lima—with no risk of being knocked to the floor by a dive-bombing insect—I reflected on our only nighttime activity at the Abiseo Aventura Paradise. Several of the workers invited CJ and me to go fishing with them. We followed them down the path to the river, where they gave us some line with a baited hook at the end.

There is an art to tossing the hook into the river and letting the current wash it gently along the shallows. On my first toss, I snagged a rock. One of the workers waded into the water and untangled the line for me. CJ tried next; he got the hook caught on the rocks behind us. By then we had lost our bait, so we asked the men for more. I made another toss and hooked one of the workers' lines, which required more wading into the water to untangle.

The subsequent tosses were different only in the details. It was clear that CJ and I had a better chance of getting a pizza delivered to us on the bank of the river than we did of catching a fish. Still, the night was breathtakingly beautiful. As we stood on the bank of the Abiseo River with no light pollution and a brilliant night sky, we both saw a bright shooting star. "You have to make a wish," I told him.

I wished for a safe return from our travels.

Chapter 6

Things Go South in South America

I had been keeping a tally of travel-related events in the back of my journal: bus rides, countries visited, and so on. That night I added a new category, Complete Family Meltdown, which would henceforth be defined as three family members crying at the same time, or one adult and one child.

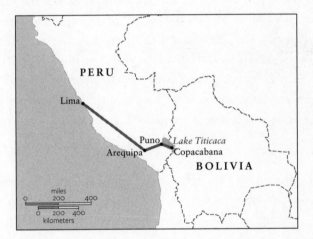

ONE OF MY FAVORITE PHOTOS from the trip is of CJ doing his schoolwork in a Lima café. It was midmorning, so the place was mostly empty. CJ was working by himself on a laptop by the window. The natural light cast a gentle glow on his solitary figure.

The fact that I took the photo from where I had opted to sit—on the other side of the café from CJ—offers some insight into our simmering introvert-extrovert conflict. CJ lost his chatter buddy when Tess returned home. As a raging extrovert, he processes the world out loud and is less comfortable in solitary activities, such as reading or keeping a journal. In contrast, I have kept a journal since I was seventeen. Katrina writes regularly in a journal. For both of us, it is a way of reflecting and processing one's thoughts.

At the beginning of the trip, I urged CJ to keep a journal, in part as a record but also as a writing exercise. This turned out to be inimical to his personality. Rather than using the daily writing as a way to decompress or to process experiences, CJ felt a need to record every detail. He was quickly overwhelmed. "What did I have for breakfast on Tuesday?" he would ask anxiously as the rest of us worked quietly. "Was that the day I had chicken empanadas? Did I have one or two? How much did they cost?" Whereas the introverts found solace in the journal, CJ found it stressful. Besides, as Katrina or I might point out sixteen hours into an eighteen-hour bus ride, CJ had already processed every single one of his thoughts out loud: "Is that a goat? Yes, it is a goat. Baby goats are really cute. Hey, guys, don't you think baby goats are really cute?"

We had now been on the road for a month. We had the travel part figured out. The family dynamics, however, were still a work in progress.

❖ ❖ ❖

While CJ did homework in the Lima café, Leah used the time to map out a route that would take us down the west coast of South America through Peru and into Bolivia. The plan was to spend a handful of days resting up in Lima, where we literally put salve on our wounds from the Amazon, and then head south to Arequipa, Peru's second largest city. There were two classes of travel on offer for that thousand-kilometer trip: the regular bus and the "VIP Coach." CJ was lobbying hard for VIP seats; the Budget Czar was skeptical. "They cost twice as much," Leah pointed out.

"Eighteen hours is a long time to be on a bus," I mused, feigning objectivity. "And it's overnight, so it saves us a night of lodging." The sybarites won a rare budget victory, and the "VIP Coach" lived up to its billing. The bus had two levels. We were in a compartment on the lower level with huge reclining seats and only a handful of other passengers. There were heavy velvet curtains on the windows, which made our little cabin feel more like a cozy salon or a garish private plane than an

Charlie, official trip photographer.

Leah and Charlie in Patagonia.

Katrina, making her views clear.

Sophie in Golden Bay, New Zealand.

CJ outside the Spanish Dancer Divers' hut in Zanzibar.

Katrina, CJ, and Sophie at the end of a short hike in New Zealand.

Road trip in New Zealand.

Geared up for the night dive on the Great Barrier Reef.

The vast openness of the Bolivian salt flats made for interesting images.

Charlie's idea for a photo in the Bolivian salt flats.

The "make it look like an album cover" photo on the road to Queenstown.

Selfie at Machu Picchu.

CJ's selfie with a lion.

A navigational dispute underwater. Only later would we realize that neither Leah nor Charlie could read the compass without glasses.

Sophie and friends at Janet's house in Dar es Salaam, Tanzania.

The trampoline on Janet's sweeping back lawn in Dar es Salaam, Tanzania, with the Indian Ocean in the background.

CJ welcomes a cold morning in Bhutan.

intercity bus. These long night bus rides had a number of advantages. First, they spared us a night of lodging, as I had deftly argued. Second, the darkness minimized our motion sickness. Finally, the time went by faster when we could sleep for six or eight hours. Still, eighteen hours is a long time to be on a bus, even one that feels like a salon.

Arequipa is a charming city, much smaller than Lima, with an archetypical plaza: a square with a fountain, gardens, and benches surrounded on four sides by government buildings, a towering colonial cathedral, and restaurants with outdoor tables. The weather was warm and sunny. On the first day, with the family still tired and cranky from the long bus ride, Leah offered up a crowd-pleaser. "Chocolate," she pronounced. "Here's what we're—"

"That sounds great," we interrupted in unison. She had us at "chocolate." One of the city's artisanal chocolate makers offered a class on how beans are transformed into bars. We had been fascinated by the chocolate business since we had seen the cacao trees on Maria's family farm. Scoop was still working on her crop substitution article. Also, we were certain that any class on making chocolate would involve eating it, too.

The four of us put on aprons and hairnets and perched at a marble counter where a charismatic guide led us through the chocolate-making process. We ground beans. We tasted different kinds of chocolate (milk, dark, etc.). We took quizzes, nibbling at chocolate chunks and trying to identify the cocoa content.* And then, of course, we made our own chocolate bars. Each of us selected a chocolate, poured it into candy molds, and added flourishes: nuts, dried fruit, wasabi, ground chili powder, and even coca leaves. We fashioned our bars with great care, each of us boasting about our unique combination of ingredients. "No one can eat mine," CJ declared.

"We all have our own," Leah assured him.

"So everyone agrees?" CJ asked.

"Yes, we heard you the first time," Katrina said.

---

* Cacao refers to the unroasted beans. Cocoa is the product of beans that have been roasted.

CJ continued, "I'm just saying, sometimes—"

"Enough," I said.

We did not appreciate the prescience of CJ's food-hoarding. It would be several days before we found ourselves in a famine-like situation.

◈ ◈ ◈

We were having a money problem in Peru. This was not a budget problem. Rather, we were literally having trouble getting money. Many businesses, such as our hostel, did not accept credit cards. We needed cash for most of our day-to-day expenses, but back in Lima a cash machine had eaten one of our ATM cards. At home, this is an easy problem to fix. The bank sends out a new card. While traveling, everything is more complicated, especially things involving access to finances. The bank would only send a replacement card to our home address. Sophie would bring that card with her, but in the meantime we had lost access to one of our checking accounts. The other account had a daily limit on ATM withdrawals. We needed more cash than usual because, in addition to our daily spending, I was stockpiling dollars to pay for our Bolivian visas: $160 per person, cash only.

The liquidity crisis came to a head at a delightful little crepe restaurant in Arequipa. I was short of Peruvian soles to pay the bill. The restaurant did not take credit cards, so the only option other than making a run for it was having Katrina withdraw cash from her personal account. We would reimburse the intrafamily loan once our liquidity crisis was over. Katrina agreed to this plan and set out to find an ATM machine. I stayed behind at the restaurant. Fifteen minutes passed, then half an hour. Arequipa is a tourist-friendly place, with ATMs all over the city. Katrina had been gone for a bizarrely long time; it was starting to feel like Medellín all over again.

After about forty-five minutes, my mild frustration grew into alarm. Eventually, I walked out into the street, at which point I saw Katrina striding past the crepe shop. I yelled, "Katrina!" loud enough to get her attention. And then, mostly out of relief, I exclaimed, "What happened?"

Katrina had become lost on the way back from the ATM—and probably would have walked past the restaurant again if I had not called out to her. She was angry at herself for getting lost, and angry at me for overreacting to the situation. She declared that I should have gotten my own money (I couldn't), or gone to the ATM myself with her card (I had offered). And then she added, "I'm eighteen years old and I can do whatever the hell I want!" One could quibble with the substance of that statement, and certainly with its relevance as we finally paid for the crepes, but Katrina's desire to be out from under her parents was plenty clear.

Meanwhile, Sophie was back home making *negative progress* on her schoolwork. How does one move backward in an academic class? If a student submits no work to a VLACS class for many weeks—not even one single quiz or discussion question—the system will automatically deny further access to the course. Once a student is "frozen out," he or she must provide some explanation to the supervising teacher in order to regain access. In other words, it takes extra work just to begin doing work again.

"I got this," Sophie insisted when we spoke to her from Arequipa. This phrase sent chills down our parental spines, as it typically signaled the opposite. For example, there was the time I spotted Sophie wheeling my bicycle out of the garage because she was late for school and did not have time to walk. I yelled from the porch, "Lock it!"

"I got this!" she replied jauntily as she rode off (without a helmet).

The bicycle was stolen that afternoon.

Leah and I could not make Sophie do VLACS from South America. We had tried bribery. We had tried threats. We had tried imploring her to think about her future. Every new strategy felt like pushing a stone with a wet noodle. To the extent there *was* good news, it was that Sophie sounded delightfully happy when we spoke to her, regaling us with stories of homecoming and other fun activities with her friends. Apparently if you take the "school" out of high school, what's left is loads of fun.

Leah and I made a strategic decision: We would give up on VLACS for the time being. We reckoned that once Sophie joined us in November, we could supervise her directly. That would leave her plenty of time to finish her classes.

❖ ❖ ❖

On our third night in Arequipa, I opted to dine on my own. I went out to a very nice restaurant for ceviche, a local specialty. The rest of the family does not like ceviche. Also, sometimes when I feel like I need time to myself, the rest of the family feels the same way. I went on Trip-Advisor and found the most highly recommended seafood restaurant in Arequipa. How did I manage to fit that in the budget? I used my "fun money," which is an accounting gimmick Leah and I invented twenty-five years earlier when we went on our first low-budget adventure. We recognized that it would be a tragedy to get to some distant part of the world and forgo a unique local activity, such as scuba diving on the Great Barrier Reef, for lack of seventy-five dollars. The solution was to give each of us a fixed amount of "fun money" over the course of the trip. We reprised the idea for our family trip: five hundred dollars per person. Every time one of us made a fun money purchase, we declared it to Leah, who kept track of our declining balances. In Arequipa, I used fun money to order ceviche, shrimp soup, and several glasses of Argentine wine. I enjoyed this delicious meal while reading the *Economist* and writing in my journal.

The next morning I awoke earlier than the rest of the family, as had become the pattern. Our hostel offered a simple breakfast on an outdoor patio: coffee, bread, juice, and cornflakes. On a whim, I opened up a file on my computer that I had not looked at in six years. It was a novel called *The Rationing*. There were forty pages or so, which I read over my coffee. *This is not terrible*, I concluded. I had been feeling the urge to write. Perhaps dusting off the novel would satisfy my writing urge while giving me a fun way to enjoy the morning solitude.

That was to be the last such solitude for some time. We had signed up for a hike to the bottom of Colca Canyon, a giant fissure running through the Andes nearly twice as deep as the Grand Canyon. The adventure began with a bus pickup from our hostel at three-thirty the next morning. We stopped at a small restaurant for breakfast—still before dawn—where our group sat shivering at a long table. The waiters brought coffee and tea and a small basket of rolls. We nibbled on the bread while awaiting more substantive food. As I wondered hungrily what might be coming out of the kitchen next to sustain us for our day of hiking, our guide declared, "Okay, back on the bus." Apparently we had just eaten breakfast: bread, butter, and jam. Meanwhile, CJ had developed a bad head cold; he was snorting and coughing and could not breathe through his nose.

If our hike were televised to a live audience, the color commentators would have pointed out that Team Wheelan was not starting the day in peak form.

> **Commentator One:** "They look tired and cranky to me, Bob."
> **Commentator Two:** "That's right, Nadine. Also, sick and hungry."
> **Commentator One:** "Are they really prepared to hike down one of the deepest canyons in the world?"
> **Commentator Two:** "I think that's what we're about to find out."

❖ ❖ ❖

Before the descent, we paused on the rim of the canyon to look for Andean condors, the largest flying bird in the world. The sun came up, casting a soft glow on the rocky precipices where the condors build their nests. The sunrise over the canyon was a reasonable payoff for getting out of bed in the dark and cold. And then the condors began soaring in front of us: first one, then two, and then many. Imagine bald eagles floating over the Grand Canyon. I perched on a rock and did my best to take photos that did justice to the condors, the sunrise, and Colca Canyon.

We began hiking down a narrow path cut into the side of the canyon. The altitude would have made the hiking rigorous under any conditions. CJ was doing it without being able to breathe through his nose, pausing every so often to rest on a rock. After a long morning, our group stopped for lunch: a half bowl of soup and a small serving of alpaca stir-fry, both of which were good. I eagerly awaited the next course. "Back to the trail," the guide announced.

"Can I get some more alpaca?" I asked.

"It's time to walk," the guide said.

"Maybe more soup?" I pleaded, as if I were in the hiking equivalent of a Charles Dickens novel.

"We go to the trail," he commanded.

Back to the trail it was. CJ had squirreled away his chocolate bars from our class in his pack. When we stopped for a break, he sat on a rock and ate one greedily, pausing between mouthfuls of chocolate to breathe through his mouth. The rest of us stared at him like jackals. Around sunset, the expedition reached the bottom of the canyon, where we would spend the night in rustic cabins arrayed around a spring-fed swimming pool. Most important, there would be dinner.

"Is there a vegetarian in the group?" the waiter asked as we crowded around an outdoor table. Katrina raised her hand. This seemed like a courteous thing to ask. In fact, it meant that none of us would get any meat. Those scraps of alpaca at lunch now felt like luxury. I devoured a plate of vegetables and rice. Still ravenous, I asked the waiter, "Can I get some more vegetables?"

"I'm sorry, no," he replied.

"How about an extra tea bag?" I implored.

"Of course," he agreed. *Finally, a small victory.* But then he never brought it.

❖ ❖ ❖

The alarm on my phone awoke us the next morning at four a.m. I have no recollection of getting any breakfast. We began hiking in the dark using our headlamps. The route out of the canyon was steeper than the descent. CJ paused around sunrise to eat the last of his chocolate bars. Again, the family looked on hungrily as he ate. "This is good," Katrina said. "We can fatten him up—like the Donner Party."

"What are they talking about?" CJ asked suspiciously. "A dinner party?"

"*Donner* Party," Katrina said.

"You're vegetarian," I said.

She shrugged. "Sometimes I make exceptions."

"What's the Donner Party?" CJ asked.

"I'll explain while we walk," Leah said.

Team Wheelan summited Colca Canyon around nine in the morning. A woman was selling snacks off a blanket laid on the ground. Leah
authorized us to spend most of that day's food budget on Snickers bars,
after which we basked in the warmth of the sun, enjoying the endorphins
from the hike and the sugar high from the candy bars. CJ had been heroic
as he struggled to breathe. The hike was beautiful. "It would have been
fine if there had been enough food," Leah remarked as we got on the bus.

"The same could be said for the siege of Leningrad," I replied. CJ
chuckled. Leah ignored me. Katrina told me I was an idiot. And Colca
Canyon entered the Wheelan family vernacular as a synonym for something at risk of going terribly awry. To this day, CJ will assess a situation
and warn, "Oh no, it's Colca Canyon!"

❖ ❖ ❖

And then another early morning, this time to catch a bus to the city of
Puno on the banks of Lake Titicaca. An enterprising company, Peru
Hop, sold us bus passes for a fixed price that allowed unlimited travel
for two weeks along their routes. We used our passes to head west in
Peru toward Lake Titicaca, one of South America's biggest lakes and the
world's highest navigable body of water. If this were a film, one might
cue the ominous music here: lingering fatigue from Colca Canyon . . .
multiple early mornings in a row . . . no rest day for a week. Also, the
rest of us had caught CJ's cold.

Puno is home of the legendary "floating islands." As the name would
suggest, these are man-made islands constructed of tightly thatched
reeds that float in Lake Titicaca. During the Inca Empire, the float-

ing islands were a clever way to survive. The inhabitants could feed themselves by fishing; if necessary, they could float the whole village to a new location. As an economist, I would argue that living on a man-made floating island in the twenty-first century is less practical. A boat dropped us off on an island the size of a football field. Several women urged us to buy souvenirs. Saying no to their handicrafts was more difficult than usual, as we were stuck on the island until the boat came back to pick us up.

I will admit that the engineering of the islands was impressive. Still, the overall experience felt like Colonial Williamsburg: an exhibition of how people used to live. In the present day, the only way people can survive on a floating island is if tourists pay to watch them live that way. We were not observing a unique culture; we were making it possible, like performance art.

That evening Katrina and I, the introverts, went to a café for a glass of wine and to write in our journals. On the walk home, we came across a concert in the central plaza. An orchestra was playing in front of a beautiful church with the moon rising behind. The central plaza was alive: families, couples, food vendors. We bought food, listened to the music, and admired the physical splendor of the moon hovering over the church and the aliveness of the plaza. The serendipitous public concert was the opposite of the floating islands: one showed us something about life in Peru five hundred years ago; the other was a charming snapshot of Puno in that moment.

That evening also gave us our first glimpse of what happens to Katrina when she gets tipsy. Katrina is wispy thin, and Puno is thirteen thousand feet above sea level. One glass of wine went straight to her head. When we arrived back at the hotel room, Katrina was abnormally chatty. She began making loud, emphatic assertions about the Ottoman Empire and other historical periods. The rest of us looked at each other in amusement as she pronounced, "Alexander the Great, really? What was so great about him?"

Some people get happy when they are buzzed. Others get mean, or funny, or weepy. Katrina becomes a truculent nerd.

❖ ❖ ❖

The next morning, the bus dropped us at the Peru-Bolivia border. As we were walking to a small hut where we would get our Bolivian visas, Katrina declared, "CJ is not allowed to sit within five rows of me on any bus ride for the rest of the trip."

"You can't do that!" CJ howled.

"You do talk a lot on the bus," I told CJ, trying to sound reasonable, but really taking the side of my fellow introvert.

"Let's just get across the border," Leah admonished, like a diplomat trying to hold a delicate peace process together. As we waited in line outside the small immigration building, Leah informed me that we were now over budget because of the Bolivian visas and the Peru Hop bus tickets; we would have to be more frugal in the coming weeks.

The Bolivian visa required a prodigious amount of paperwork: forms; photos; multiple copies of all our passports; and proof of onward travel. We had a small problem with that last one. If a scrupulous bureaucrat scrutinized our paperwork, he would find a problem with our proof of onward travel. We had no tickets out of Bolivia—only the airline tickets from Ecuador to New Zealand.

"We're missing something for our visas!" CJ said, loud enough to be heard in both Peru and Bolivia.

"*Shut your mouth*," I snarled. "Do not say *anything to anybody* until we are in Bolivia."

"What if they ask me a question?" CJ asked earnestly.

"You're not going to understand it anyway," Katrina offered. It was a perfect opportunity to appear helpful while really just criticizing CJ's poor Spanish.

"What if it's in English?" CJ asked.

"Pretend you don't speak English," I said impatiently.

"That doesn't make any sense," CJ protested. "Why wouldn't I speak English if my family is American—"

"CJ," Leah implored, "let us handle this."

A bored-looking immigration official counted our cash multiple times and then threw the paperwork into a cardboard box without looking at it. There were no questions about onward travel.

On the Bolivian side of the border, CJ stopped in front of a food stall and inspected the items for sale. "I'm hungry," he said. "Can I buy some Pringles?" This was a Western brand in a proper container that cost three dollars, not the homemade chips that cost twenty cents.

"He didn't eat his breakfast," Katrina muttered under her breath. I was thinking the same thing. CJ had eaten only half his eggs at breakfast that morning. He and Tess (now at home) had a habit of leaving food uneaten at breakfast and then complaining of being hungry around ten-thirty. Now that we had been put on budget watch, a three-dollar canister of Pringles felt like an extravagance.

Leah bought CJ the Pringles.

We walked into the Bolivian town of Copacabana, hoping that a few hours of fast Internet would improve the collective mood. Every establishment up and down the main street advertised free Wi-Fi, but as we walked from one café to the next, none of them had a strong enough signal to get our devices online. CJ was eating his Pringles; the rest of us were getting hungrier. Eventually a waiter at one of the restaurants admitted, "The Internet doesn't really work anywhere in this town."

We decided to have lunch. Leah reminded us to be cognizant of the budget. Katrina and I stared at CJ, who was licking the salt off his fingers. "Why did you let him buy the Pringles?" I asked Leah.

Like the assassination of Archduke Ferdinand, the Pringles purchase quickly exposed other fault lines. We were still tired from Colca Canyon. The Internet wasn't working. The introverts found CJ's talking to be insufferable; CJ felt that Katrina and I were being mean to him. Leah, a middle child and the peacemaker in our family, defended CJ and then felt ganged up on for doing so. Katrina and I argued that when Leah defended CJ, she abetted his annoying behavior.

When the waiter came to our table to offer us menus, we were all yelling at each other. "I will come back in a moment," he said in Spanish.

"How do you think CJ feels when you tell him that you won't sit near him on a bus?" Leah asked Katrina.

"Bad," Katrina said, her eyes welling up with tears.

"It does make me feel bad," CJ blubbered.

Leah turned to CJ. "Do you understand why Katrina finds it hard to sit next to you on the bus?" she asked.

"Sometimes I can't help talking," he said, tears streaming down his face.

Leah, still channeling her inner Oprah, looked at Katrina and me: "How do you think it makes me feel when the two of you don't want to be with the rest of us?" Katrina and I apologized. When the waiter reappeared, we were all crying.

The lunch discussion cleared the air. Sleep, a slower pace, and good Internet would help, too. Mostly, however, we had to adapt to who we all were. CJ was not going to stop talking, but he would have to become more aware of others around him. Katrina and I needed quiet time. I resolved to work on the novel every day, mostly as a solitary morning ritual. Leah would continue to hold all this together, like the conductor of a needy symphony orchestra.

I had been keeping a tally of travel-related events in the back of my journal: bus rides, countries visited, and so on. That night I added a new category, Complete Family Meltdown, which would henceforth be defined as three family members crying at the same time, or one adult and one child.

Chapter 7

Inspired by Real Events

If I were in a place with a top-notch criminal justice system, I would have called the police myself, or even grabbed the guy by the lapels and told him to walk away. Uyuni, Bolivia, is not such a place.

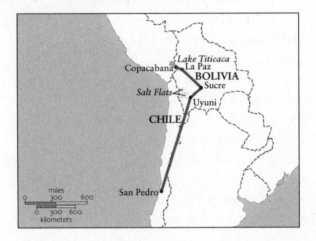

"WHAT'S THE WORST THAT COULD HAPPEN?" Leah asked. She had just Googled: WHAT HAPPENS WHEN CHILDREN INGEST POT? CJ, abnormally quiet, was sitting beside her. The two of them had just returned from a long walk in La Paz, Bolivia. Along the way, they had stopped at an organic farmers' market where there were free brownies on offer at one of the stands. CJ had helped himself. As he was wiping crumbs off his face, however, Leah noticed a large marijuana leaf displayed behind the table with the brownies. They hustled back to our apartment, where CJ's behavior seemed normal, or at least no more aberrant than the Dramamine incident in Peru.

"You didn't ask the guy at the stand if there was pot in the brownies?" I asked.

"CJ had already eaten the brownie. It either had pot in it or it didn't," Leah explained. "I wasn't going to pump his stomach at the farmers' market." She turned back to her computer. "Wow," she exclaimed as she read the online posts. "Lots of kids eat their parents' pot brownies."

"He'll talk less if he's stoned," Katrina offered.

"We're not buying him Pringles if he gets the munchies," I said.

"I'm fine," CJ insisted. "Everything is fine."

"That's exactly what a stoned person would say," I pointed out.

"I like him better this way," Katrina said.

We never found out for certain what was in the brownies. Whatever CJ had ingested, he was back to his voluble self soon enough, and La Paz would prove calming and restful, even without special brownies for the rest of us.

❖ ❖ ❖

We had made our way to La Paz after the family meltdown in Copacabana. Once all the crying had stopped, we took the Peru Hop bus for the four-hour ride along the southern shore of Lake Titicaca. It was late afternoon and clouds had settled over the lake; the jagged peaks of the Andes jutted above the clouds. There was virtually no development, just mile after mile of stark, barren beauty, especially at dusk when the setting sun cast a golden light on the lake, clouds, and mountains. After dark, the bus stopped in a small market town to make the crossing to the north side of the lake.

There was no bridge. Instead, the passengers disembarked while the bus was driven onto a barge and floated across the lake at a point where it narrowed to about a half mile. The passengers were packed into a dilapidated motorboat that sank lower and lower in the water as we climbed in. "Sit there," the driver said in Spanish as he pointed to bench seats on either side of the boat. That turned out to be the complete safety briefing as well. My head was only slightly above the waterline as we puttered to the other side.

We reboarded the bus and continued on. Bolivia was noticeably poorer than Peru. On the outskirts of La Paz, a fierce wind was blowing dust through wide, empty streets. We could see buildings with lights on, but no human inhabitants. The blowing sand shrouded everything in what looked like fog or smoke, making the little towns we drove through feel like the setting for a postapocalyptic film. Eventually La Paz came into view: points of light spilling down the side of a mountain, as if someone had draped Christmas tree lights across the Andes.

Our Airbnb apartment was in an upscale residential neighborhood across from a small park. La Paz is ten thousand feet above sea level, with steep streets; the uphill walks left us short of breath. The huffing and puffing notwithstanding, we quickly found places to do laundry and buy groceries. CJ and I ate cheap noodles at a food court on the second floor of a grocery store, which struck me as a fun snapshot of globalization: two Americans eating Chinese food in a Bolivian food court. The measure of the charm of our Bolivian neighborhood was how quickly we adopted possessive pronouns: "our apartment"; "our park"; "our grocery store"; "my café." The weather was sunny and warm, and the city was easy to explore on foot. We used the strong Internet in our apartment and FaceTime to have a video chat with my parents (once they pointed the camera on my father's phone in the right direction). I marveled that we could communicate visually across continents at no cost using a technology I had first seen on Star Trek. Most important, just a few days after the first Complete Family Meltdown, I was able to write in my journal, "The healing has begun."

Many of the storefronts in our neighborhood were advertising a concert that evening at the convention center. The orchestra would be playing music from *Star Wars*. The fact that we were reading flyers in store windows speaks to our improving Spanish and our connectedness to the neighborhood. The concert seemed like a fun thing to do. Tickets were not available online, so Leah and CJ volunteered to find the ticket office. (The pot brownie incident happened near the end of this otherwise successful walk.)

That night we made our way to the convention center. The concert hall was large and modern; the orchestra was warming up as we found our seats. For the first time in South America, we felt mildly out of place—not because we were four gringos at a concert in Bolivia, but because none of us was dressed as a *Star Wars* character. The hall was packed with families, many of whom had small children in costume. The orchestra played various pieces from the John Williams score while scenes from the Star Wars films were projected on side panels. Adults dressed as various *Star Wars* characters paraded around the stage. After the show, young kids lined up to have their photos taken with cast members. "Let's go take your picture with Jar Jar Binks," I urged CJ.

"Dad, I'm like three times as old as those kids."

"You love *Star Wars*." (True.)

I prevailed. CJ waited in line with the small children, many of whom stared up at the tall blond kid in their midst. "Don't tell them you're a marijuana user," I whispered to CJ. "They'll be very disappointed."

◈ ◈ ◈

Scoop was working on another story. La Paz has installed cable cars as a form of public transit; the cars, which look like ski gondolas, transport people by carrying them *over* the city. Cable cars are faster than buses because they can glide over traffic; they are cheaper to build than train lines because there is no need to lay tracks through densely developed neighborhoods. From a transit standpoint, the cable cars are like a bus or a train: one buys a ticket, waits in line, and then gets on the gondola when it swings through the station. Near the end of our stay in La Paz, we walked up a steep hill—steep even compared to all the other steep hills—to a cable car station. Scoop interviewed some passengers in line about how the cable cars serve neighborhoods that had that previously been cut off from the economic heart of the city. Medellín, Colombia, had also recently installed a cable car for the same purpose: connecting poor neighborhoods isolated by the mountains to parts of the city with more jobs and opportunity. Scoop loved the irony: a technology that had served wealthy skiers at mountain resorts for decades was now a poverty-fighting tool.

And then we climbed on board. The gondola gave us a bird's-eye view of La Paz as we glided over schoolyards and playgrounds and bustling streets. Our aerial tour felt almost voyeuristic as we watched people hanging laundry on rooftops or lounging in courtyards shielded from the street by high walls. From above, we could appreciate the activity, complexity, and interconnectedness of a modern city, as if we were observing the human equivalent of an ant farm.

Our travel goal at this point was the Bolivian salt flats. The city of Sucre was the next stop as we headed south and west across the country. Once again, we opted for an overnight bus, but this time Bolivia threw us a curveball. The bathrooms on Bolivian buses are always locked. The drivers are responsible for cleaning the bathrooms on their buses. Predictably—I write nonfiction books about the power of incentives— the drivers minimize their work by keeping the bathrooms locked, even on a ten- or twelve-hour trip. *There is no need to clean a bathroom that no one has used.* Instead, passengers who need to relieve themselves must ask the driver to pull the bus over to the side of the road. Leah, Katrina, and I felt self-conscious about stopping the bus to accommodate our bladders; a cranky driver might ignore the request. We chose to squirm uncomfortably in our seats until we discovered our secret weapon: CJ, the raging gringo extrovert. His Spanish was the worst among us, but he was the most eager to put it to use.

"Please tell the driver to stop," Katrina asked CJ. She does not like speaking to strangers, in English or Spanish, and was still finding that she had to work up her courage to do her *Valley News* interviews. Asking a bus driver to stop the bus so she could pee on the side of the road was beyond the pale.

"So *now* you're happy to be on the bus with me?" CJ replied.

"The pot brownies have made you much easier to be around," she said.

CJ shook his head with disapproval. Like a clerk in the bowels of a bureaucracy who suddenly finds himself in possession of an important document, a petty despot was born. "We'll be in Sucre in six hours," CJ said with faux-sympathy.

"Come on, CJ, please," Katrina pleaded.

"I'll see what I can do," CJ said. He walked to the front of the bus and asked confidently in Spanish, "Make urine on the road together?" The driver cackled at his execrable Spanish and dutifully pulled over, at which point the rest of us followed him off to "make urine."

In Sucre, for fourteen dollars a night (more good budget news) we rented two little rooms that had formerly been a doctor's office. Our tiny rooms were attached to a home, where our host lived. Sucre reminded us that spring was unfolding in the southern hemisphere, even as the days became shorter and colder back home. On our first afternoon, Katrina and I ended up separated from the others. The weather was perfect, so we decided to walk the two miles from the center of the city back to our little doctor's-office apartment. The jacaranda trees were in full bloom, creating explosions of purple all along our route. Other flowers were in bloom, too, making everything more attractive. Even the high brick walls topped with broken glass, a common security feature in South American cities, looked beautiful with red and yellow flowers spilling over them.

Perhaps Katrina and I were hungry, or maybe we were just fascinated by the impressive baked goods on display along our route. In any event, we made it our personal challenge to buy every kind of attractive street food we encountered: an enormous chocolate donut, then fresh-made potato chips, then popcorn—walk, eat, walk, eat—like two schoolkids who found ten dollars on the playground and decided to spend it all on the walk home. We laughed at our devilry when we weren't chewing. The food was so cheap that we only fibbed modestly when we reported our expenses to Leah.

I dropped off laundry at a storefront shop that would wash, dry, and fold our clothes for about a dollar per kilogram. At that price, we could afford to launder just about everything we were carrying. The proprietress told me to pick up our kilos of clothing the following afternoon. But when I showed up at the designated time, the place was shuttered. It was the middle of business hours, yet no one responded when I banged on the locked door. I lingered for fifteen minutes. There was still no sign of activity. We were leaving on a bus early the following morning. A high proportion of our wardrobe was locked inside, and this was the rare time when our itinerary did not have any slack built in.

The options were not good: we could leave Sucre without most of our clothes, or we could stay an extra day and miss the departure for a tour we had booked in the Bolivian salt flats. Leah began doing an accounting of which would be more expensive, buying a new wardrobe or losing the deposit on the tour. Our Airbnb hostess was a friendly woman who had stopped by to introduce herself when we arrived. I knocked on her door in the hope that she could offer up a more attractive option. "All of our clothes are at the laundry and it's closed," I explained, pointing to my watch to suggest that businesses should not be closed in the middle of the afternoon on a weekday. "We're leaving in the morning—"

"The game," she said with a laugh that suggested a naïveté in my question. I stared blankly at her, as if she had said "the wizard" or "the force." She explained that Bolivia was playing Ecuador in the qualifier for the World Cup. We turned on the television in our room and watched as Bolivia gave up a goal in the eighty-eighth minute for a tie. Sure enough, I returned to the laundry place a few minutes after the game ended and the owner was opening up again. She happily returned my laundry while complaining that Bolivia had let victory slip away.

◈ ◈ ◈

Our tour of the Bolivian salt flats left from Uyuni, a cold, windswept city that feels like the Bolivian Wild West. Uyuni exists mostly as a tourist launching point for the salt flats.

The streets are unpaved and comically wide. Fierce winds blow dust and dirt everywhere, even blotting out the sun at times. There is little vegetation; most of the buildings are drab cement structures. The whole place looked like it had been painted a color Benjamin Moore might euphemistically call "Wet Sand." I became persuaded that I could taste the dirt in my food.

We stayed in a room in a hostel that felt like a white-collar prison:

four beds lined up in a room with a linoleum floor and undecorated plaster walls. There was an overpowering chemical smell—some combination of smoke and cheap cleaning products. "That can't be healthy," Leah said as she inhaled through her nose. Katrina opened the window.

"It's forty degrees outside," I said.

"Would you rather be cold or die in your sleep?" Katrina asked. We opted to keep the window open, even as dust blew in and the temperature dropped near freezing.

Leah had sent e-mail queries to several tour providers asking about prices, availability, and other information for a multi-day tour of the salt flats. Only one tour provider responded while we were in Sucre. This outfitter had excellent reviews on TripAdvisor, so we booked the tour. When we got off the overnight bus in Uyuni, Leah picked up an e-mail from a different tour operator saying that he was holding four spots for us. We had never committed to book with this company; in fact, we did not know what their price for the expedition would be. Also, it had taken the company two days to reply to our e-mail inquiry, which is never a good sign in a service business. As a courtesy, we stopped by their office to tell them that we would not be joining their tour. The proprietor became belligerent and insisted that we owed him money.

"That's ridiculous," I said, and walked out. There is no legal code on the planet, not even in Bolivia, in which an inquiry about price and availability obligates one to sign up for a tour, especially when there is no reply for two days. But that was when things took a Wild West turn: The proprietor followed us out of the office and down the street, insisting that we go to the tourist police with him. The facts were on our side, but in terms of institutions I had faith in, the Uyuni tourist police did not rank up there with the FBI. The man was short and squat—not physically intimidating—but he was acting unhinged.

We walked to the end of a street with a series of small shops. He followed us. We turned and walked back on the other side of the street. "Is he still behind us?" I asked Leah. She looked quickly over her shoulder. "Yep."

If I were in a place with a top-notch criminal justice system, I would have called the police myself, or even grabbed the guy by the lapels and told him to walk away. Uyuni, Bolivia, is not such a place. We could not go back to our hostel, or he would know where we were staying. We ducked into a mini–grocery store and told the owners that the man standing outside was harassing us. There was not much of a response, probably because our Spanish was not good enough to explain this modestly complicated situation. While we were hiding inside, Leah and I began ogling the well-stocked shelves. Colca Canyon had left us with a famine mentality. As we hid from our Bolivian stalker, we bought as much junk food as we could stuff into our bags: cookies, crackers, potato chips, candy bars. No one would be pleading for extra soup in the salt flats.

The man was still waiting for us when we walked out. He continued yelling angrily that he was going to take us to the tourist police. In the Hollywood film version of our trip ("inspired by real events"), this situation could go a lot of interesting directions. Maybe I would walk out of the convenience store, apply a karate chop to a thick tree limb, cracking it in half. Then I would growl at the menacing tour operator: "Te sientes afortunado?" (Are you feeling lucky?) Or perhaps I would agree to go to the tourist police, where I would give a compelling explanation of the unanswered e-mail, and then, inspired by Jack Nicholson in *A Few Good Men*, I would challenge the tour operator, "*No puedes manejar la verdad!*" (You can't handle the truth!) What actually happened was more pedestrian—in both senses of the word. We walked around, ducking into various shops, until finally we came out and he was no longer waiting for us.

The next morning, we climbed into a Land Cruiser with our driver and guide, Marcus. We strapped our junk-food-laden luggage on the roof and drove into a salt desert the size of Belgium. We made our own path across a flat, white expanse, as if we were crossing a huge snow-covered lake. There was a ring of mountains far in the distance, including a volcano. Occasionally we would pass an "island," an outcropping of rocks and trees that rose up from the salt flat. The salt looked so much like ice that I expected to see ice-fishing huts. My brain kept warning me that our SUV might break through a hole and plunge into the depths below.

Marcus, who was a photo enthusiast, showed us how the white, endless background made it possible to take bizarre photos. He sat Leah and me on the ground, each of us with one hand stretched out flat to the side, and had Katrina and CJ stand twenty yards behind us. The photo looked as if Katrina and CJ were miniature people standing on our hands. Even the music was good. Marcus played a retro playlist from the seventies and eighties, which gave us a surreal soundtrack as we cruised across the flat white salt desert.

We spent the night in a salt lodge—a building literally constructed from salt: salt bricks for walls and salt pebbles on the floor. The white hue and the frigid temperature made it feel like we were in a large snow fort. The food was good and plentiful, rendering all our junk food unnecessary. In the morning, Marcus drove us eastward from the salt flats into a different kind of desert, more like the American Southwest. Occasionally we passed through green fields crisscrossed with streams running out of the mountains; often there were llamas grazing in these grassy areas. As we passed through one field full of llamas, CJ exclaimed, "Can we stop here and walk into the pasture?"

"It's going to be wet and full of llama poop," Marcus answered.

"That's okay," CJ assured him. "I need a selfie with a llama."

"If you step in llama shit, you're not getting back in the jeep," Katrina warned.

Five minutes later, CJ came trundling back to the Land Cruiser. "Check it out!" he said, waving the image on his iPod: CJ smiling broadly next to a llama staring bemusedly into the camera. (CJ's effort to take a selfie with a lion will be discussed in Chapter 15.)

❖ ❖ ❖

As we continued along, the vegetation gradually disappeared until there was not even the occasional cactus or scrub brush. CJ exclaimed repeatedly, "This is just like Mars!" It was unclear where CJ's Mars experience had come from, but we agreed that the terrain was unlike anything we had seen on Earth. There were vast open expanses with strange-colored lakes, curious shades of reds and greens and pinks, as if a young child had decided to color the landscape with the crayons that don't often get taken out of the box: "green tomato" and "cotton candy" and "pomegranate." Just when the colors could not get any more incongruous, we came across a large flock of flamingos gathered on a red lake, adding bright pink and watermelon-red to the palette.

We finished the second day at a bizarre field of geysers, with boiling gray mud and steam shooting out of gaps in the earth, as if we had stepped onto the set of a *Star Wars* film. CJ posed for a photo in front of a huge cloud of steam spewing from the ground. He bent over and positioned himself so that the photo made it look like the stream of gas was shooting from his rear end. This was my idea.

We had been steadily gaining altitude. La Paz was at ten thousand feet; Uyuni was at twelve thousand feet. The lodge where we would spend the night was at over fifteen thousand feet—nearly three miles above sea level. We enjoyed a glorious sunset over one of the red-hued lakes, mountains in the background. The lodge had electricity and bathrooms but no heat. After sunset, the temperature began to fall about ten degrees an hour. Our strategy for the cold was to sleep in our clothes. I took off my shoes, put on a hat, and climbed into a sleeping bag, which I then covered with layers of blankets. Eventually my shivering gave way to sleep, but then the altitude presented a different challenge. I woke up three times to go to the bathroom, stumbling through the dark and cold each time.[*] On the positive side, I was cured forever of any urge to climb Mount Everest.

The trek finished with a drive through a tableau that looked like a Salvador Dalí painting: misshapen boulders the size of small houses; curious shadows cast on the sand and rock; more lonely colors from

---

[*] One of the body's responses to altitude is to produce more red blood cells to increase the oxygen-carrying capacity of the blood. To make room for the extra cells, the body dumps fluid. The biology is remarkable—and inconvenient when one would prefer not to make repeated trips to the bathroom in the cold and dark.

the crayon box. We bade farewell to Marcus and paid our export tax to leave Bolivia—because the $160 visa fee we had paid on arrival was apparently not enough. After walking across the border into Chile, we caught a bus to the small town of San Pedro. The roads were noticeably better in Chile, which was a mixed blessing. I found myself nostalgic for giant potholes—nature's speed bumps—as our bus barreled at a crazy speed downhill out of the mountains. The driver crossed himself every time he swerved into the opposite lane to overtake a car or another bus.

In San Pedro, we had a nice meal at a restaurant with good Internet, which we all seized on ravenously. When I checked e-mail, I learned that I had sold the Czech-language rights for one of my books. When a book is published in a foreign language, the foreign publisher typically pays an advance against royalties for the books that will be sold in that language. Czechoslovakia is a small country; the advance the publisher had offered was correspondingly small—but still an unexpected windfall. "I can add this to my fun money," I declared.

"No," Leah said without looking up from her menu.

"That would be ridiculous," Katrina agreed.

"What if I gave you half?" I asked Katrina.

"Are you trying to bribe me?" she asked sanctimoniously.

"Yes," I clarified.

"Absolutely not!" she declared.

I called for a family vote to overturn Leah's budget decision. It went against me, three-to-one. However, Leah did authorize me to order "poor man's steak," which is a Chilean specialty: sirloin steak smothered with sautéed onions and french fries, all topped with a fried egg. I was happy with the compromise.

Chapter 8

To the End of the Earth (Almost)

Patagonia was the place that inspired me to figure out the panorama feature on my iPhone.

OUR BUS WAS STOPPED at a small checkpoint on the highway. Two security officials came on board. We were somewhere in southern Argentina, a country that stretches for more than two thousand miles north to south. We had passed the midpoint of South America and were headed in the direction of Ushuaia, Argentina, at the very tip of the continent. I do not know exactly where we were, as we had been on the bus for hours. Nor do I know why our bus was stopped; perhaps we were crossing some internal border, from one Argentine province to another. One of the officials walked slowly down the aisle, doing a cursory check of the cabin. Meanwhile, a dog and handler were inspecting our bags in the cargo hold below. I was listening to a podcast: Terry Gross was interviewing Bruce Springsteen on *Fresh Air*.

A few minutes later, a different official came on board and asked for the owner of a bag with a particular claim number. He read the number aloud and I ignored him. The next thing I knew, Leah was waving her hand in the air. "Please come with us," the security official said in Spanish. Leah dutifully got up and followed him off the bus.

Some have questioned whether I might have acted more bravely as Argentine security officials escorted my wife off the bus. I understand where those critics are coming from. On the other hand, Terry Gross was having a very engaging conversation with Bruce Springsteen about his recently released memoir. Also, I was reasonably confident that Leah was not trafficking narcotics or carrying huge wads of illicit cash. If that were the case, we would have had more fun money.

A Labrador retriever had gone straight to Leah's bag. The security officers led her inside a small building and opened her backpack as she looked on: clothes, shoes, books, sunscreen—and also a large Ziploc bag with more than a kilo of whitish powder. One of the officers held the bag up and looked to Leah for an explanation.

"It's pancake mix," she said.

This was true. We had been stretching our budget in Chile and Argentina by shopping at supermarkets and carrying staples with us in our packs. The mix in the bulging Ziploc bag could be combined with eggs, milk, and oil to make Swedish pancakes, a family breakfast favorite.* The officers did not fling Leah to the ground and slap on the cuffs. Apparently flour and sugar do not look like cocaine or heroin to an expert eye. Also, Leah had butter and jam in her pack, which gave credence to the pancake alibi. The drug dog, which had presumably been attracted to the food, was now lounging on the floor, wagging its tail happily. The officers searched every pocket and crevice of Leah's pack

* Wheelan family Swedish pancake recipe: Mix together batter in the following ratio: 1 cup flour, 2 tablespoons sugar, 3 eggs, 1/2 cup milk, 1/2 cup water, and 3 tablespoons oil. Batter should be thin and easily poured. Spread about a third of a cup of batter to cover the bottom of a saucepan as thinly as possible. The pancake will have the thickness of a crepe. Turn when brown and serve with lemon, sugar, fresh berries, jam, nuts, and/or Nutella.

before she was released back to the bus, by which point Terry Gross was asking Springsteen about his battles with depression and anxiety.

"All good?" I asked Leah as she walked down the aisle to her seat.

"The dog found the Swedish pancake mix," she said.

"They didn't take it away?" I asked with concern.

"No," she assured me. "The pancake mix is fine."

◈ ◈ ◈

The road to the faux-drug bust had been a long one, literally. A week earlier, after we left the salt flats and crossed from Bolivia into Chile, we had made our way to the small city of Calama, where we rented several rooms in a man's home. He was living with his son; they had one other guest, a journalist who was writing an article on the environmental harms done by Chile's copper mining industry. Our host and his son were friendly and helpful. This was the first time we had stayed in someone's home, as opposed to having our own apartment or a room with a dedicated entrance, as we had in Sucre. We had less privacy—a shared kitchen, for example—but it was interesting to speak to our hosts and the other guest about everything from politics to the local economy. There was an unexpected downside to our chats over the kitchen table, however. From these conversations, particularly our talks with the journalist, a monster was born: CJ Wheelan, Eco Warrior.

CJ had previously shown some interest in the environment, typical for a young person raised during an era of heightened environmental awareness. But in Calama, something extraordinary happened, like in those superhero movies when a normal person is bitten by a spider or exposed to radiation. As with all superpowers, CJ's fixation with the environment had a dark side. I teach public policy, lean left on environmental issues, and ran a congressional campaign in which I advocated for a carbon tax. Yet I found CJ the Eco Warrior to be remarkably grating. He brought all the subtlety of a thirteen-year-old to the issue: polluters are bad; environmentalists are good; mining companies are evil. There was not a lot of reflection on the fact, for example, that the minerals coming out of the ground were going into his iPod, or that our environmental footprint as we traveled around the world was less than admirable. CJ also had a habit of screaming excitedly whenever he saw a fancy sports car in the street. He spoke admiringly of people with huge houses and private planes. He had not, to my knowledge, reconciled his environmental sensitivity with his worship of energy-guzzling lifestyles.

Broadly speaking, CJ's environmental passion was a good thing. We can all take actions to minimize our environmental impact, many of which are simple and would collectively make a big difference. On a good day, I could let most of CJ's environmental policy illogic pass, recognizing it as a healthy passion gone overboard.

The second morning in Calama was not one of those days.

Our host had graciously invited us to use his washing machine. CJ became aggrieved when he discovered that I was washing our clothes in warm water. This was a reasonable objection—made less reasonable by the fact that I was the one who had collected the clothes and figured out how to use the washing machine, which is harder than one might think when the directions are in Spanish. The effect was like cooking dinner for someone who criticizes the food for having too much salt. It is not the kind of comment that endears one to the cook, even if the food does have too much salt.

Over a long breakfast (while the clothes were in the washing machine), CJ lectured us on various environmental factoids that he had learned on the Internet—insights that apparently escaped me while I was getting my Ph.D. in public policy. After an hour of hectoring, I took the clothes out of the washing machine. "Are you going to put those in the dryer?" CJ asked accusingly.

"I'm going to hang them on the clothesline," I answered, suppressing the urge to hurl his wet underwear into the bushes.

I opted for the bad mood cure-all: walking. I left the house, picked a random direction, and walked until I encountered something interesting. I ended up at a large shopping mall, where I parked myself in the food court. I ordered coffee, watched middle-class Chilean families enjoying themselves, and read a biography of Millard Fillmore.

One of my goals was to read a biography of every president in order. (It turns out that Millard Fillmore did not install the White House's first bathtub; that was a rumor spread by H. L. Mencken.) More important, reading about an obscure president for a long spell in a food court is a pleasant way to decompress, especially while surrounded by multigenerational families having a meal together.

When I returned to the house in a much better mood, Leah, CJ, and I had a more substantive conversation about environmental issues, including a discussion of how we can modify our own behavior to the greatest effect. I tried to underscore for CJ the importance of trade-offs: oil companies make it possible to heat our homes and drive to soccer practice; copper makes most electronics work; the sports cars he worshipped were some of the most gratuitous polluters. Still, CJ the Eco Warrior would be with us for the balance of the trip. His understanding of the issue would grow more sophisticated over time, but to my eternal frustration, he continued to shriek in excitement every time he saw a Ferrari or Maserati.

❖ ❖ ❖

I ran out of allergy medicine in Calama. This, like getting a haircut or buying a new tube of toothpaste, was a curious reminder that we had been on the road for a long time. We were now nearly halfway down the continent. Our budget was working, more or less. And I had used up all of my allergy medicine (easily replaced) as we enjoyed spring in the southern hemisphere.

We took an onward bus from Calama to Santiago: fifteen hundred kilometers, more or less, straight south along the coast of Chile. Santiago is not especially picturesque, but it is functional and easy to get around. We rented a twenty-first-floor apartment with three bedrooms and a nice kitchen. Our apartment building was in a pleasant residential neighborhood; we were able to run lots of small errands, including mailing our absentee ballots back to Hanover. Having turned eighteen earlier in the year, Katrina cast her first vote for president in a general election. We took advantage of a good kitchen to make risotto for dinner and Swedish pancakes for breakfast. (This was where the extra pancake mix was transferred to a large Ziploc bag.) One night we ordered sushi online and had it delivered. The sushi itself was mediocre, but we were pleased with ourselves for ordering in Spanish. The delivery guy showed up at our door, just like home.

As noted earlier, Leah and I had given up on Sophie doing any significant schoolwork until she joined us. In Santiago, we declared that she should at least get herself "unfrozen" from all her online courses before she left home. From five thousand miles away, we sent a parental edict: no car privileges or phone—the teenage equivalent of waterboarding—until Sophie got VLACS fixed. By afternoon, she was unfrozen in all three classes. The ongoing VLACS debacle was part of a larger debate about how to parent Sophie: Prod her along or let her learn from failure?

"We can't be threatening to take her phone away when she's in college," Leah pointed out. Like parents everywhere, we were searching for a magic formula that does not exist. Leah had been one of four children raised by a single mother who worked full-time; there was not a lot of time and energy for mollycoddling. Anyone who did not pack a lunch for school would be hungrier for dinner. One summer, Leah's mother decided to send all the kids to camp for two weeks, which was a significant family expense and the only break she would get from parenting. When they arrived at camp drop-off, the director informed them that the session had started a week earlier. "Camp is already half over," he explained. "The campers have made friends, they're on teams. The social bonding process at this age can be a delicate—"

"They'll be fine," Leah's mother said. "How about if I pick them up in the middle of the second session so they still get two weeks?" The flummoxed camp director agreed.

I, on the other hand, was raised by a Tiger Mom before the term had come into use. For example, when I received a B in gym class in seventh grade—with A's in all my academic classes—my mother demanded a conference with the PE teacher. It was, we believe, the first time in the history of the Northbrook Junior High School that a parent had ever made such a request.

"Why did Charlie get a B in gym?" my mother asked. "He gets A's in all his other classes."

To his credit, the PE teacher answered honestly: "Mrs. Wheelan, this is the first quarter and there are fifty boys in the class. I have no idea which one Charlie is." Suffice it to say, I got A's in gym for the balance of my middle school years.

The irony is that both Leah and I ended up as intrinsically motivated people. What approach would make Sophie take responsibility for her work? We considered letting her fail the online classes, which meant she would have to repeat her junior year and would not graduate with her class. That would be a valuable, if expensive, life lesson. On the other hand, we felt a parental responsibility to provide academic "bumpers"—the high school equivalent of the padding that pops up in bowling alleys and keeps the ball from rolling into the gutter. Failing three classes would definitely be an academic gutter ball. Also, we reminded ourselves that she was taking these insipid online classes because we were traveling around the world, which was not her idea. "So what are we supposed to do?" Leah asked after a long, meandering discussion of the situation.

"I don't know," I said.

◈ ◈ ◈

For reasons that should now be obvious, Leah and I were keen to visit the Concha y Toro winery on the outskirts of Santiago. Katrina was eager to go, too. Having just voted in the U.S. presidential election, she was annoyed that she was still three years away from a legal glass of wine at home, even though she could drink legally in most other countries, including Chile. She decided that America's anomalous drinking age would be the topic for her next *Valley News* article. The tourist bus to the winery cost twenty-five dollars a person. That is not a budget-busting amount on a ten-day vacation, but it was too much for us to spend, no matter how much Sophie was driving us to drink.

Leah opened her computer in our Santiago apartment and muttered, "How do the workers get there?" She found a combination of a metro ride and a public bus—sixty cents total—that got us within a mile of the winery gate. From there we walked, enjoying a warm spring day. We toured the vineyard and then settled ourselves on a lovely outdoor terrace where we spent most of our transportation savings on a delicious lunch with several flights of Chilean red wine. Katrina had me take a photo of her swilling from a big glass, which became the picture that accompanied her *Valley News* piece.

And then Katrina bade us farewell. She was heading off to meet two friends from high school, one of whom had a distant relative who owned a dairy farm in Chile and was willing to loan the three of them a decrepit old Volvo for exploring. (We learned later that they had to drive the car in reverse to get up steep inclines.)

❖ ❖ ❖

That left three: Leah, CJ the Eco Warrior, and me. The travel dynamic changed, as it had when our niece Tess went home. This time, however, I was losing my fellow introvert. The remaining three of us made our way to Gate Fourteen of the central bus terminal to catch an overnight bus south toward Patagonia. I persuaded Leah to pay an extra twenty-one dollars per person for the luxurious "full cama" (full bed) option. The bus had two levels. I was seated in the front row of the upper deck, looking out a floor-to-ceiling window at the road ahead. The seat reclined fully. When darkness fell, a steward made up my bed and closed the curtains on the front window. I settled comfortably under a thick blanket and fell into a deep sleep as our bus made its way south along a smooth Chilean highway. If anything, the trip was too short. I was still sleeping soundly when the steward gently offered me a cup of coffee as we arrived in the city of Osorno.

We parked ourselves on a bench in the bus station to wait five hours for the onward bus to Bariloche, our first stop in the Patagonia region. I read; I listened to podcasts. The aforementioned Terry Gross interview with Bruce Springsteen had prompted me to buy his book and download a few albums. (Book and music downloads fell into a gray area budgetwise, as they were much harder for Leah to monitor.) For the previous twenty years, I had thought it would be a luxury to sit idly on a bench for a long stretch of time. *It turned out to be as good as I had hoped.*

From Osorno we crossed the Chilean border into Argentina. We were now in the heart of Patagonia, an area near the tip of South America known for its extraordinary natural beauty: dense forests, turquoise lakes, and snowy peaks—all of which we were now seeing as our bus rolled along. We arrived in Bariloche, which turned out to be a prosperous ski town built on a steep hill overlooking a picturesque lake. Our Airbnb rental was a quirky, multicolored, three-story cottage. Inside, the walls were painted yellow and purple and green. I expected Willy Wonka to show up and give us instructions (in Spanish) for using the coffee maker.

Everything about Bariloche was beautiful, but as soon as we arrived the weather turned cloudy and rainy. We could see the rugged peaks of the Andes in the distance, but we were not able to do anything other than walk around town. I was getting anxious that we would miss what the region had to offer, as if Patagonia were flirting with us. Finally, the weather cleared. We bought transit cards and boarded the 20 bus out of town. It followed a route along the lake, giving us stunning views of the shimmering blue-green water and the mountains beyond. We rode to the end of the line, where we were met with a luxury hotel built on a expansive green lawn sloping down to the water. We could not afford to stay at this elegant hotel—and for the first time I wished we had the budget to do so—but we could have our picnic lunch on the sweeping lawn. Even better, Leah had struck up a conversation on the bus with a Swiss woman who told her about the Patagonia Brewing Company, a brewpub that became our destination for the afternoon.

Leah took out a bus map and determined that the 10 bus would take us somewhere near the brewpub. We waited at the designated stop. When the bus arrived, it was completely empty. The driver welcomed us aboard effusively and told us not to worry about paying the fare. We soon understood the dispensation. The number 10 bus was also the local school bus. We rumbled along a small road for a few minutes and then stopped outside an elementary school, where about fifty students came aboard. The students slapped the driver high fives; several of them perched backward against the front window of the bus, chatting amiably with the driver as we moved on. It was a joyous group, obviously accustomed to riding this bus every day. At the next stop, a group of high school students climbed aboard. No one gave us a second look. There was usually a first look—hey, three gringos are on our school bus—but then everyone went about their business. The result was a delightful combination of anonymity and acceptance.

The Patagonia Brewing Company is an architectural masterpiece. From the front, it is a warm, modern building—lots of wood and glass— that would fit comfortably in any upscale ski town. What we could not see from the front entrance, however, was the view out the back. The building is perched on the side of a mountain. Once inside, we were able to look through floor-to-ceiling windows at a turquoise lake surrounded by snowy peaks, like a giant gemstone that had been dropped into the Andes. There were even peaks that jutted up in the middle of the lake, creating picturesque islands. On the back lawn, we ordered a beer sampler and cheese fries and perched at a picnic table with Patagonia spread before us. CJ asked me to take a photo of him pointing to the Patagonia logo on his pullover while posing in Patagonia.

The next day we went to a ski resort where it was possible to take a chairlift up the mountain to a small chalet with a coffee shop and an outdoor deck with 360-degree views of the region. Again, we were blessed with sunny clear weather. We read glowing reviews of the views from the top of this peak, but the chairlift cost ten dollars a person. "There is a cheaper way," Leah asserted.

I looked up the mountain. "There's not a bus," I said skeptically.

"We can hike up," Leah said.

"It's a mountain," I pointed out.

"It's a ski hill," Leah corrected me.

"It's a ski hill on a mountain," CJ said. This was encouraging, as it suggested I might win a family vote two-to-one in favor of the chairlift. But then CJ added, "Wouldn't it be better for the environment if we walked?"

"The chairlift is running continuously, whether we're on it or not!"
I yelled. By then, Leah was already walking toward the woods. "Here's
the trail," she said without looking back. The hike was pleasant, if steep.
There was no charge for standing on the deck at the top and marveling at the 360-degree view: the lake's palette of blues and greens; the
mosaic of mountains and snow rising from the water, and sky that was a
different but complementary shade of blue. Patagonia was the place that
inspired me to figure out the panorama feature on my iPhone.

Leah and I celebrated our twenty-fourth wedding anniversary in
Bariloche. The Argentines love their beef. Having left CJ the Eco Warrior at the rental, we could enjoy an upscale steakhouse without getting a lecture from him on the environmental damage done by bovine
flatulence.* The meal was simple: two giant slabs of meat grilled over
a wood fire with a heaping bowl of mashed potatoes on the side. Our
only regret was ordering a half bottle of wine instead of a full one. We
marveled at the food, but also at the exuberance of the place, which
was full of relatively thin people—men and women alike—enjoying
prodigious quantities of meat, potatoes, and wine. We discussed the
paradox of South America: every country we visited had a robust food
culture yet relatively few overweight or obese people. My policy brain
hypothesized that this is because the diet is low in processed food and
the lifestyle is more oriented toward walking, particularly in the cities.
(If you marry a guy who teaches public policy, this is what you talk about
during your anniversary dinner.)

❖ ❖ ❖

Our goal at this point was to get as close as possible to the southern
tip of South America before we had to double back and meet Sophie in
Lima. The quest was fun; Leah chose interesting cities along the way.
In Puerto Madryn on the rugged Argentine coast, CJ persuaded us to

---

* Cow farts, which, in CJ's defense, are a major source of methane emissions and
a contributor to climate change (along with cow burps). Still, it's not the lecture
I wanted to get at an Argentine steakhouse.

go whale-watching. We joined a group led by a marine biologist aboard a small boat. For the first hour and a half, we saw nothing but a speck on the horizon that the marine biologist insisted was a whale. To me, even with my telephoto lens, it looked like a rock.

"Do you think we are going to see a whale?" CJ asked me repeatedly.

"It's not an aquarium," I reminded him each time.

"Look how beautiful the coast is," Leah offered. "What a lovely boat ride."

"Oh no," CJ lamented to me. "That's exactly the kind of thing she says if she doesn't think we're going to see a whale."

And then a mother and her calf surfaced beside us, so close that we could smell them: glistening skin, massive forked tales, and sprays of water as mother and calf exhaled loudly through their blowholes. They were majestic creatures; the baby stayed close to its mother, surfacing and frolicking beside her. CJ stood and ran to the side of the boat, screaming, "Whales! Whales!" Even the marine biologist smiled at his unadulterated joy.

◈ ◈ ◈

And then another fifteen hundred kilometers south to El Calafate, where we rented an adorable little A-frame with a sleeping loft up top. On our second evening, just as we were making dinner, there was a knock at the door. I answered, and there were two small children dressed strangely. They held out bags, as if they were pleading for something. I recognized their mother, our Airbnb host, standing at a distance and smiling pleasantly. I waved at her confusedly, and she waved back. Then one of the small kids said, "Truco o trato."

"It's Halloween!" Leah exclaimed from behind me. We rifled through our packs to find something appropriate for a treat, feeling flattered to be part of the neighborhood for that evening.

We had chosen El Calafate because it was near to the Perito Moreno Glacier: a mass of ice three miles wide and three hundred feet high pushing through a fjord into Lake Argentino like a slow-motion avalanche. The lake and glacier, which rests across the lake like a giant curtain, are part of the national park where we spent the day hiking trails and observing the glacier from different vantage points. From some perspectives, the ice took on a cool blue hue, as if it were illuminated from within. Tourist boats the size of small cruise ships floated on the lake near the glacier; the towering wall of ice made them look like toy boats in a bathtub. Near the end of the day, several condors flew overhead—just to put an exclamation point on the adventure.

That night at dinner, CJ ordered a six-hundred-gram slab of filet mignon and afterward vowed he would never eat beef again.

❖ ❖ ❖

We continued south. The roads in Argentina are long and straight, so much so that we did not need Dramamine. I was still reading Bruce Springsteen's autobiography. In the early part of the book, he writes about his passion for music and his efforts to break into the music business. I was inspired by his journey to artistic success, much of which was just dogged persistence. As a journalist and writer, I knew the drill. Now I found myself thinking about the novel I had been working on. As we rolled along on the bus, hour after hour, I resolved to finish it before the end of the trip. Maybe Bruce Springsteen was speaking to me. Maybe I just liked the alone time as I wrote every morning. In any event, I had a goal: finish the novel before we arrived home.

We crossed back into Chile to the city of Puerto Natales, which is a gateway for Torres del Paine National Park, the gem in the crown of Patagonia. Our trip into the national park began with a ride on a catamaran ferry across a lake to the main lodge. The jagged snowy peaks rising above the aquamarine lake looked as if someone had dropped the mountains of Colorado into one of the lakes of New Hampshire and then added a glacier. The weather was sunny for our crossing, but the forecast was ominous. The wind became fierce enough that I had to brace myself on deck while taking pictures. The crew warned us that the wind would get worse, an admonition I ignored until my sunglasses were nearly blown off my face.

We hiked for several hours to a large glacier as the weather grew steadily more brooding. By the time we reached the overlook for the glacier, rain was coming down hard and the temperature was falling fast. We admired the view briefly and then turned back for the lodge. I felt a pang of regret that we could not stay longer. On the other hand, with steady rain and high winds predicted for the next three days, I was happy not to be sleeping in a tent. Patagonia forced us to confront one of the trade-offs of the trip: we had opted to sample the world rather than going fewer places and staying longer. Patagonia is a place where I would have loved to spend more time, especially with a bigger budget.

We had rented a flimsy one-bedroom house in Puerto Natales that I began referring to as our "shack" after I persuaded myself that I could see the walls rattle when the wind blew. The shack did have a television, however, so we could watch the Chicago Cubs play game seven of the World Series. The games were broadcast on television with commentary in Spanish by the announcers who normally do soccer games. They treated a home run with the same enthusiasm as a soccer goal. When a hitter blasted the ball out of the park, they would yell in unison, "HOME RUUUUUUUUUUUUUUUN!"

I grew up going to games at Wrigley Field. Many of my high school friends sold concessions at the stadium as a summer job, walking the aisles peddling peanuts, or soda, or beer. I was a season ticket holder when we lived in Chicago. I vividly remember the "Bartman incident" in 2003, when a fan interfered with left fielder Moises Alou in a playoff game against the Florida Marlins and supposedly cost the Cubs a spot in the World Series. Now, in game seven, the Cubs had a chance to end the 108-year drought—a supposed "curse"—and win it all.

The game was tied at the end of regular play and went into extra innings—and then there was a rain delay. Chile is two hours ahead of the East Coast; it was nearly three o'clock in the morning for us. I gave some thought to going to bed; the rain delay could go on for hours. But I just couldn't. *The Cubs were in extra innings of game seven of the World Series.* The rain stopped, and the Cubs scored two runs in the tenth inning to win. I danced around our little shack. The rest of the family had gone to bed, but months of communal sleeping had taught us all to sleep through such disruptions.

◈ ◈ ◈

We were temporarily reunited with Katrina in Punta Arenas, Chile, a city just across the Strait of Magellan from Tierra del Fuego. She and her high school friends had driven around Chile and hiked in several national parks, including Torres del Paine. We fixed a time to meet her in a plaza near the center of the city. We arrived early and waited for her to show up. The rendezvous in a public place made me feel like I should be carrying ransom money. At the appointed time, Katrina walked casually into the plaza. CJ rushed to give her a hug. We had a lovely dinner at a quirky Croatian supper club, the kind of place where the waitress pointed at the menu and said, "Have this."

Over salmon and fried potatoes, Katrina shared her travel stories. She had made it all the way to Ushuaia—the very tip of South America (the "end of the world"). The rest of us would not make it that far. Katrina, independent adventurer that she was, insisted on staying alone in a hostel that night rather than sharing our apartment. She would be traveling north by bus on her own. Meanwhile, Leah, CJ, and I would be flying north to meet Sophie. If all went according to plan, we would see Katrina again in a week in Cusco, Peru.

Back in the U.S., Sophie was days away from beginning her journey to join us. The good news was that she seemed excited when we spoke to her. The bad news was the e-mail that we received from her VLACS chemistry teacher telling us that the assignments she had turned in— *the tiny amount of work she had managed to do*—were in an unreadable file. Sophie had also failed to deliver on a promise to clean up her room before departure. When she did finally shovel out her bedroom, a small space usually so cluttered that it was hard to open the door, *she removed twenty-three dirty towels*. I was shocked to learn that our family owns twenty-three towels, let alone that that many had been accumulating on Sophie's floor.

Leah, CJ, and I flew to Lima, a much shorter trip than the assorted bus rides that had taken us the other direction. In Lima, we made elaborate plans for Sophie's arrival so that her first experiences would be positive. CJ made a colorful sign to hold up when she emerged from customs at the airport. Leah found a bakery and ordered a cake.

Early on the morning of Election Day, Sophie texted to say that she was on the Dartmouth Coach bus headed to Logan Airport. Many hours later, she landed in Lima. We held up our multicolored sign as we waited eagerly in the arrivals hall. Sophie may not be the most enthusiastic traveler, but she is savvy. The Peruvian arrival form requires a local address. We had not given Sophie that information, since we were meeting her at the airport, and she was not able to use her phone to text us when she landed. As Sophie moved slowly in line toward the immigration officer, her many hours of binge-watching Netflix paid off. She recalled an episode of *Friends* in which Chandler claimed to be moving to Yemen. When asked by a skeptic where he was moving in Yemen, Chandler replied, "Yemen, Yemen." Sophie wrote, "Lima Street, Lima," on her form, figuring there probably was one. The official waved her through.

The happy reunion continued all the way back to our apartment, where Sophie enjoyed the chocolate cake we had bought for the occasion. "This is much better than I expected," she commented on our apartment. CJ was delighted to see his sister. At some point in the evening, he asked her if he could hug her again. Then Sophie went to bed and slept for twelve hours.

We learned over the course of the evening that Donald Trump would be the next president of the United States. It was a strange night for Americans everywhere, but it was particularly odd to be thousands of miles from home, watching the returns come in online and exchanging texts with friends. Katrina, who was making her way back to Peru, was alone in a hostel, feeling confused and lonely. As the evening progressed, we swapped texts with her, too. By the end of the night—we did stay up until Donald Trump was declared the winner—it was clear that America was entering uncharted territory.

Chapter 9

Charlie's Choice

You can try to control my whole life all you want, but you surely can't make me eat or speak, although the more I think about it the more I realize you may not be above force-feeding me.

—excerpt from the letter Sophie presented to me in the Quito airport declaring that that she was going on a hunger strike and refusing to speak.

WE WERE UP SOMEWHERE around thirteen thousand feet in the Peruvian Andes. Our guide, Juan Carlos, sidled up to me. I had a pretty good idea what he was going to say. We were doing the Salkantay Trek, a four-day hike that would take us through some of the most beautiful spots in the Andes to Machu Picchu. On this first day, we would climb over a mountain pass at fifteen thousand feet. So far, however, we were only forty-five minutes into the walk and Team Wheelan was not killing it. I knew that was what Juan Carlos wanted to discuss.

We had started before sunrise with a three-hour van ride up a winding road to the trailhead. This was a triple whammy: early morning, winding road, high altitude. Despite Dramamine, CJ and Sophie threw up so many times that we had to borrow extra plastic bags from fellow passengers. What was more surprising—and more alarming—was that neither CJ nor Sophie bounced back when we arrived at the starting point for the hike, a lovely meadow with stunning views of the Andes. The guides who would be accompanying our group set up an elaborate outdoor breakfast spread, but neither CJ nor Sophie ate anything. They both sat listlessly in the grass. Sophie showed some vigor when a local puppy came wandering over (Sorry, Rhonda), but other than that, neither of them looked prepared to hike over a fifteen-thousand-foot pass.

It was an hour later, with both Sophie and CJ struggling along the trail, when Juan Carlos pulled me aside. We had four days of rigorous hiking ahead. "Señor Charles," Juan Carlos said as we walked, "you have a choice to make. We have one horse, and there are two people who need a horse." It wasn't exactly *Sophie's Choice*, but Juan Carlos was making explicit the dilemma I had been confronting in my own mind. Our tents and gear were being hauled by packhorses. There was one spare horse to help out, if necessary. I could put Sophie on a horse, or I could put CJ on a horse. But not both.

The trek had been majestic from the moment we began walking through a meadow along a bubbling creek into the jagged, snowcapped Andes. But what if we did not make it through the first day? If CJ and Sophie were motion sick, they would get better. But if one or both of them had altitude sickness, the only safe option would be to turn back. Leah or I would have to go, too. "Who goes on the horse, Señor Charles?" Juan Carlos prodded.

The parenting books do not say anything about which child should get the horse when two of them are pale, weak, and unhappy at thirteen thousand feet. I tried to be strategic. CJ and Sophie each get unhappy in their own way. With CJ, physical discomfort drives his mood. If he began to feel better, his mood would bounce back quickly. He had, after all, powered up and down Colca Canyon with a massive cold, in large part because Leah helped him find a comfortable pace. Sophie is the opposite: her moods tend to dominate how she feels physically.

If she grew grumpier, everything would spiral in a bad direction. My best play—the one that might salvage the trek—was to give Sophie the horse in the hope that it would improve her state of mind. Also, she likes horses. Meanwhile, Leah offered CJ a brilliant suggestion: put on headphones and listen to music while hiking.

CJ plugged in. Sophie mounted up. The horse was relatively short; Sophie is tall, with long legs. Sophie's feet seemed oddly close to the ground as the horse walked slowly along the trail; it was like an adult riding a pony at a petting zoo. Katrina had bounded ahead of us. As a cross-country runner and Nordic skier, she was in the best shape of the family. When she saw tall Sophie come around a bend on the short horse, she burst out laughing—not a chuckle, but a roar. CJ began to make jokes about Sophie on the horse. I was delighted that he was feeling good enough to malign his sister, but I told both Katrina and CJ to zip the horse jokes. The last thing we needed was Sophie dismounting in protest.

We hiked on. CJ began to feel better and the music made the hiking more enjoyable for him. Sophie and the horse took a different path on occasion; we would look across a small canyon and see Sophie on her horse, plodding along with the other pack animals. I would wave and she would wave back jauntily. She looked better, too.

After lunch, Sophie declared she would not be using the horse in the afternoon. "That's good news for the horse," CJ declared. We traversed the fifteen-thousand-foot pass, pausing for a group photo at the top. Everyone was now on foot. No one had altitude sickness. The rest of the trek would be lower and easier. Leah, who grew up in Colorado and has hiked across New England and the Alps, proclaimed, "This is the most beautiful hike I have ever been on."

❖ ❖ ❖

The parenting gods gave us only moments of respite. The bright sun was reflecting off the snow. Leah, Katrina, CJ, and I had slathered ourselves with sunscreen. Sophie had refused. "I don't get sunburned," she insisted. Our children are one-eighth Armenian, which makes them slighter darker than the average white person. But the notion that Sophie would not get sunburned from twelve hours of exposure at high altitude was ludicrous.

"We have another four hours in intense sun," I pointed out.

"It doesn't affect me," Sophie repeated. "I don't need sunscreen." There were two possible explanations for this claim. Perhaps Sophie had some miracle genetic endowment that made her impervious to the rays of the sun. If so, we might be able to commercialize this genetic good fortune and make billions. Or maybe Sophie was a stubborn teenager with a prefrontal cortex that had not fully developed, leading to impulsive acts and poor decision making.

Which one could it be?

I lost the sunscreen battle. We camped that night in a meadow ringed by mountains. I savored the sensation of crawling into a warm sleeping bag after a long day of hiking. We had aggressively hydrated all day; crawling out of a warm sleeping bag to find an outhouse in the dark is less pleasant. I fumbled around for my headlamp, put on flip-flops, unzipped the tent, and tried to squeeze through the small opening without stepping on Leah or pulling a muscle. What greeted me outside was a full moon casting a bright glow on the snow-covered mountains encircling us. The campsite was quiet and still but for the gentle stirring of the horses. I stood marveling at the peaks, which were nearly as bright as they had been by day. The stillness of the camp made it feel as if I were the only one in the universe given license to appreciate the beauty of that moment. When I turned off my headlamp, I noticed that the moon was casting shadows. The horses, gently lit in the pasture by moonlight, looked like a painting of the American West.

My three subsequent trips to the outhouse were progressively less enrapturing.

The next day the terrain went from cold and mountainous to semi-temperate as the trail led us back down to five thousand feet. As with the Amazon, we were in a totally different ecosystem. I spotted one flower after another that I had never seen before: domes the size of a tennis ball with tiny pink, orange, and yellow petals; tall stalks with furry indigo and white nubs; flaming red tubes the size of chili peppers that hung downward like bananas in bright clumps. I took photos of them all; sometimes I pleaded with a family member to pose in the frame. "Katrina, can you stand near those purple flowers?"

"How many flower photos do you need?"

"Can you just stand there?"

"No."

"I'll give you some of my fun money," I offered.

"Your fun money ran out like two countries ago," she said. (This was inaccurate, though I was spending somewhat recklessly.) If I got lucky, Leah would happen along and corral one or two of the kids into a picture. "Look how pretty these red ones are," she would say.

"It's his ninety-seventh flower picture," one of them would point out.

"I'm an artist," I explained. As they laughed at me, I got the shot.

At our campsite that evening, we had a view across a canyon of the Sun Gate at Machu Picchu. Juan Carlos loaned us binoculars and in the soft evening sun we could make out the structures of Machu Picchu. One more day of hiking and we would be there.

❖ ❖ ❖

We set out the next morning on the final stretch of the Salkantay Trek, which runs along a set of railroad tracks into the city of Aguas Calientes, gateway to Machu Picchu. The hiking was flat and short compared to earlier days, but we had two new issues on our hands. First, Sophie's face was peeling off because of her earlier decision not to use sunscreen—dashing my plans to pay for college by commercializing her extraordinary genetic resistance to sunburn. Second, the whole town of Aguas Calientes was on strike—every restaurant, hotel, and business. The strike had started with the workers on the railroad that operates between Cusco and Aguas Calientes. Other businesses soon closed, both in sympathy with the strikers and because any business that stayed open risked getting a brick through the window. The whole city was effectively shut down.

The final six miles into Aguas Calientes were on a trail that ran along a railroad bed. The hike felt postapocalyptic: scores of people fleeing in the other direction with their possessions. Most of the tourists streaming past us had expected to take the train back to Cusco; now they were walking. Some clutched bags to their chests. Others were trying to pull wheelie-board suitcases along the bumpy railroad tracks. Many looked unfit to hike a long distance. Some of the women were in high heels. We, of course, were going the other direction—past the fleeing hordes into a city that had been closed by a general strike. What if Machu Picchu was closed, like Walley World at the end of the movie *Vacation*?

When we arrived in Aguas Calientes, every business along the main street was shuttered. Strikers and police officers mingled uneasily. We sat on the sidewalk while Juan Carlos set off to take stock of the situation. He returned half an hour later with good news: we would be able to check into our hotel. "But don't enter as a group," he instructed us. "Go in one or two at a time." When we found the hotel, we lingered on the other side of the street. The lights in the lobby were off. Sophie and I walked to the entrance, where there was a handwritten sign on the front door expressing solidarity with the strikers. "Is it open?" I asked.

"I don't think so," Sophie said, peering into the dark, empty lobby. She tried the door and it was open.

"Go in quickly," I said. She disappeared inside and I walked in behind her. A minute later, the rest of the family crossed the street and entered the hotel as unobtrusively as possible.

Once inside, we spotted a woman standing in the dark behind the front desk. She quickly dispatched us upstairs to our rooms. That evening, Juan Carlos summoned us and the other trekkers to a meeting in the lobby, where the lights were still off. "Everything is okay," he offered in a tone suggesting that most things were not okay. We would be able to see Machu Picchu the next day, he pledged. After that, we would return by train to Cusco, either when the strike was resolved or on a special train the government was sending for stranded tourists.

In the meantime, we had to find food. Juan Carlos led us through the empty streets to a restaurant that looked as closed as everything else. We looked through the front window: the lights were off; there was not a soul inside; the chairs were stacked on the tables. Juan Carlos pointed to a door on the side of the building. He told us to enter in groups of one or two and take a stairway up to the second floor, as if we were going to a 1920s speakeasy. On the second floor at the back of the darkened restaurant, there was a long table set for us. The lights stayed dimmed as the waitstaff served the meal in the dark. We left as we had arrived, sneaking out the side door, one or two at a time.

Each briefing from Juan Carlos seemed to bring grimmer news. The strike was going on longer than expected, he told us. The special government train to retrieve stranded tourists was postponed. On the other hand, Machu Picchu was open—and nearly empty. We took a small bus to the entrance early the next morning and spent much of the next day exploring the beautiful and enigmatic Inca city, with its terraces, stone walls, and canals, all juxtaposed against mountains so steep and lush that the sprawling site was not discovered until the twentieth century. The weather was warm and sunny. The rail strike had given us a gift: we had a World Heritage site almost to ourselves.

Machu Picchu is a lot of things: a geographic wonder; an example of an extraordinary pre-Columbian civilization; and, perhaps most ominously, a reminder that even great civilizations can collapse precipitously. I had read Jared Diamond's excellent book *Collapse*, which documents the factors most likely to cause advanced societies to unravel (e.g., climate change and feckless governing elites). The awe-inspiring grandeur of Machu Picchu makes its abandonment all the more sobering. For reasons we do not understand, five hundred years ago all the inhabitants died or left; the jungle began reclaiming the magnificent structures.

Our visit was not entirely angst-ridden. At one point, Katrina tried to take a close-up photo of a llama. The llama smelled a granola bar in her pocket and tried to grab it. Katrina panicked and ran. The rest of us watched with amusement as Katrina sprinted across a flat grassy area with the llama in close pursuit, like two cartoon characters. Leah and I enjoyed having all three children reunited and in good spirits. They posed happily for selfies in the matching ugly green T-shirts that Juan Carlos had given us to promote his trekking company.

All the while, there were vicious little mosquitoes swarming about. Unlike the mosquitoes back home, these creatures were hard to see and they bit aggressively by day. Leah, Katrina, CJ, and I sprayed any exposed skin with mosquito repellant. "These mosquitoes don't bite me," Sophie declared when I offered her the bug spray.

"They bite anyone who has blood," I said.

"Not me," said Sophie.

Leah and I looked at each other in amazement. Sophie's face was still peeling from the sunburn debacle. "Are we in some kind of parenting reality show that no one told me about?" I asked. I pretended to look around the trees for television cameras. "When does the host jump out of bushes and say, 'Smile, You're on the *Teenager Show*'?"

The teen obstinacy was frustrating; Leah and I were also mildly concerned because every mosquito bite carries some health risk: the Zika virus, dengue fever, encephalitis. Once again, we found ourselves trying to figure out where we ought to draw the line between forcing sensible behavior and letting her learn on her own. We were enjoying a pleasant day together on Machu Picchu. I had no interest in chasing Sophie around with mosquito repellant.

When we returned to Aguas Calientes that afternoon, about two hundred strikers were marching through a main street toward the depot where the tourist buses were parked. The police had set up a cordon to stop the protesters from getting that far. At first the demonstration felt like a parade. The protesters were chanting, singing, and waving placards. Sophie opted to head back to the hotel. The rest of us stopped to watch the demonstration as it moved steadily toward the phalanx of officers in riot gear arrayed shoulder to shoulder across the road. When the protesters did not stop, the police fired tear gas. Suddenly it no longer felt like a parade. The strikers and their supporters dispersed in every direction, running and screaming and crying. Katrina plunged into the crowd, pushing against the panicked tide to take photos of the reaction to the tear gas. This became her next *Valley News* article.

Meanwhile, CJ had a panic attack, literally. He began crying and hyperventilating. Leah tried to calm him. "Breathe . . . breathe . . . breathe," she urged. CJ was traumatized that the police had fired on the crowd. He did not realize in the moment—with people screaming and crying and running—that tear gas does not cause long-term harm.

The protest eventually petered out without any serious injuries. We now had two challenges. First, Sophie was tormented by her mosquito bites. Suffice it to say that the mosquitos in Peru do bite her. (She ended up with so many bites on her ankles that she still had scars at the end of the trip.) Second, the strike had been extended yet again. Juan Carlos called another meeting in the darkened lobby of our hotel and informed us that the government rescue train would be coming . . . never. He laid out a different option: We could hike out of the city, reversing our six-mile walk along the train tracks. The tour company would send a van to pick us up at a point where the railroad tracks intersected a highway. From there, the ride to Cusco would be seven to nine hours on winding roads (which is why most people take the train).

This plan was no sure thing. Juan Carlos warned that the strike was spreading. Protesters in neighboring towns might barricade the highway, preventing the van from reaching our rendezvous point. If we were to hike out, Juan Carlos advised, we should leave early the following morning under the cover of darkness to reach our van before the strikers barricaded the road to Cusco. Obviously we would have to take our bags with us. This was fine for Team Wheelan, of course: *we had drilled for such contingencies.* Okay, we hadn't drilled for anything, but we weren't carrying a lot of extra crap. Others at the hotel began scrambling to find porters to carry their bags; we could easily carry everything we had.

We assembled the following morning in the hotel restaurant at four-thirty. There was an elegant buffet set up for us, which felt incongruous. On the other hand, if all the guests were sneaking out of town before sunrise, it made sense to offer them a nice breakfast. We ate a little and then walked out into the darkened streets before five. The city was eerily quiet; we walked in silence, even CJ. When we reached the edge of town, the police checked our passports, prompting me to wonder why one needs travel documents to walk out of town. They waved us on. The sun was coming up by the time we reached the railroad tracks.

The morning was much cooler than our midday walk going the other direction. Also, the tracks had a slight grade and we were now walking downhill. All five of us walked fast, almost effortlessly. Our collective mood was ebullient, some combination of endorphins from the brisk hike and excitement from the early morning escape. We covered six miles in just over two hours and reached the hydroelectric station—our rendezvous point with the van—at about seven-fifteen. This was the moment of truth: Was the road blocked or not? If the van had not made it from Cusco, we would have to find a place to stay, or perhaps reverse course and walk six miles back to Aguas Calientes.

As we emerged from the tracks, we saw vans and buses. Juan Carlos urged us to waste no time in getting aboard, as a barricade could go up at any minute. We loaded our stuff in the back of the van and rode off. The driver was good; the road was not as precarious as I had feared. We were going to make it to Cusco.

Team Wheelan had fired on all cylinders. The day before, CJ had thrown a hissy fit over a pair of lost headphones. Sophie's poor judgment and chronic stubbornness have been thoroughly documented. But on that morning, when we needed to execute—get up early, carry all our stuff, and hike briskly for six miles—every family member rose to the challenge. It is even possible, though I am not certain of it, that Sophie put on mosquito repellant for the walk.

◈ ◈ ◈

The escape from Aguas Calientes suggested that we were getting pretty good at the travel part of the traveling. The homeschooling piece, however, was a work in progress. Leah was teaching CJ geometry; he grumbled about the work but tended to get it done. I had the task of teaching him writing. We were making less progress, in part because there were no online assignments that I could direct him to do. In Peru, I figured out something that should have been obvious from the beginning: CJ needed to write about things that interested him—like street food. For his first assignment, I told him to write a restaurant review of a small open-air Middle Eastern restaurant in Lima. He had gone back repeatedly, met the owner, and raved about the food. "I don't know how to write a restaurant review," he complained.

"Just describe it," I instructed. "Tell me why you like it so much." He did:

> Amid the chaotic streets of downtown Lima, there sits a peaceful open-air café, with a juicy spit of shawarma outside, calling for the hungry pedestrian. Just twenty feet off of the sidewalk, one can escape the diesel spewing trucks and sit down in a comfortable Middle Eastern café. With help from the pillows, music, and paintings, it almost feels like a real shawarma stand in downtown Jerusalem.

Not bad, right? The bigger project I would have to supervise was an eighth-grade research paper. I did not want CJ to reach high school without doing a proper research project: discerning data from Internet trivia; organizing an extensive amount of information; and writing it all up in a coherent manner. We agreed to channel CJ the Eco Warrior for the project. He would write about deforestation: causes, consequences, and potential remedies. The paper would be due by the end of the trip, with intermediate deadlines along the way (outline, list of sources, rough draft, and so on).

Sophie's schooling was turning out to be as frustrating in person as it had been from afar. We set several deadlines for VLACS assignments, all of which she missed. This was especially frustrating because now we could observe her watching Netflix and chatting with friends as the work went undone. We threatened to take the phone away until Sophie finished some work. "I want to be treated like an adult," she challenged.

"Adults use sunscreen," Leah replied.

"And insect repellent," I piled on.

"That's true," Sophie said. We waited for some quibble or rejoinder, but there was none. She admitted that it had been foolish not to use sunscreen on the trek. "I thought that if I didn't use bug spray at Machu Picchu and it worked out okay, then it would make up for the sunscreen," she explained. The candor was refreshing, even if the logic was horrifying.

Sophie agreed to do more VLACS work. We agreed to nag less and evaluate her on the results. *Everybody would be happy if she got her work done without us being involved.* The first task, a trial of sorts, would be for Sophie to e-mail a thank-you note to my brother-in-law and sister-in-law for looking after her in Hanover for two months. We would not remind her; she would just get it done by a specified time. This would be a small step forward—like one of those confidence-building measures that the Israelis and Palestinians periodically agree to.

Sophie spent the subsequent twenty-four hours texting, posting on Facebook, watching Netflix—everything but sending the thank-you note, which would have taken between two and four minutes. The details of the subsequent screaming match are uninteresting, except that it culminated in the letter Sophie handed me in the waiting area of the Quito airport.

It began: "To Whom It May Concern (although I'm not sure if that includes you)." The note included several paragraphs on being the unappreciated child. The pièce de résistance was a declaration: "You can try to control my whole life all you want, but you surely can't make me eat or speak, although the more I think about it the more I realize you may not be above force-feeding me." (For the record, we did not force-feed her.) Then there was the final line: "Sorry for being harsh, but you needed to hear the truth." The irony, of course, is that the protest letter took about twenty times as long to write as the thank-you note would have.

When CJ learned about Sophie's civil disobedience, he began comparing her to Mahatma Gandhi, who had also refused to speak or eat as a form of protest. As Sophie sulked in the corner of the boarding gate for our flight to the Galapagos, CJ began yelling, "Viva Mahatma! Viva Mahatma!" This was unhelpful, though I was impressed with his historical fluency. I sat next to Sophie on the plane and wrote a six-page response to her letter. We were both crying by the time letters had been exchanged. Leah kept looking across the aisle, trying to figure out what was going on.

We had hit bottom with Sophie, in terms of both the homeschooling and the broader maturity issues. The good thing about hitting bottom is that things tend to get better. Sophie recognized that she needed deadlines from us to get her work done. We agreed not to harass her about her work if she hit those deadlines. And we all recognized that the deadlines needed to be more specific than most business contracts. Gone were phrases like "significant progress in pre-calc"—replaced with clauses such as "two assignments, uploaded to the portal in a format accessible to the teacher by midnight, local time as determined by Dad's iPhone." I kept a small notebook in my back pocket in which we recorded the details of each agreement. At one point, we considered videotaping our conversations.

The combination of crystal-clear agreements and firm deadlines, with the phone to be confiscated for missing them, turned out to work surprisingly well. There were several occasions on which Sophie's recollections of our agreements were more accurate than ours. I would open the notebook like a lawyer consulting a statute and say, "She's right." Sophie began speaking to us again. Leah persuaded her that using self-starvation as a weapon was a scary and unhealthy thing. CJ continued to yell, "Viva Mahatma!" whenever he felt the urge to annoy Sophie.

◈ ◈ ◈

We took a break from early mornings and grueling bus rides and the tight budget. My brother Pete and his wife have two boys close in age to Sophie and CJ. When Leah and I began planning our adventure, Pete proposed meeting us with his family in the Galapagos for Thanksgiving. At the appointed time, my brother and his family's taxi pulled into the parking lot of a tortoise reserve. As when we reunited with Katrina in Chile, there was something exciting about picking a spot on the map—an arbitrary place, previously unknown—and having everyone show up as planned.

Our rental house was on an outlying island accessible only by ferry. As we waited to board the boat, seals lounged beneath the benches on the dock. Huge lizards crawled across nearby rocks. CJ and his cousins spotted a small shark swimming in the shallow water. CJ, who had been talking incessantly about sharks ("misunderstood creatures"), began running up and down the dock, shrieking in excitement: "Shark! Shark! Shark!"

"He's so happy," Leah said admiringly.

"What if he pees on himself?" I replied.

The ferry deposited us on Isabela Island, a beautiful but remote place with one town and no paved roads. The house we rented had a hammock on the back deck; the beach and the ocean were beyond that. We did not have to go looking for nature; it found us: colorful lizards lounging on rocks; sea lions frolicking in the harbor; exotic birds hunting in the water and sand. I took a short walk along a wooded trail and stumbled upon an estuary full of bright pink flamingos.

We snorkeled in the shallow, clear water. The world underwater was as exciting and diverse as what we were seeing on land: stingrays, a bright blue starfish, a moray eel, and giant sea turtles that drifted so close we could see the algae on their shells swaying gently in the current. A small shark darted past in the distance, prompting a frisson of excitement.

The next day a guide took us to a murky canal just offshore, where we dropped into the water and began floating with masks and snorkels along the warm channel. The guide told us that the reef sharks are most often found in caves or under large rocks. He proposed a plan: I would dive down to the bottom of the canal, about six feet, and peer into a cave. Since the human body is naturally buoyant, he would assist me by putting his foot on my back when I reached the bottom so I could look into the cave without popping up to the surface.

I took a big breath and dived down. Per our agreement, the guide put his foot on my back, holding me against the bottom of the canal. I looked under the gap in the rocks. At first I saw nothing. My eyes slowly adjusted, at which point I saw two eyes looking back at me. As my brain caught up, I realized the eyes belonged to the long body of a reef shark. These sharks are harmless creatures if not disturbed. Still, the human brain is wired to react to the unique shape of a shark, particularly a large one. Also, I was pinned to the bottom with someone's foot on my back, which is a curious sensation under any circumstances but particularly alarming when one is staring at a shark. I calmed myself and spent ten seconds admiring the beautiful creature in its natural environment. Like so much in life, the shark felt less scary up close than it had from afar.

We continued snorkeling through the shallow, murky channel. Enormous sea turtles swam under and around us. Some had small transmitters attached to their shells, presumably to monitor their movement and health. I spotted another long shark lounging on the bottom. And then, as my brain made sense of the contours on the muddy bottom, I realized there were multiple sharks lying next to one another: more than I could count, all six or eight feet long. Some of the sharks began swimming around; at one point, I had to abruptly change course to avoid drifting into one.

Isabela Island was small enough that we could turn the cousins loose: to swim on the beach; to snorkel in the harbor; to go out for pizza together at night. CJ had a blast with his boy cousins. Sophie had fun, too. There was a single bakery down the street that produced fresh banana bread every afternoon around three o'clock. I was the first to discover this treat; every slice I brought home was immediately consumed by hungry teens. The next day I bought more; again, there was nothing left but crumbs. By the end of our stay, we became more proactive: one family member was dispatched to the shop around two forty-five to buy every loaf the proprietress produced. It was like a cross between American tourists and a bank robbery: one of us waving U.S. dollars and declaring, *"We want it all. Every loaf."*

We celebrated Thanksgiving at an outdoor seafood restaurant. My parents were delighted that two branches of the family were together in this special place; every time we spoke to them they offered us more money to subsidize our meals and adventures. I may be fifty years old, but a free meal from my parents is still a free meal. The Galapagos turned out to be a remarkable travel destination, a successful family reunion, and a relaxing and semi-luxurious break from our backpacking regime.

❖ ❖ ❖

Team Wheelan was now firing on every travel cylinder except the homeschooling one. Sophie missed her first VLACS deadline, prompting two and a half hours of arguing, crying, and, eventually, a confiscated phone. She admitted that she had trouble completing work that she did not care about. That was progress. She agreed to do an hour of work each morning before doing anything else (namely getting on her phone, which had been returned). She and Leah would work together on math. The real breakthrough, however, came when Sophie began working on something she did care about: writing. She did a long Facebook post from the Galapagos that reminded me of her writing talent. She can write quickly, almost effortlessly, and has a great ear for teen dialogue. On the first leg of the flight to New Zealand, she began writing a novel; she had several chapters done by the time we reached our layover in Santiago. The writing put her in a good mood, as it does for me. Now two of us were writing novels, though Sophie's was arguably more practical. Her high school offers an opportunity for seniors to do an independent project that can substitute for class credit. Sophie proposed that the novel would be her independent project. *Oh, the irony: the child doing her best to fail junior year was looking ahead excitedly to doing independent work senior year.*

We had a long time to kill in the Santiago airport—hours and hours. We found a Johnny Rockets restaurant and lingered over the meal. We were all in good moods. The conversation wandered: movies; then sex; then sex in movies. "I got my first erection while watching *Bad Teacher!*" CJ blurted out. We laughed; the discussion moved on. As we were walking to the gate, though, Katrina pulled me aside. "Dad, is he normal?" she asked earnestly. "I'm really worried about him."

"Which part: the sexual behavior, or his willingness to talk about it?" I asked.

"*Both*," she said.

"The sexual behavior is normal. His eagerness to talk about it—less so," I said. "But he does talk a lot about everything."

"Yeah, I guess that's true," Katrina agreed.

"He'll be fine," I assured her.

With that, we bade farewell to South America. We boarded a 787 Dreamliner for the overnight flight to Auckland, New Zealand—the flight I had booked with trepidation on the screened porch many months earlier. We were in a good place as a family as we prepared to cross the Pacific Ocean, with one modest exception. Katrina had a dime-sized sore on the top of her left foot. The wound was bizarrely symmetrical—a perfect circle. We had originally assumed it was the remnant of a blister from the Machu Picchu trek, but the sore did not appear to be healing. If anything, it was getting bigger.

Chapter 10

The Left Side of the Road

I had been keeping a tally in the back of my journal:

Countries: 8	*Horse rides: 2*
Bus trips: 28	*Incidents of motion sickness: 7*
Flights: 13	*Search parties looking for us: 2*
Boat rides: 6	*Family meltdowns: 5*
Jeep rides: 7	*Books read (by me): 25*

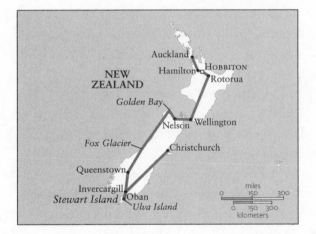

OUR PLAN FOR NEW ZEALAND was a long road trip, steadily south. When Leah and I visited New Zealand in 1988, we landed in Auckland on the North Island. Everyone we encountered, tourists and locals alike, told us to make sure we left enough time to explore the South Island. We did not. We became absorbed by the bucolic North Island and never made it to the most scenic spots in the south.

This time we resolved not to make that mistake. Katrina and I pulled out a map of New Zealand and began planning a route to the southern tip of the South Island. Then we read about Stewart Island, just to the south of the South Island, a place where kiwis can still be spotted in the wild. "What about Ulva Island?" I asked, pointing to a tiny speck on the map near Stewart Island.

"We can make it to Ulva Island," Katrina declared.

The plan was hatched. *We would make it to the island to the east of the island to the south of the South Island.*

◇ ◇ ◇

Our road trip began in Auckland around six in the morning, after we had flown overnight from South America. We picked up our rental car and headed out of the airport—on the left side of the road. Leah had so little interest in driving that we did not put her on the rental agreement. Her job was to yell loudly from the passenger seat whenever I instinctively ended up on the right side of the road, which was the wrong side of the road.

Our first destination was the central post office. In particular, we needed to find the poste restante window. Poste restante is a holdover from the days when anyone without a fixed address could have mail held for them at a post office. Only a few post offices in the world still offer the service. Fewer still accept packages, but the central post office in Auckland was one of them. I had mailed a pouch of books there before leaving Hanover. Back then, it was just a meaningless address on the other side of the world. As I handed the pouch to the clerk in the Hanover post office, I had wondered: *Would we make it that far?*

In downtown Auckland, we found the main post office and then the poste restante window. I presented my driver's license and a friendly woman retrieved the parcel. I was happy to have new books; I was even more excited that the poste restante experiment had worked and that we had made it far enough to pick them up. In theory, there would be more books waiting for me in Tasmania and Mumbai.

New Zealand felt familiar, especially the prices. On that first day, we exceeded our food budget before dinner. The rental car would have to be folded into the budget, too. Every accommodation in Auckland was too expensive, even the hostels. We drove about an hour and a half to the smaller city of Hamilton, where we rented a small Airbnb apartment adjacent to a miniature golf course and driving range. Driving on the left side of the road was exhausting. We got lost on the way, making the drive even longer. Also, the last time any of us had slept in a bed was in Quito, about thirty-six hours earlier. I de-stressed by paying eight dollars to hit a bucket of golf balls at the driving range, which was really just an open field with sheep grazing on it. (No sheep were harmed.) Still, we were not able to escape Complete Family Meltdown #4.[*]

The blowup happened in the parking lot of a grocery store. Katrina, Sophie, and CJ were sitting in the backseat of our rental car while Leah and I were inside buying provisions. Having them in a confined space after traveling for thirty-six hours was like chain-smoking in a fireworks factory. A dispute arose when someone impinged on someone else's space—typical five-year-old stuff. In the heat of the argument, CJ yelled at Sophie, "Freedom is never voluntarily given by the oppressor; it must be demanded by the oppressed!"[†] Katrina began laughing hysterically, causing Sophie to declare that she was being ganged up on. By the time Leah and I returned to the car with groceries, the pushing and shoving had morphed into a tearful discussion of pent-up grievances.

There was a volatile combination of personalities squeezed in the backseat. CJ tends to provoke, sometimes intentionally but often not. Regardless of how a dispute begins, however, he is unable to bring it to resolution without proving himself right. Sophie gets stubborn and belligerent when she is angry, escalating the situation. Katrina is quiet and withdrawn, hiding her annoyance until the dam bursts, at which point there is a cascade of emotions. All three of them are *terrible* at apologizing.

---

[*] Complete Family Meltdown #2 was as the result of Sophie's protest in the Quito airport. I noted Complete Family Meltdown #3 in my journal but not the details, and now I can no longer remember anything about it.

[†] Martin Luther King, Jr.

From the front seat, Leah led the de-escalation. She asked Katrina and CJ, "How do you think Sophie felt when you were laughing at her?"

Katrina said, "Sophie, I'm sorry that you're so sensitive."

"Try again," Leah demanded.

Katrina doubled down. "Sophie, I'm sorry you misunderstood—"

"Nope," Leah said.

"I'm sorry we laughed at you," Katrina said earnestly.

"Okay, good," Leah said. "Now CJ."

"Sorry, Sophie," CJ complied.

"Thank you. Now we're all okay?" Leah asked.

There were nods of agreement from the backseat. I started the car and began backing out of the parking spot, at which point CJ said, "But Sophie was in my space."

"Oh my god!" Leah screamed. The process began anew.

We celebrated the eventual reconciliation with a round of miniature golf, which came free with our Airbnb. The whole trip was a process of family self-discovery, but in this moment we learned that Katrina is an unbelievably bad miniature golf player—worse than anything I ever thought possible. She began the round by taking a near-full swing with the putter, sending the ball far off the course. Even after we urged her to putt rather than swing, she continued to hit the ball into the surrounding bushes and gravel. Because Katrina is also stubborn, she then tried to hit the ball back onto the course, which usually involved sending it farther into the New Zealand countryside. Soon she was far enough away from the course, still flailing away with the putter, that other mini-golfers began to stop and watch. "Just don't hurt anyone," I said loudly, trying to project so that she could hear me from the other side of the parking lot. The levity helped our collective mood, as did sleep.

◈ ◈ ◈

We drove south to Hobbiton, the film location for *The Hobbit* and other *Lord of the Rings* films. Hobbiton epitomizes both the bucolic beauty of the North Island and the filmmaking genius of Peter Jackson, the New Zealander who directed the *Lord of the Rings* trilogy. My economist brain was impressed by how a film location deliberately chosen for its remoteness had been turned into a huge, ongoing tourist attraction. Also, what's not to love about an entire village built for hobbits? In the afternoon, we continued south to Rotorua, a city famous for its hot springs and outdoor activities. The weather was sunny and warm and we had many hours of daylight as the first day of summer in the southern hemisphere drew nearer. We rented a cozy basement in a suburban home and parked our rental SUV in the driveway. Our basement apartment had a galley kitchen and a microwave, and we could drive to a nearby supermarket. Yet even when we tried to survive on bread, cheese, and fruit we consistently spent more than our daily food budget. Restaurants were worse. On the other hand, the outdoor activities were relatively cheap. We lounged for a day in the outdoor hot springs. Leah, Katrina, and I took a peaceful hike on a forested trail, admiring wildflowers and scenic views of Lake Rotorua along the way.

CJ and Sophie found a brochure for a recreation area that offered trapshooting. I was designated as their chaperone. For a nominal amount, a guide drove us in an ATV up a mountain path to a rickety plywood shooting shack. CJ and Sophie each got ten shots with an over-under twelve-gauge shotgun. The clay pigeons were fired away from us from beneath the shooting platform: straight, right, or left. CJ eventually got the hang of it and hit two. Sophie, on the other hand, was alarmingly good. By the end, she had hit five clays in a row: left, left, right, center, right. She looked like a natural as she blasted away with the shotgun. I was both impressed and slightly afraid.

The things that made New Zealand familiar also made it less culturally interesting. Katrina said at one point without irony: "New Zealand is cute. Like Vermont without snow." The rental car gave us great flexibility, but we missed wandering on foot. The places where we were staying felt more cut off than the urban neighborhoods we had become accustomed to. Our mission remained moving quickly to the South Island. We drove the final leg to Wellington, which sits at the southern tip of the North Island. Along the way, the terrain changed repeatedly: rolling green hills; snow-covered mountains; a high, steep vol-

cano; brown scrub grass (site of an army training facility); and finally
the city of Wellington, nestled on the rocky coast. Wellington stirred
two powerful emotions. First, our one night in a hostel cured me of
any lingering regret that we were not staying in more hostels. We had
reserved a "family room," but no such private room was available at
check-in. Instead, our family was spread all over the hostel. Leah and
I shared a four-person room with a young European couple who had
claimed the two bottom bunks. I suspect our roommates were no more
excited to be sharing a room with a fifty-year-old couple than I was to be
climbing up the ladder to the top bunk. I shall not describe the sounds
of gastrointestinal distress that I heard in the communal bathroom as
I queued up to brush my teeth the next morning.

Second, Wellington was where I decided that one of my life goals
was to see a kiwi. I will admit that when we arrived in New Zealand, I
thought kiwis were extinct. Once I learned that spotting a kiwi is a rare
and exciting event, however, I was all in for the kiwi hunt. The rest of the
family did not share my newfound passion, so the next morning I awoke
early and drove alone to Zealandia, a giant conservation area known for
its kiwi population and other indigenous bird life. As I entered Zealandia, an officious woman searched my camera bag, not for alcohol or
weapons or drugs, but to make sure that a ravenous rodent was not lurking inside. New Zealand has no indigenous ground-dwelling mammals.
Over millions of years, many of New Zealand's birds lost their ability
to fly. This was Darwinism at work: Why exert the energy to fly when
it is easier to walk, eat, and sleep on the ground? Alas, predators eventually found their way to New Zealand. More Darwinism: the newly
introduced mammals, the fiercest of which is a weasel-like animal called
a stoat, began devouring the flightless birds, including kiwis. My bag
was searched at Zealandia to keep it as a "predator-free" forest. I walked
for hours as a light rain grew into a steady downpour: many interesting
and colorful birds, but, alas, no kiwis.

❖ ❖ ❖

A ferry carried us across the Cook Strait to the South Island, where we picked up a new rental car and made our way to Nelson, a sleepy town with lovely ocean views and some of New Zealand's best wine country. (Nelson is adjacent to the world-famous Marlborough Region.) In Nelson, we had our only modestly creepy Airbnb experience. We rented an apartment overlooking the ocean from a man who lived in a separate unit just below ours. He was gracious and helpful but also tended to linger awkwardly. One evening he knocked on our door and invited us to visit his home. "I'm not going down there," Sophie declared after he left.

"It'll be fine," I assured her. "He seems nice enough."

"I'll be the designated survivor," Sophie said. "When you don't come back, I'll alert the authorities." As the rest of us were walking out of the apartment, she said dramatically, "I love you all."

Our host welcomed us at the door and ushered us into a darkened living room. As our eyes adjusted, he pointed out the room's most prominent feature: a piano-sized hole in the floor covered by plexiglass. "There's a hole in the floor?" CJ asked.

"Go take a look," our host invited. We peered through the plastic: There was a skeleton lying in a four-foot hole on a bed of sand. We stared uncomfortably at the bones, which I assumed—though could not be certain—were plastic.

"A skeleton," CJ said, capturing the full essence of the moment.

"Yep," our host said proudly.

"Oh my," Leah added, which in Leah-speak means, "Oh my ▮▮▮ ▮▮ God!"

I looked across the room and noticed a woman sitting silently in a dark corner. Our host had not mentioned her, nor had he introduced us. This woman was alive but unmoving, staring back at me with a vacant expression. "Hello," I said instinctively as we made eye contact. She blinked but did not reply. Our host still did not acknowledge her. "Would you like to see the bathroom?" he asked. "I've just fixed it up."

"I know that Sophie is anxious for us to get back," I said.

"She stayed behind," Katrina said.

"She's our sister," CJ said.

"Who's waiting for us to get back," Katrina repeated.

We bade our host farewell and walked briskly back to our apartment. Sophie nodded knowingly as we described the visit. "Just what I thought," she said. "You're alive because of me."

"He's just a quirky guy," I said.

"Was there room in the hole for four more skeletons?" Sophie asked.

"It was a pretty big hole," CJ answered.

"You're welcome," Sophie declared.

❖ ❖ ❖

Leah, Katrina, and I decided to go wine tasting, mostly as a way to explore. Leah opened the "wine map" and chose two vineyards on a scenic peninsula. The tasting at our first stop was ten dollars, or free with the purchase of a bottle of wine. *Not a hard decision.* An older woman was the only person looking after the place. She explained the history of the vineyard while we sampled wine and ate a picnic lunch on a deck overlooking the sloping vineyards. The second stop was another family-owned vineyard, again with an outdoor deck that looked out over a field of grapes and the shimmering blue sea. We were the only ones tasting; the proprietress told us the story of the property, which had originally been an apple orchard. In both places, we felt like we had stopped by someone's beautiful home to have a glass of wine.

Left behind, Sophie and CJ walked into town to get lunch. "Are you guys wagging?" a young clerk at a sandwich shop asked them. The two kids looked at her blankly. "You know, skipping school," she said.

CJ and Sophie exchanged a glance. "Yeah," CJ answered. "We are."

"Totally," Sophie agreed. "We don't go to school."

"Cool," the clerk replied.

❖ ❖ ❖

Sophie's behavior was improving steadily. In fact, she had become downright pleasant. Some of that was sleep; one semi-intended benefit of the trip was that we could all sleep as much as we needed. The family meltdowns tended to come when we deviated from that. Some of it was due to VLACS; we had figured out a system of weekly deadlines that was causing less anguish for all of us. But much of the newfound sweetness was strategic. Sophie was angling for our permission to get a tattoo in Christchurch, which would be our final stop on the South Island.

Back in the U.S., Sophie had expressed vague interest in getting a tattoo, but it was a nonstarter. She needed to be eighteen or have parental consent; she was not eighteen and no parental consent was forthcoming. Once we made our travel plans, however, Sophie discovered that the legal age for getting a tattoo in some parts of the world is sixteen. New Zealand is one of those places. How ironic: Sophie would be able to get a tattoo legally because we had taken her to a place she did not want to go. Neither Leah nor I were keen on the tattoo; on the other hand, what Sophie had in mind was a pea-sized semicolon, the symbol for mental health awareness, just below her rib cage. She had us over a barrel: in Christchurch, where there are lots of tattoo parlors, she would be able to get in a taxi and have it done without our permission. To her credit, she was acting excessively kind and polite to get us on board with the idea. Leah and I considered that a step forward: The mere fact that she was acting with forethought—trying to make us happy in order to get what she wanted—was a sign of maturity. Christchurch was about ten days away; we had some parenting decisions to make before then.

At the one-third point in the trip, I offered reflections in my journal while drinking our New Zealand wine outdoors on a warm, sunny evening. There were no great life epiphanies. I felt no urge to quit my job or sell my possessions. If anything, I was looking forward to returning to Dartmouth and teaching. I missed my regular nonfiction writing; the novel-in-progress was helping to fill that void.

I had been keeping a tally in the back of my journal:

Countries: 8
Bus trips: 28
Flights: 13
Boat rides: 6
Jeep rides: 7

Horse rides: 2

Incidents of motion sickness: 7

Search parties looking for us: 2

Family meltdowns: 5

Books read (by me): 25.

◈ ◈ ◈

Our drive grew progressively more beautiful as we made it farther south. We were also getting better at the road-trip mindset. We took turns picking music playlists (with general agreement). One evening, as we approached a campground where we had a reservation for the night, the song playing as we drove down the final hill was "Hallelujah." I turned up the volume. It was about eight o'clock in the evening; the late spring day was still bright and beautiful. The kids spontaneously began to sing along: three heartfelt but off-key renditions of the refrain. It made for a magical finish to the drive—one of those great, unscripted travel moments: *Hallelujah . . . Hallelujah . . .*

As we made our way toward Queenstown, the hub for outdoor activities near the south end of the South Island, the road snaked around huge lakes with snowy peaks jutting up behind them. We passed fields of white, purple, and pink wildflowers. I pulled to the side of the road periodically to take photos. The family yelled at me each time, which, I will admit, incited me to pull over more often. I was the guy with the camera. More important, I was the guy with the steering wheel. It was on the last stretch to Queenstown that I got my "album cover photo."

We had been driving for five hours, all three kids wedged in the backseat. We were approaching the longest day of the year in the southern hemisphere. The terrain was lovely, but the drive was beginning to feel long. The collective mood in our small SUV was cranky. And then we hit what I can only describe as one of the most visually stunning stretches of road I have ever seen: an open field with snowy mountains in the distance and no signs of development anywhere. The evening sun bathed everything in a gentle light. This photo opportunity was too good to pass up. I swerved onto the shoulder and pleaded for a picture. The family dutifully complied, lining up against the white rental car, each of them displaying a bit of attitude in their own way.

What I was seeing through the lens was gold. *I mean it was literally golden*, in that the soft evening light was casting a golden glow on the four of them and everything in the background. Sophie was wearing sunglasses. Katrina had her arms crossed, as if she would rather be anywhere other than on the side of a remote road in New Zealand posing for a family picture. Leah and CJ were standing patiently, waiting for the photo to be over. What I was seeing through the viewfinder—the collective family attitude with the soft light and the stunning mountainous background—was a moment. I did not want smiles and giggles; I wanted exactly what I was seeing. "Okay, make it look like an album cover," I said.

I snapped my photo. We got back in the car and drove on.

❖ ❖ ❖

Queenstown was our point of departure for the Routeburn Track, a three-day hike. We would stay in huts along the way—the spots Leah had reserved for us while watching *Modern Family* in our living room nearly a year earlier. We slept late on the day of departure, parked at the trailhead, and set off on a gentle four-hour uphill hike to our first hut. Some of the most beautiful things were the subtlest: the moss, the little waterfalls, the intriguing rock formations. Our "hut" for the evening was perched on a scenic overlook—a flat river plain with mountains in the background. "Hut" is a misnomer; these cabins along the trail are large comfortable buildings with huge kitchens, cozy common areas, and communal bunk rooms. We cooked pasta and sauce, played cards, read, and chatted with the other hikers. After dark, we climbed into our sleeping bags as the temperature plunged.

In the morning, Leah made pancakes using the pans she was able to find in the communal kitchen. One of the pancakes happened to burn just as CJ strolled into the kitchen. "Did you burn them all?" he asked loudly. His question was so rude and obnoxious as to be immediately funny. One of our ongoing tasks was dealing with thirteen-year-old boy behavior. Every day presented teachable moments: no interrupting; no talking with your mouth full; no farting loudly in the presence of others; and no saying ridiculously insensitive things to people who have just cooked your breakfast while you were sleeping. It was a slog.*

On day two, we crossed an alpine meadow surrounded by mountains. We climbed steadily to a mountain pass and then down along a river valley toward our hut on the edge of a beautiful mountain lake. The final half hour of the hike took us through an enchanted forest. Every surface was covered by green moss of different hues: dark green, light green, emerald, lime. It was eerie and beautiful at the same time, as if a set designer had built a forest path for the next *Avatar* film.

That evening an Australian school group showed up at the hut: thirty high school students. For Sophie and Katrina, this was manna from heaven. They were suddenly surrounded by scores of English-speaking teens. Better yet, as Americans on a global adventure, they were a curiosity. The Aussies were keen to hear about the American high school experience and how it compared to what they had seen in movies like *High School Musical* and *Mean Girls*. Katrina and Sophie parked themselves at a table with the Aussie students for much of the evening.

On our final morning, we stood on the porch of the hut looking out at the sheets of rain blowing sideways. The weather report was posted on the front door of the hut. It showed rain (and snow at high altitudes) for the next five days. We covered our packs as best we could and set out. In places the path was covered with inches of water, forcing us to step along on rocks. We reached a point where the trail was blocked

---

* There are rumors that CJ's puerile behavior sometimes prompted a "Code Red" in which I would subtly tap my chest, giving Sophie a signal that she could pummel CJ while we looked away. I will not dignify such rumors. I will acknowledge that whenever I look at Sophie and tap my chest, CJ runs screaming out of the room. You can draw your own conclusions.

by a flood; water was spilling down the mountain and across the path with such force that anyone trying to pass might be swept over a steep embankment on the other side. A sign pointed us to an alternate route through the woods. As we began the detour, a distraught young woman came running up the trail. "My boyfriend is missing!" she exclaimed. "He tried to go that way," she said, pointing to the waterfall crashing down on the trail. "Now I can't find him!"

"I'll go look for him," I said.

Was I concerned for my life? Perhaps. Was I a hero? That's not for me to judge. The woman described her boyfriend's rain jacket, and I set off. The water was shin-deep in places. There was a deafening roar as the waterfall pounded me from above. More ominously, the current from the water rushing over the side of the trail made it hard to keep my footing. Visibility was terrible, but I did not see any bright rain jacket. I moved carefully to the side of the trail to see if perhaps the guy had been washed onto the rocks below. Nothing.

I made my way back to the detour to tell the woman that she might need a new boyfriend, perhaps a smarter one. I would explain—with great sensitivity, of course—how evolution weeds out those whose genes may not be best suited for the long-term survival of the species. "Never mind," the woman said when I reached her. "I found him. It turns out he did take the bypass."

After four hours of hiking through the steady rain, we arrived at our finishing point and drove to a motor lodge with good Internet and a coin-operated washer and dryer. In ninety minutes, we were able to satisfy what we now recognized as our basic travel needs: good food, hot tea, clean clothes, and dependable Wi-Fi.

◈ ◈ ◈

The next day we continued on to Invercargill—*the south end of the South Island*. The road trip was effectively done; we'd made it as far as we could drive. I had yet to see a kiwi. The rest of the family did not seem to have the same burning desire as I did to see the national bird of New Zealand. Only Katrina and I had any interest in continuing on to Stewart Island.

The two of us took an early morning ferry across the Foveaux Strait and checked into a hostel in the tiny but picturesque town of Oban. I immediately signed up for a guided kiwi safari, a multi-hour night walk with naturalists through areas where one is most likely to spot a kiwi.

The safari departed at sunset, leaving Katrina and me the day to explore Ulva Island, a predator-free nature sanctuary. We took a small boat to the island. Once again our bags were searched for mammals; the boat driver pointed out an electric cable running through the water to zap any rat that might try to swim from Stewart Island to Ulva Island— more than a mile. The birdlife along the scenic trails was extraordinary. We saw keas, the colorful parrots indigenous to New Zealand, and a host of other interesting creatures. *And then, as we were strolling along on the trail, two kiwis ran out of the bush.*

Words fail me as I try to describe my excitement. I began taking photos as fast as I could shoot: thirty or forty shots from every possible angle. The kiwis paused to feed, pecking at the ground. I changed lenses and took more pictures. I hugged Katrina and then went back to taking photos. What could be more perfect? Here we were—on the island to the east of the island to the south of the South Island—and we had spotted not one, but two kiwis. And we had encountered them during the day, which is highly unusual.

As I snapped away—*the kiwis were still right in front of us*—a group of people came over the bluff. I held up my hand to slow them down. "Kiwis!" I whispered. The group approached slowly. One of the guys said, "That looks like a weka." He came closer. "Yeah, those are wekas. Sorry, mate."

Let's just say that a weka is to a kiwi as a seagull is to a bald eagle.

"So you're still going to do the kiwi safari tonight?" Katrina asked.

"Yeah," I said forlornly.

"You got a lot of good weka pictures," she offered.

❖ ❖ ❖

Katrina had no interest in hunting kiwis after dark. I would be alone: the final survivor in the Wheelan family kiwi hunt. My adventure began at eight o'clock at the ferry terminal. It was the solstice, so the sun was still bright. A naturalist gave a brief introduction during which she told us that there is no shame in confusing a weka for a kiwi—*she really said that, unprompted by me*. The group boarded a boat that wound through various channels on a calm, beautiful evening. We disembarked around dusk and hiked for an hour along forest paths, pausing periodically in response to noises in the bush. Nothing. We made our way to the beach. (At night, kiwis eat the bugs that eat the seaweed; I learned this at the orientation.) Still nothing.

We walked for several more hours in complete silence, six or eight of us in a single-file line. The temperature was falling, and I was starting to shake from the chill. I tried to reconcile myself to the fact that I would likely leave New Zealand without seeing a kiwi. I ticked off rationalizations in my head: Stewart Island was a lot of fun; Katrina and I had enjoyed a great meal at the local pub; the boat ride and the hike were memorably beautiful; the other birds were interesting; the tour company offered our money back if we did not see a kiwi; and we had made it to the island to the east of the island to the south of the South Island. We had done everything we wanted in New Zealand, other than seeing a kiwi.

The money-back guarantee meant that the organizers had an incentive to stay out as long as possible. The hike stretched on; the temperature continued to fall. I was now shivering uncontrollably. And then, somewhere around two in the morning, a kiwi walked across our path—*a real kiwi*. It was a strange-looking creature, like a rodent with bird legs and a bizarrely long beak. We were not allowed to take pictures—the flash would spook the kiwi—but that was no matter. I was like a fisherman who lands a giant catch and then immediately tosses it back. The joy was in the quest, which had been made all the more glorious by the long, dark, cold hike through the night. A few minutes later, another kiwi scurried across the trail in front of us. That was just extra frosting.

Katrina and I caught the morning ferry back to the South Island. No one else in the family seemed distraught that they had missed the kiwis, though Leah was mildly suspicious as Katrina and I described our dinner in the Oban pub.

"It was so good," Katrina gushed. "We had mussels and salmon and a really nice sauvignon blanc."

"And only twenty-three dollars for the both of you?" Leah said.

"You wouldn't believe how funny-looking kiwis are," I said quickly.

◇ ◇ ◇

Our New Zealand adventure was complete, but New Zealand was not done with us. We had an eight-hour drive north to Christchurch, where we would catch our flight to Australia. Christchurch was also where Sophie was planning to get the semicolon tattoo. Katrina, a fount of free parenting advice, told us that we should call Sophie's bluff. Katrina insisted that if we did not drive Sophie to the tattoo parlor, she would be too lazy to get there on her own. Katrina's logic had two flaws. First, Sophie was plenty industrious when it suited her needs—even if online chemistry and pre-calculus were not among those needs. Second, the last thing we wanted was for Sophie to end up at some sketchy tattoo parlor. A tattoo is permanent; so is hepatitis C. Before we left Invercargill, Leah and I used some of our fun money to go out for dinner, where we discussed the issue. We opted for a "consent without approval" approach: We would continue to discourage the tattoo, but if necessary, we would make sure she had it done safely.

The drive to Christchurch was one of the most enjoyable legs of our road trip. We stopped frequently: for chicken peri peri (on my New Zealand bucket list); at the gift shop of a Cadbury chocolate factory; at a great used bookstore. Katrina and I discussed the role of institutions in economic development. As this scintillating conversation stretched into its second hour, Sophie exclaimed, "If this conversation goes on any longer, I'm going to jump from the moving vehicle." She persuaded us to play a sex education trivia game instead. Each child competed to answer age-appropriate sex-related questions. The questions grew steadily harder with each round. CJ began weeping when he lost all his points on a menstruation question.

Sophie did not relent on the tattoo. In Christchurch, I was assigned the task of driving her to Jolly Octopus Tattoo. The tattoo artist was a chatty guy originally from Minnesota. Sophie was on her best behavior. The semicolon tattoo was so small that I had trouble seeing it without my glasses on. It was, all things considered, an anticlimax. Meanwhile, Katrina had noticed a round sore on her calf that was nearly identical to the one on the top of her foot, which was still not healing. While I was chatting up the tattoo artist, Leah went with Katrina to a health clinic to have the sores inspected. The doctor diagnosed a staph infection and prescribed a round of antibiotics.

❖ ❖ ❖

The South Island had been the beautiful adventure we had hoped for. We saw and did many of the things Leah and I had missed on our first trip. We hiked one of the most scenic trails in the world. We had pointed to Ulva Island on the map and then made it there, all with me driving on the left side of the road. We had a diagnosis for Katrina's strange sores.

And I even saw a kiwi.

Chapter 11

The Exploding Penis

The crew warned about seasickness and began passing out pills to ward it off. Because Team Wheelan gets motion sick on any moving vehicle bigger than a donkey cart, we eagerly took the medicine—except Sophie. "I don't get seasick," she declared.

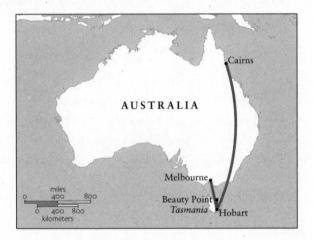

OUR PLAN FOR AUSTRALIA WAS to make our way to the scuba mecca of Cairns, where we would stay long enough for Sophie and CJ to do a scuba certification course. (Leah and I were already certified.) After that, we would head out onto the Great Barrier Reef on a "live aboard" dive boat for three days and two nights. Katrina had plans to travel separately with a high school friend, Bevin. She and Bevin would do the same scuba course as CJ and Sophie, but a few days behind, so that they could have their scuba live aboard experience unencumbered by the rest of us.

It was during the scuba certification class that CJ became concerned that his penis might explode on the ocean floor. For several days, CJ and Sophie spent mornings in a classroom and afternoons in a pool getting used to diving with equipment. Scuba is dangerous in part because of changes in pressure underwater. Gases are compressed as one descends; they expand as one returns to the surface. The first hours of the scuba certification course are full of warnings. If you hold your breath while ascending, your lungs may explode. If you do not properly pressurize your ears, your eardrums will blow out. And so on. Hour after hour on contracting and expanding gases, with CJ dutifully taking notes.

I was sitting in the back of the room doing other work. At the end of the first day, I sidled up to CJ. "They probably won't tell you this," I said, "but if you get an erection on the bottom of the ocean and then ascend too quickly, your penis will explode."

"That doesn't make any sense," CJ protested, but I could sense a glimmer of doubt. "You're joking, right?"

I kept a straight face. "Fine. Don't believe me," I said. "It's your penis."

The next morning, I pulled aside the course instructor, Adam, who was a young guy with exactly the personality one would expect from someone who teaches scuba to beginners: fun, enthusiastic, kind—and with a great Australian sense of humor. I explained what I had told CJ about the penis pressure problem (which, if you are wondering, is *not* true). Might Adam mention this pressure issue to the whole class? "Absolutely, mate!" Adam replied enthusiastically. At the beginning of class, Adam explained "for the benefit of the guys in the group" what might happen if one gets an erection on the ocean floor and then ascends too quickly. The adults in the class recognized the joke. CJ did not. He came home that night and said, "Wow, Dad, I thought you were joking about the exploding penis, but Adam told us the same thing."

And then both Adam and I forgot what we had told him.

❖ ❖ ❖

Our Australian adventure had begun several weeks earlier in Melbourne. We arrived from New Zealand on December 23, just in time for Christmas. All five of us wanted to do "a real Christmas," even if the ninety-degree weather felt more like the Fourth of July. We spent Christmas Eve shopping for stocking stuffers and Secret Santa gifts.

Each of us was assigned to buy a gift for another family member with a ten-dollar limit. We joined the hordes of last-minute shoppers and admired the Christmas windows in the big stores, complete with snow scenes. I bought Leah a Nalgene water bottle. She got me four airplane-size bottles of scotch. Katrina got CJ a pouch of freeze-dried Mexican food. And so on. That night in our Airbnb apartment, we made holiday cookies with homemade frosting, a family tradition passed down from my grandmother to my mother and now to us. Leah bought food coloring at the supermarket and made different frostings, which the kids used to make a flag cookie for each country we had visited. We had cheese fondue for dinner and opened a bottle of white wine. Katrina had two glasses and started dancing happily around the apartment. We played Christmas music on portable speakers we had bought in some airport along the way.

I found myself thinking nostalgically about the rituals of the holiday: visiting my grandparents as a young boy; decorating the tree and sledding in their backyard; putting out cookies for Santa and carrots for the reindeer; and then, decades later, doing the same things with our children in my parents' home. Leah and I made stockings using bags recycled from the Secret Santa shopping and filled them with practical odds and ends: Band-Aids, ibuprofen, antibiotic cream. We gave the kids each a Swiss Army knife and reminded them repeatedly to put the knives in their checked baggage on all future flights. (The first knife would be confiscated by airport security roughly two weeks later.) Our splurge for Christmas Day was an afternoon buffet at the InterContinental Melbourne. We cobbled together the nicest outfits we could conjure from our packs. The temperature was close to a hundred degrees at mealtime; we were bathed in sweat after walking to the hotel. Once we arrived, however, we were transported from our low-budget world to someplace far more elegant.

The InterContinental has a beautiful Gothic stone façade, redolent of an earlier era when hotels represented the height of luxury. On our travel budget, it was not a place we could afford to have coffee, let alone a meal. But this was Christmas. The dining room was enormous, with a high ceiling and a skylight that bathed the tables in natural light. And then there was the buffet, or, more accurately, the buffets: a seafood line with oysters, shrimp, and lobster; a carvery station with roast beef and lamb and ham; a long line of salads and fresh vegetables; and *an entire room of desserts*. As we settled at our table, Santa Claus stopped by to pose for a photo with the children. The meal was the travel equivalent of a snow day—a glorious, if fleeting, escape from a routine to which we would soon return.

❖ ❖ ❖

The only affordable flight to Hobart, Tasmania, left at six a.m. on the day after Christmas. Tasmania (an Australian state) is an island south of Melbourne about the size of Ireland. We awoke in the dark and caught a bus to the airport for the short flight. Upon landing, we filled out paperwork at the rental car desk and then walked out to the lot to pick up our "SUV." The vehicle was so small that it was physically impossible to fit our five modestly sized packs inside and still have room for passengers. Obviously, this did not stop us from trying. The family, having awakened at three-thirty in the morning, was not in top form. I fit four of the bags in the cargo area but could not get the hatch closed. I kicked one of the bags in frustration. "Maybe if you kick it harder," Leah said.

"The bags need to go sideways," Katrina declared.

"It won't make any difference," I said.

"Try putting the big ones on the bottom," Leah instructed.

"It's physics," I yelled. "*These* bags will not fit in *this* car in *this* universe."

"Not with that kind of attitude," Sophie said.

"It has nothing to do with my attitude!" I yelled. "It's a space constraint!"

"Somebody didn't get their coffee this morning," Sophie replied.

As we were squabbling, another family loaded up a larger vehicle and drove off. "Why didn't we rent that car?" CJ asked.

I went back inside to the rental counter and threw money at the problem. We had been consistently missing our daily spending targets since arriving in New Zealand. The upgrade to a larger vehicle was more bad budget news. I managed to save a few bucks by declining the optional insurance coverage. This gave me even more incentive to drive carefully—still on the left side of the road. The only thing worse than driving this expensive SUV would be crashing it.

The weather in Tasmania, which is cooled by winds blowing from the South Pole, was blessedly more pleasant than in Melbourne. We stayed in a small town outside the capital of Hobart with a charming main street and a stone bridge across a meandering river. There was a monument in the center of town to the soldiers who died in the Great War (World War I). I never saw a corresponding monument for World War II, which contributed to the feeling that the town had somehow been frozen around 1920. The cool weather and the idyllic town screamed out for a picnic. We bought bread and cheese at a small shop and settled on a knoll overlooking the stone bridge and the river. I could envision the same picnic in the same place a hundred years earlier, except that the girls would be in fancy hats and hoop skirts, nibbling at fruit and cheese while waiting for a suitor to invite them on a stroll.

For all Tasmania's sleepiness, Hobart is home to a delightfully provocative modern art museum: the Museum of Old and New Art (MONA). I will admit that I am a modern art skeptic; I find a lot of it incomprehensible and silly. Why is it art if you put a knife in a bowl with two live goldfish? On the other hand, we were captivated by the "fat car": a life-sized obese Ferrari. Rather than the sleek lines of a sports car, the flabby Ferrari's frame was bulging and inelegant, like an obese person or animal. "Is that supposed to be us? Like our culture?" I asked Leah. "Overindulgence?"

"I have no idea," she said. We stared at the bizarre car for a while and then wandered over to where a live man with a bare, tattooed back was sitting on a pedestal.

"That's what he does every day?" I whispered.

"It's performance art," Leah explained.

"He's just a guy with a lot of tattoos sitting on a pedestal," I said.

"He can hear you," Leah reminded me.

"Isn't that part of the job?" I said. "He's the one who decided to be a museum exhibit." Eventually the tattooed guy went on his hourly ten-minute break. "Do you think he has a union?" I mused as he walked away.

It was the *Great Wall of Vagina* that rendered CJ speechless. As the name might suggest, the exhibit was a wall of four hundred vaginas: plaster molds of vaginas made from volunteers, young and old. All were displayed along the wall of a corridor, vagina after vagina. CJ wanted to talk about this, but he could not formulate a specific question. "That thing with the vaginas . . ." he began. "Like, who . . ." Still, no complete thought. He stared in silence for a while and then went back to the flabby Ferrari.

◈ ◈ ◈

We took our second vacation from travel in Tasmania. We made our way to Beauty Point, several hours north from Hobart on the opposite side of the island. There we would have a large, lovely estate to ourselves for a week. One of our college friends, Pam, married a guy from Tasmania, Mark. The two of them arranged an invitation for us to stay in Mark's parents' home while they were away for a stretch. We followed the directions and eventually found ourselves outside an electric gate. We entered a code and the gate swung slowly open.

"Is that a tennis court?" CJ exclaimed as we drove up the driveway. It was. There was also a pasture with cattle, lovely flower gardens around the house, and a meadow overlooking a river. We had arrived in the lodging equivalent of the Christmas buffet: a lovely, comfortable house with big bedrooms, a full kitchen, a living room, and another sitting room in a distant wing of the house. The books I had mailed to myself were waiting for me on the dining room table, along with a welcome letter and a bottle of wine from Mark's parents.

We made ourselves at home—because it felt like home. On our first night, we made a baked potato bar and played Scrabble at the dining room table. We celebrated New Year's Day by swimming at a nearby beach. Sophie stayed up late into the night texting with friends back home. Katrina was outside taking extraordinary time-lapse photos of the night sky. I parked myself in the distant wing of the house, where I enjoyed my airplane bottles of Johnnie Walker and wrote about the previous year in my journal. We came together in the living room at midnight to welcome the New Year, sixteen hours ahead of our friends back home.

Beauty Point was surrounded by a tall electric fence to keep the wallabies out. Wallabies look like small kangaroos. As tourists, we were thrilled to spot them jumping across the road or in the bush. *Hey, we're in Australia!* For the locals, wallabies are nuisances. They eat flower gardens and destroy the natural vegetation. Every time we drove in or out of Mark's parents' property, we had to open the electric gate and then close it behind us. Early in our stay, there was a massive electrical storm. During the storm, the electronic gate stopped working, which I discovered only after driving from the house to the gate. There was not enough room to turn around, so I put the SUV in reverse and began backing up. After about thirty yards, I heard a loud scraping noise. I stopped and pulled slowly forward, causing more scraping.

The SUV had grinded against a short light post. The light post was fine, but there was a scratch on the vehicle running across two side panels. *This was going to be a four-digit repair.* How sadly ironic: For all my driving on the left side of the road in New Zealand and Australia, I did the damage while going slowly in reverse. Leah and I expected the budget situation to get better in Asia; the question was how much damage we would do before then—literally and figuratively.

When we returned to Hobart, I dropped the rental car at the airport and reported the damage to a cheerful agent. "Did you sign up for the insurance coverage, Mr. Wheelan?" she asked. And then before I could answer, "Oh, I see that you did not."

"No," I acknowledged, reflecting on the forty-five dollars I had saved by declining the coverage.

"It sure comes in handy sometimes," she said jauntily. "You'll get an e-mail from the company with the charge for the repairs. Shall we put that on the same credit card?" she asked.

"Why not?" I said.

❖ ❖ ❖

We bade farewell to Katrina once again. She flew to Sydney to meet Bevin. Katrina's departure coincided with a major VLACS deadline for Sophie. Per our negotiated agreement, a rigidly defined quantity of work was due at midnight local time. At six o'clock, Sophie informed us that she would be submitting an extra criminal justice assignment—the one class she enjoyed—instead of a chemistry assignment. "It's the same amount of net progress," she pointed out.

"You have to submit an assignment *in chemistry*," Leah replied.

"Either one is fine," Sophie argued.

"Let's consult the text of the agreement," I offered. I retrieved my little blue notebook, as if we were diplomats trying to resolve an international dispute. Thankfully, the particulars of this treaty were clear: Sophie's bid to substitute criminal justice work for chemistry was rejected.

From seven o'clock to nine o'clock, Sophie took advantage of the excellent Wi-Fi to watch *Friends*. Then, as I struggled to uphold my pledge not to nag, she began looking at colleges on the Internet. She stumbled across John Jay College of Criminal Justice in New York, which is part of the City University of New York (CUNY) system. One of Sophie's abiding interests for years had been criminal justice. At ten o'clock, Sophie discovered that John Jay had a volleyball team; she began watching video of the team's matches against other CUNY schools. "I can definitely play there," she said. At ten-thirty, she sent an e-mail to the John Jay volleyball coach expressing an interest in the program.

And then, miraculously, she made her midnight VLACS deadline with reasonably high-quality work.

❖ ❖ ❖

We flew to Cairns for our family scuba adventure. The weather was hot and humid, with rain nearly every afternoon. At times, we could not discern if it was raining or not; everything just felt steamy and wet. The only affordable apartment felt like the kind of place we might end up after getting evicted from our home. Legions of ants drilled regularly on the kitchen counters. The grilling utensils were chained to the grill; the swimming pool had an alarming greenish hue. (We used both.) Mostly, we were killing time while CJ and Sophie finished their scuba certification course.

Katrina and Bevin arrived in town just as we were preparing to leave for the Great Barrier Reef. They rented their own apartment and began the scuba course that CJ and Sophie had just finished. "How are the sores?" we asked Katrina over dinner.

"They're getting better," she insisted nonchalantly. Leah and I inspected her foot and calf. To our eyes, the two round sores were not healing; if anything, they looked larger. Katrina agreed begrudgingly to go to a travel clinic in Cairns if the sores were not better after her dive trip, which would be just a few days behind ours.

The next morning, Leah, Sophie, CJ, and I boarded the eighty-foot ship on which we would be living for three days with fifteen other divers. As the ship left harbor, several small false killer whales surfaced and began playing in our wake, an auspicious beginning to our ocean adventure. The sea quickly grew rough, however. The crew warned about seasickness and began passing out pills to ward it off. Because Team Wheelan gets motion sick on any moving vehicle bigger than a donkey cart, we eagerly took the medicine—except Sophie. "I don't get seasick," she declared. I had given up on changing her behavior. My best hope was that she would throw up overboard rather than in the lounge.

Fortunately, CJ's idiot behavior gave Sophie cover to change her mind. On their first dive, the two of them were required to do certain exercises with the instructor to complete their certification: maintain neutral buoyancy underwater; practice using the auxiliary breathing device; do an emergency ascent; and so on. Sophie, CJ, and the rest of their group assembled on the ocean floor for their drills. As CJ tried to maneuver himself into position, he kicked Sophie in the face and knocked out her regulator—the device that enables one to breathe underwater. Nobody likes to be kicked in the face, especially underwa-ter. *And Sophie really does not like to be kicked in the face by CJ.* To her credit, Sophie did not panic. She retrieved her regulator, using the procedure she had been taught during the certification course, and continued with the dive. When she arrived on the surface, she pointed an accusing fin-ger at CJ: *"You endangered my life!"*

CJ replied calmly, "That's why we did the drills." It was a fair point, though not the response Sophie was looking for. The two of them patched up their dispute, and we all applauded Sophie for staying calm underwater. More important for the seasickness situation, Sophie told us that she had might have swallowed seawater during the regu-lator incident and was going to take Dramamine to avoid getting sick. Needless to say, taking Dramamine does not protect against seawater-induced nausea—but it gave Sophie cover to do the sensible thing, which was progress.

◈ ◈ ◈

Before each dive, we assembled on the top deck for a dive briefing. The dive master described where we would be going underwater and what we would be seeing. These pre-dive meetings had the feel of a military briefing: compass headings, warnings about the current, and so on. There were instructions like, "Do eighty kicks at a compass bearing of fifty degrees and then turn left at the giant mushroom coral." I have a prodigiously poor sense of direction *aboveground*. Underwater, it was worse. All the visual signposts that seemed obvious on the whiteboard were difficult to discern. There are a lot of corals, and many of them look like mushrooms. Leah was nearly as bad at navigating underwater as I was. Getting lost on a coral reef is not as ominous as it sounds; there is always the option of swimming to the surface and looking around. On our first dive, Leah and I popped up two hundred yards from the boat. We signaled to the dive master that we were okay and then opted for a long swim back to the ship rather than having the crew pick us up in the dinghy—a little rubber raft nicknamed "The Dinghy of Shame."

Once CJ and Sophie finished their certification drills, we could dive as a family. On the second day, I buddied up with Sophie. The dive began well. We saw a massive barracuda lurking under the boat. We glided over a reef shark lounging on the sand. I had rented an underwater camera for the dive, so we were able to get photos of the extraordinary things we were seeing, such as a beautiful jellyfish floating near the surface—a stunning translucent pink, almost like a painting. At about the midpoint of the dive, however, Sophie and I had a navigational dispute. One feature of scuba diving, obviously, is that there is no verbal communication. I was pointing to a sandy wedge in the reef that I believed was a reference point. Sophie was gesticulating strenuously that we should go in a different direction. The underwater argument grew more animated: pointing and waving and assorted facial gestures. (Eye-rolling underwater is even more dramatic because the water and mask magnify the eyes, making them look gigantic.) I prevailed in the end and led us farther in what turned out to be the wrong direction.

After a dive in which Leah and I surfaced even farther from the boat than usual, CJ probed the source of our poor navigation skills. He held up a black plastic gauge attached to his tank with two round dials: the compass and the pressure gauge (which indicates how much oxygen is left in the tank). "Can you read the compass without your glasses on?" he challenged me.

I stared at the two blurry gauges. "Which one is the compass?" I asked eventually.

"Oh, Jesus!" Sophie exclaimed.

"What about you, Mom?" CJ probed.

"That one is the compass," she said, correctly indicating the compass.

"What is our current heading?" CJ asked, pointing at the needle on the compass.

"Is that a fifty or an eighty?" Leah replied.

Mystery solved. Leah commented near the end of our dive adventure, "It's neat to see the kids get better at things than we are."

Later that day we engaged in one of life's great adventures: the night dive. As with the other dives, we assembled on the top deck for a briefing, only now we were enveloped by darkness. The boat's underwater lights cast rays of light into the black water, which attracted schools of little fish. The little fish attracted bigger fish. *During the dive briefing, we looked overboard and saw reef sharks circling the boat.* We geared up, each of us attaching a fluorescent glow stick to our oxygen tank, and then lined up on the dive platform at the back of the boat. A crewmember handed us flashlights, and one at a time we plunged into the dark ocean: a big step into the water, the okay sign while bobbing on the surface, and then a descent down the anchor line.

During the day, one can look down the rope while descending and see the bottom. At night, one can only see the flashlight beam for five feet or so as it illuminates the green algae waving gently on the anchor rope. Beyond that: darkness. We descended to the bottom and swam in a row, each of us following the glow light on the tank of the diver ahead. Slowly our eyes adjusted, making it possible to see beyond the beams of our flashlights. The diver ahead of me motioned to a wall of coral, where a moray eel was jutting out, its mouth snapping open and shut. We made our way around reef formations, where the giant sea turtles were sleeping with their heads in crevices and their giant bodies sticking out, like small children who cover their eyes and think that no one can see them. A large gray reef shark—with a thick body, not unlike that of a great white—appeared out of the darkness, glided above us, and then disappeared back into the darkness, once again invisible to us. I fought the impulse to wave my flashlight in all directions, looking for that shark or others that might be lurking in the darkness. Instead, I clung tightly to the advice from the dive briefing: "Just admire their beauty. If you don't do anything stupid, they won't hurt you."

◈ ◈ ◈

Every dive on the Great Barrier Reef presents some surprise: a hawks-bill turtle, a giant clam, a whitetip reef shark. As a boy growing up in Chicago, one of my favorite places was the Shedd Aquarium, which has a huge coral reef exhibit. I remember standing at the window gaping at the teeming life, especially at the posted times when a diver would plunge into the tank and feed the fascinating creatures. Now we were

living for days on the real thing. The experience was tinged with sad-
ness, however. On some dives, we navigated through large dead areas,
the underwater equivalent of a forest decimated by fire. Both Leah and
I concluded independently that the Great Barrier Reef had more barren
patches than we remembered from our diving twenty-five years earlier.

When we reached shore, the dive instructor Adam pulled me aside.
"Did you ever tell CJ that we were just joking about his penis blowing
up?" he asked.

"No. Did you?"

"I assumed you did, mate."

The two of us pulled CJ aside and informed him of the joke. He
smiled admiringly. "You had me," he said. "There was one time I was
really worried. About ten minutes into the fourth dive—"

"Stop there, mate," Adam said. "We don't need the details."

Chapter 12

Do You Have What It Takes to Cross Four Lanes of Saigon Traffic?

One must marvel at the resiliency of the place—the remarkable fact that less than fifty years after that gruesome conflict we could return as American tourists. Will there be tourists in a vibrant, thriving Syria in less than half a century?

WE WERE A LONG WAY FROM AUSTRALIA, having made our way through Southeast Asia to Cambodia. Katrina and I were sitting on the back deck of a long, thin motorboat as we traveled from Phnom Penh to Siem Reap, a journey that takes the better part of a day. Our boat was headed north in the Tonlé Sap Lake, which serves as a transportation route between the two cities, as well as a source of fish and water (and sewage disposal) for all the villages along the banks.

Leah, Sophie, and CJ were in the cabin where there was a modicum of air-conditioning. Katrina and I were taking photos: families in little boats who waved excitedly; fishermen casting nets in the shallows;

clusters of simple wooden houses on stilts; groups of schoolchildren walking to or from school along the riverbanks. Katrina was wearing flip-flops, and I noticed that her left foot was red and swollen. She had gone to an urgent care clinic in Cairns, as promised, where a doctor had diagnosed the sores as tropical ulcers—not a staph infection, as she had been told in New Zealand—and prescribed an antibiotic ointment. But now the ulcers were as big as ever; the redness and swelling suggested a secondary infection. Katrina's red foot would be alarming anywhere, but we were in the middle of a lake in Cambodia.

"How long has it been like that?" I asked Katrina.

"Just today," she said.

I went inside the cabin to confer with Leah. We decided to take Katrina to a clinic or hospital as soon as we arrived in Siem Reap. The boat felt even slower for those last hours, as I stared at Katrina's foot trying to persuade myself that the redness was not getting worse.

We docked in Siem Reap and hired a small van to take us into the city. During the ride, Sophie and CJ speculated that Katrina would most likely have her foot amputated. "You'll kill it at the Paralympics," Sophie said.

"But you have to get one of those new prosthetic limbs—the kind that can receive signals from the brain," CJ advised. The levity helped a little. Katrina seemed surprisingly unconcerned—naïvely so, to my mind.

Meanwhile, I called our travel insurance company for guidance. The company keeps a database of vetted medical providers around the world. The person we reached on the phone gave us an address for an international clinic. Once in the city, we hired a tuk-tuk, a small motorized cart with bench seats in the back, to take us there. When we arrived, the clinic looked like it had been shuttered for months, if not years.

There was no more jovial banter. We instructed the tuk-tuk driver to take us to the Angkor Hospital for Children. By remarkable coincidence, I had visited this hospital with graduate students nine years earlier. I had been impressed by the hospital's work with children harmed by the millions of land mines left over from the brutal civil war in the

1970s. But never in my wildest nightmares did I think that I would return to the Angkor Hospital for Children with one of my children as a patient.

A guard met us at the entrance to the hospital, and we showed him Katrina's foot. "How old is she?" he asked.

"She's a child," I said. "We're her parents." For once, Katrina did not quibble.

The man asked to see her passport. "She's eighteen," he said. "I'm sorry. That's too old." The Angkor Hospital for Children only treats children up to age sixteen.

We returned to the waiting tuk-tuk. "I got carded," Katrina told her siblings. The driver suggested that we go to the city's main hospital. Our tuk-tuk pulled into the ambulance bay of the Royal Angkor International Hospital, a huge, brightly lit building on one of the city's main avenues. The lobby was clean and orderly, and Katrina saw a doctor immediately. He assured us that the infection around her sores could be treated with antibiotics. The nurses recommended that Katrina keep the ulcers covered—the opposite of what she had been told in Australia.

The redness and swelling went away once Katrina began taking the antibiotic, but the underlying medical issue was still there: these two puzzling, circular sores. I texted my parents from the hospital to update them. My mother hectored me to take Katrina's wounds seriously—an understandable if unhelpful sentiment. For the first time, Leah and I contemplated flying with Katrina to someplace with a top-notch tropical disease clinic, perhaps Singapore or Bangkok. Katrina insisted her leg would be fine, though with less conviction than in the past.

❖ ❖ ❖

Leah, Sophie, CJ, and I had arrived in Southeast Asia two weeks earlier, having flown to Hong Kong from Australia. (Katrina was finishing up her scuba trip with Bevin and planned to meet us in Vietnam after a stop on her own in Singapore.) The density of Hong Kong is striking. Our barely affordable guesthouse was on the thirteenth floor of a high-rise. There was a sign near the entrance warning visitors to keep the windows closed so rats would not climb in. *On the thirteenth floor!* The four of us had a single room with two undersized double beds that took up nearly all the floor space. The bathroom was so small that the easiest way to shower was to sit on the toilet.

The Wi-Fi was good, which made up for the lack of space. Sophie took a criminal justice exam—VLACS progress! As promised, the Tasmanian rental car company sent me an e-mail with a bill for the SUV damage: $1,125.29. In the U.S., many credit card companies will pay for rental car damage if the car was rented using their card. (Full disclosure: This was not the first time I had backed a rental car into a fixed object.) I dialed the number on my American Airlines Mastercard and explained the accident. "This happened to me once before, and the credit card company paid the deductible on my auto insurance," I said.

"That was in the U.S.?" the woman asked.

"Yes," I admitted.

"But the accident you're telling me about was an international rental?" she asked.

"Yes, in Australia," I said.

"Then we'll pay for the whole thing," the woman said without any emotion or inflection.

"I'm sorry?" I said, even though the line was perfectly clear.

"Since it's an international rental, we will pay for all the damage to the car," she repeated.

"The whole deductible?" I asked. "Whatever my auto insurance won't pay?"

"No. *All of the damage to the car*," she said slowly and loudly. "Just forward me the claim from the rental car company."

With one click, the bill for $1,125.29 went away. That was a good budget day.

❖ ❖ ❖

The fourteenth of January was CJ's birthday. He opted to celebrate by eating "the best dumplings in all of Hong Kong." CJ's fastidious research on TripAdvisor led us to a restaurant with a Michelin star in an ultramodern shopping mall. CJ, now fancying himself as something of a food critic, described the dumplings as "the perfect blend of spice, flavor, and texture." We bought him a slice of birthday cake at the Starbucks next door.

CJ's birthday took a sadder turn the next day when we went in search of a used bookstore that we had read about online. We took a ferry across the harbor from the Kowloon side of the city to the Hong Kong side, where the neighborhoods are older and more traditionally Chinese. As we wandered toward the bookstore, we passed many small, decrepit storefronts. Sometimes we could identify the items for sale: fruit, spices, flowers. Often, the stinky, dried objects in large bins were unidentifiable.

Unfortunately, the shark fins were easy to spot. Our time on the Great Barrier Reef had inspired CJ the Eco Warrior to embrace the crusade against shark fin soup, a notorious Chinese delicacy. The shark fins are harvested by cutting them off living sharks, which are then dumped back into the ocean to die. Tens of millions of sharks are killed this way every year. Many upscale hotel chains have taken shark fin soup off their menus, but it is still a common delicacy in Hong Kong and China. CJ grew increasingly distraught as we passed store after store with mounds of dried fins for sale. Eventually he started to cry. "Why do they do this?" he asked as the tears rolled down his face.

"It's getting better," I said. This was true, but inadequate in the moment.

❖ ❖ ❖

From Hong Kong, we flew south and west to Ho Chi Minh City (Saigon), Vietnam. Our guesthouse was in a dense tourist area, with scores of restaurants less than a hundred paces from our front door. On the first morning, I wandered down the chaotic little street and had a delicious breakfast for $4: fresh fruit, great coffee, and a baguette with jam and butter. I will not defend French involvement in Indochina. I will point out that they left a legacy of great food, particularly the pastries and baguettes. I was also optimistic that Southeast Asia would be good for our budget.

The homeschooling efforts were in a decent place, too. CJ and I watched *War Horse* to finish up his study of World War I. Sophie finished a paper on *The Crucible*. Before Saigon, I had tried to give Sophie and CJ an overview of the Vietnam War, but I found myself struggling to explain the complexity of the conflict. It is hard to explain the rationale for a failed war when the impetus for that war, the rise of communism, is no longer a threat. That changed dramatically once we were in Vietnam. Our first outing was to the War Remnants Museum, which tells the story of the war from the Vietnamese perspective. (Prior to the normalization of relations between the United States and Vietnam in 1995, it was called the Exhibition House for Crimes of War and Aggression.)

We opted to walk to the museum, giving us our first exposure to Saigon's frenetic streets. Every square inch of sidewalk is packed with stalls and parked motorbikes. If the city were an amusement park, the feature ride would be the Street Crosser™. *"Do you have what it takes to cross four lanes of Saigon traffic?"* The dominant form of transportation is the motorbike; there are often ten or fifteen riding abreast. Rarely does the traffic come to a complete stop. As a result, crossing the street requires a leap of faith: step off the curb; walk predictably; and hope that all fifty motorcycles will steer around you, like a school of fish swimming around a fixed object. *And never, never stop or turn around.*

The War Remnants Museum shook us even before we entered the building. The courtyard has a collection of captured American tanks, planes, and helicopters. One realizes almost immediately that the Americans who flew or drove these war machines likely ended up dead or in Vietnamese prisons. The smallest details had the biggest impact, such as the stickers on the planes offering safety warnings: Do NOT STEP HERE and FILL THIS TANK FIRST. I could envision American soldiers adhering to (or ignoring) these little warnings as they fought a war nine thousand miles from home. And then one day their luck ran out.

My conversations with CJ about Vietnam made the work we had done on World War I feel more relevant, too. The defining feature of that conflict was the folly of it all: the alliances that precipitated it, the gruesome trench warfare, the punitive Treaty of Versailles that made future conflict with Germany more likely. CJ and I had watched films like Stanley Kubrick's *Paths of Glory* and read books like *All Quiet on the Western Front* that were brilliant because of the way they portrayed the human costs of World War I, just like the War Remnants Museum does for Vietnam.

At the same time, we were surrounded by the miracle of postwar Vietnam. The vibrant streets are testimony to how the nation has been transformed in the decades after the war. One must marvel at the resiliency of the place—the remarkable fact that less than fifty years after that gruesome conflict we could return as American tourists. Will there be tourists in a vibrant, thriving Syria in less than half a century?

The ABC Bakery (that's really what it was called) became my morning ritual. After months of counting every penny, it was a luxury to buy a heaping tray of pastries—baguettes and croissants and chocolate-covered things—for only a few dollars. *And if I wanted a second cup of coffee while I was writing, I could go back and get one!* I made my way to the ABC Bakery every morning to write for an hour and a half or so. After that, I would take a bag of pastries back to our rooms, where the rest of the family was just waking up.

We made a day trip from Saigon to see the Cu Chi tunnels. During the war, the guerrillas built underground encampments: sleeping areas, cooking areas, and ammunition depots, all connected by narrow, maze-like passages. Part of the tunnel network has been preserved, and it offers a fascinating, if horrifying, snapshot of the war. For example, the U.S. Army had soldiers known as "tunnel rats," whose job it was to drop into the narrow tunnels and destroy everything inside while avoiding mines, booby traps, and enemy fire. We were invited to crawl through a stretch of tunnel; it immediately gave me claustrophobia and I turned around. I could not imagine doing it in the dark with people shooting at me.

There were displays of the spiked pits that were used during the war to impale the unlucky soldiers who stepped in the wrong place. Our guide took great pleasure in describing the gore of each booby trap. I found it strange, and eventually annoying, that both our guide and the video we were forced to watch at the visitors' center described only "Vietnamese patriots" and "American invaders." There was no mention of the South Vietnamese Army. One can argue at length about U.S. involvement in Vietnam, but the conflict was first and foremost a civil war between North and South Vietnam. Many of the soldiers falling into the gory traps that our guide took such pride in describing were members of the South Vietnamese Army, which suffered enormous casualties at the hands of the North. My quibbles notwithstanding, the Vietnam War no longer felt like a chapter in a U.S. history textbook.

❖ ❖ ❖

Once Katrina arrived in Saigon, we all boarded a bus for the five-hour trip to Phnom Penh, Cambodia. It was the beginning of Tet, the Vietnamese New Year. The holiday is celebrated for a week during which young people travel to visit extended family—like Thanksgiving and Christmas rolled into one. Every seat on the bus was full; the cargo hold was packed with electronics and other gifts. I settled into a tiny seat, made even less comfortable by the bags of coffee beans wedged where my feet were supposed to go.

After several hours, we crossed from Vietnam into Cambodia. The Cambodian countryside has a unique rural beauty: glimmering rice paddies; water buffalos plowing the fields; myriad shades of green and brown; ponds with pink and lavender lily pads. As we rolled toward Phnom Penh, the setting sun cast a warm light on these bucolic scenes, as if they had been painted by French impressionists. Even the view from the men's room at our rest stop was bucolic, as the bathroom was open to the fields beyond. I was so taken by the lovely view from the urinal that I snapped a photo.

The rest of the family was buying snacks when I returned from the men's room. Katrina has the best photo sense of the group. I showed her the display on my camera. "Look at this artistic photo," I said. "I'm calling it, *The Cambodian Countryside as Seen from the Men's Urinal*."

"That's disgusting," she said.

"It's actually kind of pretty," Leah offered.

"Don't encourage him," Katrina admonished.

◈ ◈ ◈

Cambodia offers up both wonder and horror. The wonder is ancient: Angkor Wat, the stunning complex of temples built in the twelfth century as the capital of the Khmer Empire. The various temples of Angkor Wat are spread over an expansive territory, often miles apart. Some are so enmeshed in the jungle that they have only recently been discovered. Despite that, the entrance to the main temple, the one that shows up on posters and postcards, is chaotic and crowded. "We can rent a tuk-tuk for half a day to escape the craziness," Leah advised.

The tuk-tuk whisked us to the more remote temples, like hiking into the Grand Canyon rather than standing on the observation platform. With that, the experience was transformed from a battle against the tour bus hordes into a peaceful family adventure. Many of the temples were made more interesting by the way huge trees have grown up, around, and sometimes through the ancient stone structures. We climbed and explored at our own pace, pausing for reflection in some of the quiet, solitary spots. CJ and Sophie appreciated the Indiana Jones quality of the ancient structures nestled in the jungle. Katrina and I tried to take photos that captured the light playing on the stone and moss and tangled trees.

If Angkor Wat reflects the wonder of Cambodia, the genocide— sadly, far more recent—is the horror. In the 1970s, the nominally Marxist Khmer Rouge killed several million people—roughly a quarter of the Cambodian population. Led by the notorious Pol Pot, the Khmer Rouge emerged from the jungles and ultimately took over the country. To the extent that the Khmer Rouge had any coherent ideology, it was an emphasis on agricultural self-sufficiency that targeted educated, urban elites as the enemy. At the height of the insanity, anyone with eyeglasses—a sign of education—was at risk of arrest or murder.

The most effective memorial to this murderous period is the Tuol Sleng Genocide Museum, which was built on the site of a notorious Khmer Rouge prison. The prison complex was a high school before the guerrillas took it over. Some reminders of that more pleasant era are still there: three-story buildings with outdoor hallways that surround a green courtyard with flowering trees. When the Khmer Rouge moved into the complex, they converted the classrooms into torture chambers and prison cells. A gallows was erected in the courtyard for hanging prisoners.

Each prisoner was photographed upon arrival at Tuol Sleng. Those photos are now part of the museum: hundreds of black-and-white head-shots posted on the walls of the old prison cells—row after row of those who fell victim to the place. When I looked closely at the photos, I was certain I could see fear in the prisoners' eyes.

I wish I could report that exposure to these horrors prompted the young members of the Wheelan family to reflect on their privilege and good fortune. In fact, Cambodia was the site of CJ's most epic melt-down. He and Sophie had been squabbling for some time over petty things, such as whether CJ had blocked Sophie's path to the bathroom with his backpack. "Figure it out yourselves," Leah and I said in unison when they tried to raise their respective grievances. However, CJ's bad mood escalated during an outdoor dinner at an Indian restaurant. We were seated at a table on a patio beneath an overhead fan. The temperature was near-perfect and we were enjoying our outdoor meal. The overhead light attracted some black bugs that looked like grasshoppers and were jumping around in an unpredictable way.

One of these grasshopper-like bugs landed on CJ's plate. He jumped out of his seat, screaming and waving his arms. He was unable to calm himself. Instead, he became hypersensitive to the other insects buzzing harmlessly about. Soon his hysteria became unbearable, and the rest of us came to a unanimous decision. "You're out," I said, waving my thumb like an umpire.

"What's that's supposed to mean?" CJ asked.

"You've been evicted from the table," I said.

Leah concurred. "Take your plate somewhere else," she said.

"You can't do that!" CJ protested.

"We just did," I said.

"Where am I supposed to go?" CJ asked.

Leah pointed inside the restaurant. "There are plenty of tables."

CJ picked up his plate and walked away. When we looked in the restaurant ten minutes later, he was eating happily with an older English couple.

CJ's ridiculous behavior inspired some humorous healing. The rest of us wanted an apology. Also, we were looking for a way to remind the friends and family following our trip that life on the road was not all roses. I offered up the idea of holding a videotaped "press conference" in which CJ would abase himself for his actions, like a disgraced politician. The next day, with one of the Angkor Wat temples as a backdrop, CJ read from a script while Katrina filmed the statement with her phone. I used my camera to make clicking noises to approximate a press conference. He looked somberly into the camera and said:

> I deeply regret many of my actions yesterday. At times, my behavior did not conform to the high standards I set for myself. Mistakes were made. I have now seen the error in my ways. I realize that the presence of small crickets should not be a cause for hysteria at dinner. I should not have used foul language when Sophie moved my possessions to clear a path to the bathroom. I am committed to better behavior today, tomorrow, and for the remainder of the trip. Thank you for your attention. I will not be taking questions at this time.

We posted the clip on Facebook (where it has over eighteen hundred views).*

---

* https://www.facebook.com/charles.wheelan/videos/10210605581607606/.

❖ ❖ ❖

Our plan was to visit northern Vietnam, which has a distinctly different culture and history than the south. The most efficient way to get there was to return to Hanoi and then travel north. (In a region character-ized by impenetrable jungle—other than for opium traffickers—the fastest way between two points is not always a straight line.) We had booked a "sleeper bus" from Saigon to the coastal city of Nha Trang. If the overnight buses in South America were like business class on a fine airline, the Vietnamese buses were more like a convict ship. The "sleepers" were not seats that reclined to a comfortable position. Rather, they were fixed bunks, an upper and a lower. One line of bunks ran the length of the bus along the right side, one ran along the left side, and one was squeezed in the middle (where I was). Lying down was the only option; passengers were essentially stacked on the bus. Just as I managed to fall asleep, the bright fluorescent lights snapped on as we stopped for a bathroom break.

At the end of the trip we were dropped on a dark street corner in Nha Trang at five-fifteen a.m. We had all slept poorly on the cramped bus. Now we had another problem: no hotel room. Leah had not been able to find any rooms online because of the Tet holiday, which is Vietnam's busiest travel period. As we stood in the dark, she laid out our options. We could travel on; this would require booking an overnight bus on to Hoi An—two sleepers in a row. Even that was not a sure thing, however. With all the Tet travel, there was a good chance that the bus would be sold out, in which case we would end up sleeping on the beach. Or we could search for a hotel in Nha Trang—but the longer we waited to buy onward bus tickets, the more likely they were to be sold out.

"We need to buy bus tickets *immediately*," Katrina declared. "We'll never find a hotel room."

"Why wasn't I consulted about any of this?" Sophie asked accus-ingly. Under different circumstances, this would have been laugh-out-loud funny. Sophie had not been consulted on any decision in the last five months, nor had she expressed any interest. CJ was surprisingly calm and quiet, perhaps because of the predawn hour.

"Give me a little time," I pleaded. There were large hotels in every direction. All we needed was one cancellation. Also, the thought of two overnight buses in a row was miserable.

"The tickets are going to sell out," Katrina warned.

Leah is the family member best suited to put down a rebellion, like the Jimmy Stewart character in *It's a Wonderful Life* when he climbs on the counter of the Bailey Building and Loan and calms the depositors to ward off a run on the bank. "Let's try to find a room," she urged. "It's a big city." The kids warily agreed.

Having been raised in the pre-Internet era, I set out to find a hotel room the old-fashioned way: I walked in and asked the desk clerk if there was a room available. The first two hotels I tried were full. But the third—still only two hundred yards from where the family was standing sullenly with our luggage—had a "penthouse" free. The room slept five; for an extra twenty dollars the proprietress agreed to let us check in right away.

"It's a penthouse and we can check in now!" I reported back to the group.

"How far?" Katrina asked skeptically.

"Right there," I said, pointing to a modern high-rise across the street. For one brief moment, I basked in their adulation and respect.

Nha Trang is nestled on the coast of the South China Sea with lovely swimming beaches running the length of the city. We walked on the beach; we swam. The city is a popular tourist destination for Russians, perhaps going back to the Cold War. In a culture-bending evening, we had dinner at a German brewhouse surrounded by Russian tourists as a Vietnamese cover band played Pink Floyd and Amy Winehouse. It was a relaxing place to pause before stacking ourselves on another overnight bus to Hoi An.

Vietnam is long and narrow, just over a thousand miles from south to north, but only thirty miles wide at its narrowest point (and three hundred at its widest). Hoi An, one of Vietnam's most picturesque cities, is about halfway up the country. The historic district, a World Heritage site, has no motorized traffic, which allowed us to stroll past the ancient wooden buildings in relative peace. At night, the narrow streets were lit by the colorful glow of silk lanterns.

This was all lovely. But to me as a policy guy, the most striking feature of Hoi An was the clothing industry: shop after shop offering made-to-order suits, jackets, dresses, shoes, shirts. There were fifty or sixty stores, many of them in a row, with mannequins in the window and touts darting out the door to offer great deals to passersby. Every store offered a variation on the same basic service: Order the item (pants, suit, shirt, etc.); get measured; choose a fabric and style; and come back in a few hours for a fitting. The result was custom-made clothing overnight, or on the same day for a little extra.

"What exactly makes this country Communist?" Katrina asked as she observed the hustling entrepreneurs. The efficiency was brilliant—right down to the woman who would show up on a motorcycle with a scale and boxes to ship the items anywhere in the world.

Hoi An was where we finally made progress in treating Katrina's bizarre ulcers. The improbable hero was my mother. "Send me a picture of them," she demanded when we called from Hoi An. "I'm going to the dermatologist tomorrow, and I'll ask her what they are." To placate her—remember the conference with the middle school gym teacher—I snapped photos of the sores and texted them along. I can only imagine my mother's conversation with her doctor: "While I'm here, could you look at this photo of my granddaughter's foot? She's in Vietnam." How does Medicare bill for that?

Everything about the situation was ridiculous—except that it worked. My mother's dermatologist made a diagnosis from the photo: leishmaniasis, a potentially dangerous flesh-eating parasite spread by the bite of a sand fly. We immediately went to the Centers for Disease Control website and learned there are two strains of leishmaniasis, one more dangerous than the other. Katrina would need a biopsy to determine which strain she had. This became our top priority for Hanoi, which was our next stop and a much bigger city.

We flew to Hanoi rather than taking another overnight bus. On our first morning, Katrina and I set off in a taxi to the International SOS clinic, an impressive facility that appeared to serve mostly expatriates. A doctor from Singapore confirmed the leishmaniasis diagnosis. "Can we get a biopsy done here to determine the strain?" I asked.

"It would have to be done in a local hospital," the doctor said. After a moment, he continued uncomfortably, "I would not recommend that." The biopsy is an invasive procedure, he explained. Having it done in a Hanoi hospital would present risks of its own. Still, we finally knew what we were dealing with, if not necessarily the strain. The Singaporean doctor was a member of an online community of tropical disease specialists. He offered to solicit information from the group and e-mail us any helpful information.

◈ ◈ ◈

From a historical perspective, the capstone to Vietnam was a visit to the Hoa Lo Prison, better known as the "Hanoi Hilton" and the place where former Senator John McCain was held as a prisoner of war for more than five years. The former prison is fascinating—though not in the way the Vietnamese authorities intend. It is the clumsy and self-serving propaganda, rather than the exhibits, that make the place so revealing. We watched a video running on a loop that explained how "lucky" the American prisoners were to have ended up at this fine institution and how "grateful" they were to their captors. There was even a reference to the nickname "Hanoi Hilton"—*but without the irony*, as if the U.S. prisoners really had come to think of the place as a high-end hotel. There were photos of the prison staff giving gifts to the POWs upon their release.

At the same time, the Hanoi Hilton offers powerful lessons in forgiveness. In 2000, Senator John McCain visited the place where he had been imprisoned and tortured. It was an inspiring gesture of reconciliation, both by him as a person and between the United States and Vietnam. Pete Peterson, America's first postwar ambassador to Vietnam, had also been a POW at the Hanoi Hilton. Like McCain, he was tortured there. As much as the war permeates an American's visit to Vietnam, so, too, does this remarkable eagerness to heal—not to forget the conflict, but to move beyond it.

As we contemplated our departure from Vietnam, the travel planning grew more complex. One urgent goal was to get Katrina to a tropical disease clinic. The most logical option was the School of Tropical Medicine in Calcutta, where there were doctors with experience in treating leishmaniasis. We were headed west toward India and could get there reasonably quickly. The only complication with the Calcutta plan was that we would need a multiple-entry Indian visa rather than a single-entry visa. We had plans to visit friends in Mumbai later in the spring; we would likely leave India after treatment in Calcutta and enter the country a second time.

A multi-entry Indian visa may seem like a mere formality. In fact, we had put ourselves on a collision course with one of the most formidable and officious institutions in the world: the Indian bureaucracy.

Chapter 13

Indian Bureaucracy 2, Wheelan Family 1

The visas were ready, the consular official informed us. There was just one formality left, he said. Both of us would have to be fingerprinted. All ten digits. For most families, this might seem like a formality. For ours, it was not.

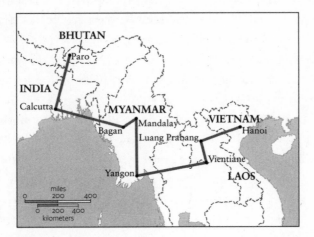

THE VISA SECTION OF THE INDIAN EMBASSY in Yangon, Myanmar, is open every weekday from nine-thirty to eleven a.m. Katrina and I arrived at 10:50, figuring we would pick up the forms and then return the next day with our documents in order. The first visit would be a reconnaissance mission. What we failed to realize is that even reconnaissance planes get shot down from time to time. Poised just inside the entrance of the visa section was a gatekeeper in the literal sense of the word: an Indian woman whose sole job consisted of letting people in or out—but mostly keeping them out.

The woman pointed to the sign on the door saying the office was closed. I pointed vigorously to the sign next to the door indicating that the visa section was open until eleven, and then to my watch, which showed that it was 10:51. As I was gesticulating on the stoop, a man arrived carrying some forms and a stack of crisp American bills. The woman let him in. As she went to close the door, I stuck my foot in it. There were more pantomimes on both sides, with my foot still wedged in the door.

I explained that if I could get the forms and ask one simple question— a ninety-second undertaking—then we would be prepared to return the next day with everything in order. At that point, a sanctimonious European gentleman* told me that I was being rude. He was technically correct. But his criticism would have carried more weight *if he were not already standing inside, looking at me over the shoulder of the gatekeeper.* It was like someone sitting in a lifeboat reprimanding me for splashing and yelling as I tried to climb in.

I did not get the rest of my body inside the door before eleven. Katrina and I returned to the hotel and downloaded the requisite forms. The next day we returned to the embassy well before the posted opening time of nine-thirty a.m. When the office opened, Nasty Woman in a Sari was once again standing guard. We watched in horror as she slammed the door on an elderly Japanese man *who was there for his fifth visit.* As I looked around at the other supplicants in line, I began to have a bad feeling. Everyone else had electronically uploaded their photos to the visa form. Our photos were attached with a paper clip; the instructions online had said that uploading the photos was optional.

After an hour and fifteen minutes of waiting outside in brutal heat, we were admitted to the promised land: the air-conditioned antechamber of the visa section. In an adjacent room, the clerks distributing visas were standing behind windows like bank tellers. A male official asked to see our paperwork. I presented him the forms and the required cash. He shook his head disapprovingly. "The photos must be uploaded to the form," he said. "Also, these dollar bills are not acceptable."

---

* In my journal, I referred to him slightly differently, but there is no reason to dwell here on the part of the human anatomy he most closely resembled.

Each visa cost $102. All of the bills, including the singles, had to be crisp and not issued before 2013. Our $100 bills were fine, the man told us, but the singles were too wrinkled. It was now 10:40. Katrina and I rushed outside to find a business center with good enough Internet to upload our photos, and then a money changer who could give us four crisp American dollar bills. We wandered for ten minutes and found neither. "We can run around in the heat," I said, "but that's just confusing motion for action. We'll never make it back by eleven."

"We're going to give up?" Katrina said.

"We didn't give up when the Germans bombed Pearl Harbor," I answered—a sarcastic reference to a famous scene in *Animal House*.

"*What are you talking about?*" she asked. Apparently she hadn't seen the movie.

Eventually eleven o'clock arrived and the argument became irrelevant.

This was a Friday. The visa section would not open again until Monday, leaving us the weekend to enjoy Yangon without being consumed by the visa quest. It was too hot to explore on foot during the day, but in the late afternoon the temperature became more tolerable and we set out walking to the Shwedagon Pagoda, the most sacred Buddhist pagoda in Myanmar. We were back in our travel comfort zone, wandering through a city to a place of interest—until one of Katrina's bandages came off. The prospect of an open wound on the streets of Myanmar was terrifying. Fortunately, we were standing in front of a supermarket. I went inside to buy gauze and tape. We rewrapped Katrina's foot and continued on our walk. The open wound was a reminder that we really needed to get an Indian visa.

We had a strategic decision to make. We could return to the Indian Embassy on Monday and continue to do battle. The image of the Japanese man returning for his fifth visit loomed large in my mind. Or we could try something radically different. "The Indian consulate in Mandalay gets great reviews," CJ pointed out. He read aloud some of the reviews: "Easy . . . efficient . . . friendly."

"That's four hundred miles away," I pointed out.

CJ shrugged. "How are things working out for you here?"

"It's only a ten-hour bus ride," Leah offered.

We decided to go with the positive reviews. Katrina and I booked an overnight bus to Mandalay. Leah, CJ, and Sophie would go to Bagan, which was in the same general direction. We would meet up later.

❖ ❖ ❖

The main Yangon bus station was the size of a small college campus. There were hundreds of identical-looking buses in long rows. If the taxi driver had not dropped us off in front of our bus, we would never have found it. The hot air was thick with mosquitoes as Katrina and I waited to board. When we did get on, the bus was almost ninety degrees, according to the digital thermostat at the front. By the time it cooled down, I was coated in sweat and furiously scratching my mosquito bites.

Sometime around four a.m., when I had finally settled into a deep sleep, the lights went on and the driver yelled, "Mandalay! Mandalay!" Katrina and I got off at a dusty, dark, modestly foreboding station. We hired a taxi to take us to the hotel we had booked. Luckily, given our physical and mental condition after the hot, mosquito-infested overnight bus ride, we were able to check into our room right away. We dropped off our laundry with a woman who ran her business from under a tree. She instructed us to return to pick it up at the end of the day. We had an excellent lunch, explored the city, and visited a temple on top of a small mountain to watch the sun set. When we returned to the woman under the tree, our laundry was ready: a stack of clean clothes, neatly folded and still warm. Mandalay was lovely when we were not thinking about why we were there: getting Katrina to India for treatment.

That night, Katrina went online and began doing more research on leishmaniasis, a disease that can do great harm if left untreated. Katrina scrolled through photos of people whose faces had been eaten away by the parasite. She found a blogger who had lost several toes to "█████ leishmaniasis." She read about an internal strain of the disease that can be deadly. Katrina, never voluble, grew more silent and brooding. "Those are people who didn't get treatment," I said.

"How do you know?" Katrina replied worriedly. She sent a text to a high school friend of hers, Kati, who was living in Munich and studying biology at a German university. The two of them had planned to travel together in India and Nepal. Katrina informed her that the leishmaniasis might force a detour and disrupt their travel plans. Kati responded to Katrina's text immediately and said she would contact the Tropeninstitut in Munich, one of the world's preeminent institutes for the study and treatment of tropical diseases, to learn what the doctors there had to say about leishmaniasis.

The next morning, we took a taxi ride to the consulate, making sure to arrive early. Shortly after nine, we were shown into a small office, where an official interviewed us about our travel plans. The process was smooth; the officials were friendly. We paid our fee and were told to return to pick up our passports with the new visas in three days. The rest of the family had made it to Bagan, five hours away. Our plan was to join them and then return to Mandalay to pick up the visas at the appointed time. Katrina and I took a hot, cramped minibus from Mandalay to Bagan. As I stumbled off the bus, trying to reinvigorate the circulation to my legs, I began to wonder if I had a finite number of long bus rides in me.

◈ ◈ ◈

Bagan is one of Myanmar's most picturesque cities. Thousands of temples and pagodas dot the landscape, which is a UNESCO World Heritage site. Exploring this ancient kingdom, however, was not our top priority. Kati called from Germany with an update: the Munich clinic had an expertise in leishmaniasis (great news), but the treatment could take as long as eight weeks (less great news). The Germans were using a new medicine that had not yet been approved by the FDA for use in the United States. Kati had even procured the cell phone number of a doctor at the Tropeninstitut.

Katrina phoned the doctor to gauge how quickly she needed to get to Munich. We had a trek planned in Bhutan that she really wanted to do. "You can wait a week," the doctor told her. "And then you need to get here." Separately, we had heard back from a doctor in Calcutta that the clinic there did not specialize in the "New World" strain of leishmaniasis that Katrina had most likely picked up in South America. Months of confusion and uncertainty finally gave way to a plan: Katrina would fly to Germany for treatment. The irony, of course, was that we had set in motion an elaborate process to get our multiple-entry Indian visas, which we no longer needed.

Our passports were in Mandalay, but there was no way I was getting back into a minibus for the five-hour trip *each way*. For a modest sum, I hired a taxi for the day. The driver picked us up at our hotel at six forty-five in the morning. The relative comfort of the backseat of the car was delightful; the drive turned out to be my favorite day in Myanmar. As the sun rose, we watched the country pass slowly, like a good train ride: men and women working their fields, children walking to school, little roadside villages bustling with activity. At one point, a herd of cattle blocked the road for an extended period of time before they finally parted and let us through.

We arrived at the Indian consulate in time for the visa pickup. The visas were ready, the consular official informed us. There was just one formality left, he said. Both of us would have to be fingerprinted. All ten digits.

For most families, this would be a formality. For ours, it was not. Katrina has only nine fingers, having lost one in a car accident when she was very young. I went first and placed each finger, one at a time, on an electronic print reader. How was this going to work with only nine digits? Katrina stepped up and pressed one finger at a time on the machine, leaving the index finger on her right hand blank. The software demanded ten fingerprints. The visa could not be processed without them. The Indian bureaucracy was playing its final card.

The consular official fiddled with the fingerprint machine but could not get it to accept any fewer than ten digits. Eventually he said, "We'll just skip it." He pasted the visas in our passports. This, too, was a lesson in bureaucracies. This gentleman had already decided that we were going to get our visas; therefore, he became our partner in the process rather than our enemy. We walked out of the Indian consulate in Mandalay with two multiple-entry Indian visas. Never mind that we no longer needed them; we had taken on the Indian bureaucracy and prevailed!

Katrina and I basked in victory on the drive back—until the taxi overheated halfway to Bagan. The driver pulled over to the side of the road in a tiny hamlet and told us that we had to wait for the engine to cool. "Maybe we eat?" he said, pointing to an open-air restaurant with a thatched roof. As Katrina and I walked in, the other patrons stared as if our spaceship had broken down while we were passing through their galaxy. We could not read the menu, and the taxi driver did not speak enough English to explain it to us. Katrina pointed to what looked like a large flatbread on a patron's plate at a nearby table. "How about that?" she said. We soon had two enormous slabs of soft, warm bread with a chickpea sauce that was so good, we ordered more the moment we tasted it. The other customers watched intently as we ate, smiling and laughing when it became apparent that we were enjoying the food. Our driver was relieved that the breakdown had evolved into a culinary adventure. Eventually the taxi's engine cooled sufficiently for us to continue on. We arrived back in Bagan roughly twelve hours after we had set out on our visa retrieval mission.

The next day, we were finally able to be tourists. We borrowed bicycles from our hotel to explore the temples spread across the city, some of which are a thousand years old. Bagan was center of a kingdom from the ninth to thirteenth centuries that eventually would become Myanmar (formerly Burma). There are over three thousand remaining temples spread across the flat landscape, like elegantly carved artifacts spread on a huge table for display. As the temperature cooled down in the afternoon, bicycling was the perfect way to get around. We rode along dusty roads past the small temples and pagodas and stopped to go inside some of the big ones. Near sunset, Leah and I climbed up one of the largest temples, giving us a remarkable view as the sun set behind temples on the horizon. I turned around and looked behind me: scores more temples were brightly illuminated by the golden, almost orange light of the setting sun.

❖ ❖ ❖

The logistics for getting to our trek in Bhutan were modestly complicated. We would fly from Yangon to Calcutta in the evening and then to Bhutan the following morning. However, since only Katrina and I had visas to enter India, Leah, Sophie, and CJ would have to spend the night in the transit area of the Calcutta airport. We had spent extensive amounts of time in airports in Dubai and London; these places are like shopping malls with airline gates attached. The three of them would be able to get something to eat, perhaps do some shopping, and then find a comfortable place to sleep for the night.

That was not how the night unfolded.

Upon arrival in Calcutta, Katrina and I, armed with our multiple-entry visas *that we had worked very hard to get*, went through immigration and entered India. Our job was to retrieve the luggage, which could not be checked all the way to Bhutan. We passed through immigration and collected the bags, after which we had a nice dinner and settled into a "retiring room" that was convenient, clean, and comfortable. As Katrina and I drifted off to sleep in our private sleeping quarters, we wondered why the rest of the family had not texted us to offer an update.

Apparently there is no Wi-Fi in the bowels of the Calcutta airport. Nor, it turns out, are there restaurants. Or shops. Or chairs. Or carpeting.

The Calcutta airport does have some rudimentary transit facilities, but Leah, Sophie, and CJ were not able to access these facilities because they did not have a boarding pass for the morning flight to Bhutan. The attendant who was supposed to issue these boarding passes was not at his post. As a result, the three of them were relegated to a hyper-air-conditioned, mosquito-infested hallway. They put on whatever clothing they had to protect against the cold and the mosquitoes. (Remember, their luggage was with Katrina and me.) CJ covered his extremities with a towel and went to sleep on the tile floor. The others struggled to get any sleep at all.

The next morning, Katrina and I still had not heard from the rest of the family. We checked in for the Bhutan flight and passed through immigration and security. In theory, the others, having spent the night in the airport, should have been waiting for us at the gate. They were not. I asked a representative of Bhutan Airlines where they could be. He pointed down a long staircase that led into darkness. "They're probably down there," he said.

"How do we get them out?" I asked.

He spoke rapidly in Hindi into a walkie-talkie. "They are coming," he told me. Minutes went by, and then half an hour. Still, the rest of the family did not appear. From time to time, the man would speak into the walkie-talkie, his voice growing more agitated.

Eventually Leah, Sophie, and CJ appeared at the top of the staircase, escorted by a woman in some kind of uniform. They looked as if they had spent the night in an Indian prison. CJ's face was covered with mosquito bites.

"Katrina and I were able to get the bags," I offered. "How was it?"

"It was horrible—a living nightmare," Sophie said.

"It was a frozen-over hell with mosquitoes—the worst night of my life," CJ added.

Leah, the most chronically upbeat person I have ever met, said, "It was long. It was miserable. It was freezing cold."

❖ ❖ ❖

Our plane took off and climbed toward the Himalayas. The day was clear. Not long after we reached altitude, the pilot announced that Mount Everest was visible out the left side of the plane. There it was: the distinctive sharp peak jutting up above the clouds. We crowded around the window and stared admiringly at the highest mountain in the world, a view that went a long way toward erasing memories of a night spent in the bowels of the Calcutta airport.

Chapter 14

A Punjabi Shortcut

I did manage to get a photo of two monkeys having sex, which had been on my bucket list. In that respect, Sundarbans was not a complete bust.

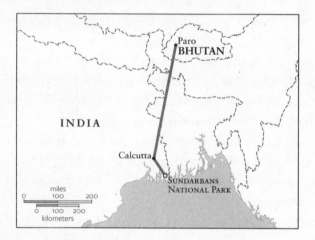

THE INDIAN GOVERNMENT had not played its last card. Our plan from the beginning of the trip had been to spend time in Mumbai with our longtime friends Sumer and Sonali Shankardass and their twin daughters, Saira and Simran. We'd met the Shankardass family when they lived in Chicago for a stretch; Saira and Simran went to school with Sophie from kindergarten through third grade. After their family moved back to Mumbai, we visited them there and had a lovely time. As a result, we fixed a date for a return visit; we scheduled the Mumbai stop after Saira and Simran's national exams—tests that are required of all high school students in India. Who or what could disrupt this plan? *The entire government of India.*

First, the Election Commission in the Indian state of Uttar Pradesh (UP) called elections. India has a parliamentary system, both at the national level and in its twenty-nine states. As in most parliamentary systems, there is a window of time during which elections can be held, rather than a fixed date. The Election Commission scheduled elections earlier than expected. Roughly a hundred million people in UP, India's most populous state, would be voting. The government needed schools as voting centers, but many of those schools were already booked to be testing sites for the annual Indian Certificate of Secondary Education (ICSE) exam. Therefore, Indian Prime Minister Modi postponed the ICSE exam to facilitate the UP elections. The Shankardass twins would be taking their exams a month later than expected.

At the end of this long chain of events were the Wheelans. We would have to put off our visit to Mumbai and do something in the meantime. "You should take a Punjabi shortcut," Sumer Shankardass advised.*

"What is a 'Punjabi shortcut'?" I asked.

"It's the shortest distance between two points via any third point in the opposite direction," he explained. (I suspect the Punjabis may not use this term.) We had a new plan: India to Africa and back to India again.

❖ ❖ ❖

The Punjabi shortcut still lay in our future as we prepared to trek in Bhutan and then dispatch Katrina to Germany for treatment. Bhutan, a small kingdom in the Himalayas, is one of the more beautiful and untraveled places on the planet. The Bhutanese government limits the number of tourists by requiring that every visitor spend a minimum of two hundred and fifty dollars per day. We could afford to visit Bhutan—just not for long. Sumer, architect of the Punjabi shortcut, had connected us with a university friend of his who ran a tour company. We booked a three-day trek leaving from the city of Paro, not far from the capital Thimphu.

* Punjab is one of the Indian states.

The Bhutanese government requires every trekker to buy a license; there is a steep discount for students. CJ and Sophie were traveling with their school IDs, but Katrina was in student limbo. She had graduated from high school but did not yet have a college ID from Williams. Neither the tour company nor the Bhutanese government grasped the concept of a gap year. In a series of e-mails with the tour company, I struggled to explain how Katrina could be a student without being a student. "Perhaps you can obtain a provisional ID from her college," my contact suggested.

"Of course," I wrote back. I told Katrina that she needed to procure an ID indicating that she would be enrolled at Williams College in the fall.

"How am I supposed to do that?" she asked.

"You're going to make one," I instructed. Ten minutes later, Katrina presented me with an "Accepted Student Identification Card" from Williams College: a college logo, her smiling photo, some purple writing, a series of random numbers, and even a bar code that she had cut-and-pasted from the Internet. I forwarded it on to the trekking company.

"Well done, sir!" the representative e-mailed back. I don't think he appreciated how apt his choice of language was.

Our first impression of Bhutan was delightful: clean air, no mosquitoes, cool weather, and a general calmness. The minimum daily spending requirement gave us no choice but to stay in an upscale hotel with cozy rooms and lots of wood and stone. The three members of the family who had spent the previous night in the Calcutta airport were particularly appreciative of this luxury. For the first time in a long time, we slept in a cool room without air-conditioning.

We began hiking the next morning at seven thousand feet on steep terrain. I noticed Sophie was struggling, so I dropped back to hike with her. She insisted that we carry on a conversation to pass the time. We talked hour after hour: about her college plans, her friends back home, our family history—anything and everything to pass the time. I described the plot of the novel I was writing, including some ideas for how it might end. Sophie encouraged me enthusiastically. Eventually she found her stride and was a delightful hiking companion.

The scenery was intriguingly diverse: forested paths, distant mountain views, prayer flags fluttering on the top of rocky peaks. We stopped on occasion to look down at the river valley we had left behind. The fields were fallow for winter—lovely geometric patterns of brown and black. There were several large Buddhist temples set amid the empty fields, which gave the country a medieval feel. There were no signs of industrial activity. From our vantage point, we could have been in the twenty-first century or the twelfth. The walled encampments surrounded by the mosaic of fields looked a lot like a diorama on feudalism I did in middle school.

We reached camp while the sun was still high. We basked in the warmth, enjoying our post-exercise high. The cold arrived quickly when darkness fell. We put on wool hats (bought cheaply in South America) and retreated to the comfort of our tents, each of which had a brass bed inside with layers of blankets. The porters working at the campsite brought us hot-water bottles to nestle under the blankets. The temperature fell low enough during the night that my camera battery discharged. I switched to a backup battery and slept with it under my covers the next night.

We awoke to snow flurries. As we waited for the bright sun to dispatch the cold, I decided to spend the morning trying to photograph the Himalayan monal, a turkey-sized bird in the pheasant family that struts along the ground and looks like a peacock. I invited the family to join me in this exciting quest; each one demurred. "Why not?" I prodded.

"You'll never see one." (CJ)

"I'd rather clean the outhouse." (Sophie)

"I don't have to answer that question." (Katrina)

"I'm sure you'll get a great picture that I'll be able to look at." (Leah)

Then one of them made a weka joke and they all cracked up.

The monals have vibrant blue and green feathers, with patches of red and orange. One website for birding enthusiasts describes them as "so beautiful that it's hard to believe they are real." I had seen one scurry into the brush near our camp and was determined to get a good photo. The rest of the family—no more excited about seeing a monal than they were about spotting a kiwi—waved disparagingly from lounge chairs as I set off.

I meandered along a narrow path, reacting excitedly to every noise. I saw a flash of bright colors on the ground in the distance—definitely a monal—but it disappeared before I could get a photo. I walked on. Eventually I came over a rise and encountered four monals feeding in the long grass no more than ten yards in front of me, their exotic plumage glistening in the bright sun. I crouched down and snapped photos until I was certain I had captured an image that did justice to these majestic creatures. (No, they did not turn out to be wekas.)

The second day of trekking took us higher into the mountains, past temples and religious sites to a peak adorned with rows of prayer flags. Buddhists believe that these fluttering flags send compassion, goodwill, and wisdom to all places the wind reaches. The scenery was dry and mountainous, with broad stretches of forest at lower elevations. There were none of the signs of deforestation that we had seen in South America and Southeast Asia. Bhutan's approach to economic development is unique. In 1972, the king of Bhutan pronounced that gross national happiness (GNH) would be the metric of success for the country, rather than a traditional measure of economic output like gross domestic product (GDP). To that end, the king promulgated a series of policies that were intended to make the nation's citizens happier but not necessarily richer. One pillar of that approach is sustainable economic development. For example, sixty-two percent of the country's territory must remain forested.

CJ the Eco Warrior was predictably enamored of this policy. I was less persuaded of its merits. On the one hand, we ought to measure well-being using a measure that is broader than aggregate production. Gross national happiness, or something like it, is a step in the right direction. There is ample evidence that rising incomes in the developed world have not led to correspondingly large increases in well-being. On the other hand, Bhutan remains a poor country whose people might benefit handsomely from more development. There are only seven hundred thousand people in the country—about the same population as Vermont—and yet large numbers of young people migrate to neighboring countries every year in search of work. The scenery is lovely and relatively untouched, but there is no obvious long-term path to prosperity.

I am also skeptical that governments can easily determine what makes individuals happy. One pillar of gross national happiness is preservation of culture and tradition, which sounds appealing except that it is achieved through policies that are relatively illiberal (in the classic sense of the word). For example, Bhutanese citizens must wear national dress when visiting temples, schools, government offices, and on national holidays. *Just imagine the government in the United States dictating what Americans are required to wear in public on the Fourth of July.*

❖ ❖ ❖

The final day of the trek led us toward Tiger's Nest, a seventeenth century temple and monastery built on the side of a steep mountain face. The walk was pleasant, taking us along gentle forest paths. With all in good spirits, we paused for a group photo beneath a string of fluttering prayer flags. This became one of my favorite images from the trip, as each of our personalities seemed to leap from the photo in this lovely, exotic place. Shortly before we arrived at Tiger's Nest, our guide changed into national dress, as required by law. The monastery is tantalizing from every angle, as it appears to be hanging off the side of the mountain. The sky was a brilliant blue, which threw into sharp relief the thousands of colorful prayer flags flapping in the wind. We spent several hours exploring the Buddhist temples inside, a labyrinth of dark, incense-filled rooms where monks still live and work.

Reaching Tiger's Nest felt like a special accomplishment, even relative to the other extraordinary places we had seen along the way. Bhutan is one of the more exotic countries on the planet. We had made it more than halfway around the world, and we had walked three days to reach this mystical, gravity-defying monastery. From now on, we would be moving in the direction of home, and the five of us would be together for only a few more days. As we contemplated these thoughts, every flutter of every prayer flag dispatched compassion, wisdom, and goodwill to all corners of the earth.

◈ ◈ ◈

Bhutan had offered us a hiatus from the reality that Katrina would soon be flying to Germany to be treated for a flesh-eating parasite. We flew back to Calcutta, where we had one day to spend with her before she continued on to Munich. "Let's go *full Calcutta,*" Leah suggested when we landed. She asked two tourism officials at the airport, "If we could go to any restaurant in the city, what should it be?" The two officials took this challenge seriously. They had an animated conversation that we could not understand. Eventually they recommended a restaurant half an hour away by car. It was late morning; we could be there for lunch.

We loaded our luggage into two flimsy Ambassador taxis and took off on a ride through the heart of Calcutta. India is one of the most bustling and unpredictable places in the world; Calcutta is one of the most bustling and unpredictable places in India. Calcutta, which is in the state of West Bengal, is also curious because it is run by democratically elected Communists. While most of the rest of the world ditched their Communist leaders when given the opportunity, the West Bengalis elected them to power again and again.

The Indian Communists have rejected the kinds of policies adopted elsewhere in the country to promote growth—as evidenced by our dilapidated Ambassador taxis. These boxy vehicles were manufactured by Hindustan Motors beginning in the 1950s, back when India was determined to promote its domestic auto industry and exclude foreign competition. Like the East German Trabant and the Soviet Lada, the Ambassador did not fare well when consumers were offered alternatives. Hyundais and Toyotas replaced Ambassadors across India when the economy was opened up in the early 1990s. But not in Calcutta, where the Ambassador is still the dominant taxicab, presumably because of some regulatory concession granted by the West Bengal government.

Many of these were queued up outside the Calcutta airport and looked to be thirty years old, with parts literally taped or wired in place.

We gave the two taxi drivers the name of the restaurant, and off we went, weaving our way through people, cars, trucks, carts, animals. The Ambassadors could not go more than about thirty-five miles an hour before we began to worry that a door or some other important component might fall off. The soundtrack for our cross-city trip was an incessant honking, to which our drivers contributed aggressively. We found the restaurant and stacked our bags around a table. A large chalkboard on the wall displayed the Bengali dishes on offer. Periodically a waiter would go to the board and erase an item. The food was distinctive and delicious—well worth a ride across the city. India's chaos felt more familiar and less off-putting than what we had experienced in other crowded cities in Southeast Asia. Perhaps it was because English is a unifying language in India, making us feel less cut off. Or maybe it was because we had spent time in the country before. Whatever the reasons, the "full Calcutta"—broadly consistent with what we had drawn up in the airport—left the family in good spirits.

That evening we sequestered ourselves in a Calcutta hotel, where the cacophony of noise from the street was muffled but still audible. Katrina, who was killing time with us before I took her back to the airport around midnight, grew progressively more morose. She had a cold—her third in a month—and she had lost weight. The leishmaniasis was likely sapping her immune system. The anti-malaria medicine may have had that effect, too. (One side benefit of getting to Germany was that she would be able to ditch the malaria pills.) Mostly, though, Katrina was nervous about the impending treatment. Katrina was working for a stretch on Leah's computer. When she returned it, Leah noticed that there were multiple tabs open related to leishmaniasis.

Leah and I had offered repeatedly to fly to Munich with Katrina for her treatment. She adamantly refused that offer; there seemed no point in forcing it. If necessary, one of us could hop on a plane later. Katrina would be staying in Munich with her friend Kati, who had found the leishmaniasis doctor and was fluent in German. Katrina did agree to let me take her to the airport. A little before midnight, I called an Uber. Our driver had a "real car," as opposed to a flimsy Ambassador. It was not clear which was more terrifying: an Ambassador taxi traveling slowly but at risk of falling apart; or a modern car driving excessively fast through darkened streets as peddlers and stray dogs appeared suddenly from the shadows.

A dense fog had settled over the city by the time we reached the airport, making it look like an eerie film set. A security official stopped Katrina and me as we entered the terminal. "Tickets," he demanded. Katrina showed him her ticket. "Okay," he said, waving her inside. As I went to follow her, he stopped me.

"I'm dropping her off," I explained.

"Not without a ticket," the man answered. Katrina and I stood awkwardly on the sidewalk.

"I should go," Katrina said.

"We love you, hon," I said, giving her a hug. She turned and went through the automatic doors into the airport: our oldest daughter, headed to Munich to be treated for a flesh-eating parasite. I hailed an Ambassador taxi from the queue and headed back to the hotel.

◈ ◈ ◈

The remaining four of us visited a travel agent on a busy Calcutta side street to book an excursion to Sundarbans National Park, a coastal mangrove forest several hours from Calcutta that is the natural habitat for Bengal tigers. A sprightly woman who was at least seventy years old suggested that we take an overnight trip to a tourist lodge there. She crowed about the luxurious accommodations, the delicious food, the boat cruise to spot tigers, and the all-inclusive nature of the resort. "You will not be reaching for your wallet!" she assured us. We liked her. We appreciated her enthusiasm and salesmanship. We booked the excursion. Yes, we would be staying at a government-run tourist lodge. And yes, the Communists had run the West Bengal government for decades, making it slightly less efficient and consumer-friendly than the rest of the Indian government. But maybe we would see tigers.

Sundarbans is on the Bay of Bengal, where four major rivers converge. The land is flat and many of the fields were flooded. On the drive from Calcutta, we shared the road with every manner of wheeled vehicles: scooters, trucks, bicycles, and even tricycles with platforms mounted on the back, transforming them into the Indian equivalent of a pickup. We passed ducks, pigs, cows, goats, sheep, and dogs. Everyone was in motion: walking, pushing, pounding, stacking, selling. That is part of the wonder of India; there is no idleness. The place somehow lurches along, with the saris and bright school uniforms adding color to it all.

As foretold, I did not reach for my wallet at the "resort." There was nothing to spend money on. Our luxury lodge consisted of several cement bunkhouses surrounded by pools of stagnant water. The bunkhouses reeked of mildew, and the mattresses felt like plywood. CJ and Sophie shared a room with two beds, one of which was so badly stained that they agreed to share the other. But we were not in Sundarbans for the luxury; we were there to see tigers.

We set out the following morning in a boat that meandered through the coastal waterways, searching the shore for the elusive Bengal tiger. The gnarled roots of the mangroves formed a web along the water's edge. I saw some interesting birds. Once I saw a deer walking alone in a clearing. I focused my telephoto lens on it, eagerly anticipating the moment when a tiger would leap from the bushes and attack. That did not happen. We stopped at a small preserve to climb an observation tower. Our guide pointed to marks in the mud below. "Wild boar prints," he said.

"Maybe the tigers will come eat the boars," I suggested.

"Yes," the guide assured me without conviction.

We did not see a tiger, or even a boar. There were monkeys everywhere, which had long since ceased being a novelty for us. I did manage to get a photo of two monkeys having sex, which had been on my bucket list. In that respect, Sundarbans was not a complete bust.

We took an evening cruise and saw less, at least in terms of wildlife. The main channel was full of freighters making their way to the ocean: a parade of enormous cargo ships, each the length of a city block, stretching as far as we could see. We had set out looking for tigers. We got a snapshot of the global economy instead.

The drive back to Calcutta was one of the worst three vehicle rides of my life—not the three most unpleasant rides, but the three during which I felt most at risk of dying in a fiery wreck. Our driver, who had been needlessly aggressive in overtaking cars and vehicles on the way to Sundarbans, became downright crazy on the way back. I think he was under the influence of some substance. We roared through small villages just as school was letting out and students were walking on the side of the road. At one point, he swerved toward the middle of the road and hit a duck square on, killing it instantly. I tried to convince myself that the driver, recognizing that he was going to hit the duck, had tried to hit it squarely to avoid unnecessary pain. But when he deliberated swerved toward a dog that was not in our path, nearly hitting it before turning away at the last minute, I realized that he was doing this for fun. I yelled at him to slow down, which he did for thirty seconds. This became the pattern all the way to Calcutta. He drove like a lunatic. I screamed at him. He slowed down for less than a minute—and then he sped up again.

When we arrived back in Calcutta, I called the woman who had sold us on the trip to complain about the driver. "Oh yes, the driving in India is so chaotic," she replied merrily, as if I were a naïf who had been caught off guard by India's bustling roads.

"He's a psychopath," I said.

"Hah! These drivers are so crazy!" she said.

"He was trying to kill things," I pointed out.

"The roads are so busy with animals," she agreed. By then, I knew the driver's job was secure. I did not have the energy to point out that the "luxury lodge" was a complete dump.

❖ ❖ ❖

Katrina sent us an update from Munich. A biopsy at the tropical disease clinic confirmed that she had the "New World" strain of leishmaniasis. She began a twenty-eight-day regimen of pills. The medicine was fairly toxic; there were some comparisons to chemo. Katrina would have to report to the clinic once a week to have blood drawn in order to check for side effects. She moved into Kati's student apartment, and the two of them made plans to travel around Europe between the weekly appointments. Leah and I were enormously relieved that Katrina was finally in a place where she had a clear diagnosis and was getting proper treatment.

Back in Calcutta, we used our final day in the city to plan for our return to India, after the Punjabi shortcut to Africa.* In addition to our stay with the Shankardass family in Mumbai, we planned to visit the state of Kerala in the south of India. Sophie's friend from home, Isabel, would be joining us for that stretch. Isabel had never been out of the United States, and we wanted her to have "an authentic Indian experience." To that end, we decided that we would travel from Kerala to Mumbai on an overnight train. The sleeper cars on the overnight trains fill up weeks in advance. We found a travel agent (different than the one who booked our Sundarbans adventure) to book our rail reservations. We informed him that we wanted to buy overnight train tickets for the twenty-seven-hour trip from Kochi (a city in the state of Kerala) to Mumbai. He looked confused. "It's faster to fly," he said.

"Yes, I know," I acknowledged.

"It's cheaper also," he said.

"That's right," I agreed.

"So do you want to fly?" he asked. "Because it's faster and cheaper."

"No," I said. I tried to explain to him that the overnight train would offer a more complete Indian experience for our family and for Sophie's friend Isabel. He looked at me as if I had told him that I was hoping to contract syphilis in order to better understand what it was like to have a venereal disease. We filled out lots of forms and returned later to pick

---

* Although Leah, CJ, and Sophie were returning to India, enough time had passed after our first visit to the country that they were able to apply for another single-entry visa, which is relatively easy to get online.

up our tickets. It turns out that taking the train is not just longer and more expensive than flying; the tickets are also harder to book. Eventually we secured our reserved berths.

I suspect that even our skeptical travel agent did not envision what would go wrong in the middle of the night on that rail journey.

Chapter 15

One Afternoon in Tanzania

I was responsible for buying the tickets for the lunch buffet, which cost seven thousand shillings, or about three dollars a person. "Why do you think it's so expensive?" I asked Leah.

"I think we've just been traveling for a long time," Leah pointed out. "Because that's really not very much money for a full buffet."

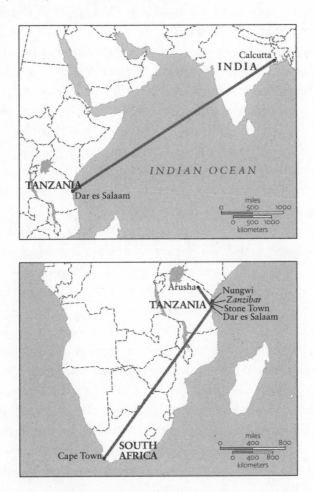

WE WOULD RETURN TO INDIA for our train trip. In the meantime, the Punjabi shortcut (Calcutta to Mumbai via Africa) took us across the Indian Ocean to Tanzania on the east coast of Africa. We rented a spacious and affordable two-bedroom apartment in a middle-class area of the capital, Dar es Salaam. The apartment had a serviceable kitchen, decent air-conditioning, and a washing machine. As is typical in much of the world, there was no dryer. The landlord instructed us to hang our wet laundry on the roof, a task that fell to me. After we did a load of wash, I climbed up a ladder in the hallway on the top floor of the building and then through a hatch in the ceiling. Once I was on the roof, I leaned down and Leah handed me the basket of clothes from below. The clothesline was on the far end of the roof. I began pinning our wet clothes to the line using a bucket of clothespins I found nearby.

The day was hot, but there was a pleasant cooling breeze from the Indian Ocean. Tanzania is a place where the Middle East meets Africa. From the roof, I had a sweeping view of Dar es Salaam: minarets rising along the skyline in one direction, and the glimmering blue ocean in the other. I had two thoughts as I hung the family laundry. The first was picayune: *Use lots of clothespins.* The family would excoriate me if our wet clothing blew off the roof into the streets below. The second was a burst of awareness: *I am standing on a roof in Africa, looking out over Dar es Salaam and the Indian Ocean, pinning our laundry to a clothesline.*

The manager of our Airbnb apartment was a woman named Janet. When she stopped by to inquire if everything was okay, we got to talking. Sophie mentioned that she had an interest in schools and children; Janet seemed excited by the topic. She invited us to visit a facility she operates for children with special needs. We eagerly accepted the invitation. Janet warned in vague terms that many of the children had physical handicaps. We assured her that we were comfortable with that. She offered to send her driver for us at two o'clock that afternoon.

The driver showed up without Janet and said very little. He drove us through a more affluent part of the city, where apartment buildings gave way to estates with razor wire atop their high walls. Eventually we turned into a small complex that we learned was a residential facility for roughly twenty children of various ages with profound physical disabilities—far beyond anything we had encountered at home. Several of the children had no physical disabilities but were afflicted with albinism, an absence of skin pigment. Albinos are persecuted in parts of Africa because people believe them to be cursed.

There was no sign of Janet. The children huddled around us: in wheelchairs, on scooters, or, in a few cases, having dragged themselves along the ground. They looked at us; we looked at them. We asked a few basic questions in English, and one or two of the students answered awkwardly. Soon a large van arrived with several young men who worked at the facility. "We are going to Janet's house," one of them told us. The children scrambled excitedly into the van. The young men carried those who were not able to climb in by themselves. Wheelchairs were collapsed and loaded up. And then the Wheelan family climbed in, wondering where Janet's house was and what were we going to do when we got there.

Janet's house turned out to be a modest ranch not far away. As the van pulled up in front, it was clear the kids had been there many times before. They climbed out, or were carried out, and immediately scrambled through the front door into Janet's home. We followed them through the house to a back patio that overlooked a large, sprawling lawn and then the ocean. Some of the children settled comfortably on the lawn, where there was a trampoline and a bicycle. Some headed straight through the backyard to a gate with access to a rocky beach and swimming area in a protected cove. We realized that for the kids with the most severe disabilities, swimming with a flotation device was easier than getting around on land.

Janet invited us to join her on the patio with her brother and sister. The siblings were in town because their mother had died recently. A family friend was there, too—an economist who had done development work across East Africa. The patio, with its shade and ocean breeze, was ten or fifteen degrees cooler than the rest of the city. We drank tea and talked about Tanzania, about the children, and about politics in Tanzania and the U.S.

As we sipped our tea, Janet told us about the children. She was not paid to take care of them. She was not running a government program or even a nonprofit organization. She had, for lack of a better description, begun collecting children who had been discarded by Tanzanian society. I assume she had personal money to fund all this, though we never asked. In a country without a serious social safety net, Janet had built a home for children who would otherwise be living on the street. She pointed at the lawn and described where each child had come from. Most had been cast out because their families felt they were too expensive, or cursed, or both. Some of the children had been begging by the side of the road when Janet found them. Some had been brought to her. Albinism runs in families, so in one case she had taken in siblings.

What these children had in common was that Janet had rescued them from destitution. She funded the residential facility we had seen. She connected each child with the best available schooling. And she opened her home to all of them every weekend. As Janet explained all this to us on the cool patio, Sophie sat down on the lawn and opened a simple game on her phone. She invited several of the girls to join her. Soon she had a crowd of laughing children gathered around her. This led to other games that went on for hours.

CJ climbed on the trampoline and attracted a different group, mostly boys. They were fascinated with his straight blondish hair and insisted on running their hands through it. I loaned CJ my phone so he and the children could take photos and videos. They would snap a photo or video on the trampoline and then crowd around the phone to look and laugh at it. (I spent a long time the next day deleting about five hundred pictures and videos—but I kept a few.) There was a tremendous amount of joy and laughter coming from the lawn. CJ and Sophie were in the middle of it.

I was struck by the resilience and joy of these kids, who were among the most disadvantaged humans on the planet. It is tough to be born without legs in the U.S. or in Europe; it is orders of magnitude more difficult to confront that challenge in Tanzania. These children comported themselves with remarkable dignity. I was also awed by what

Janet had chosen to do. I am not a religious person, yet I found religious language to be the only way to describe that afternoon. We were surrounded on the lawn by God's children and Janet was doing God's work. To be honest, it also made me feel small. Her profound generosity shone a light on what the rest of us might do to make the world better. And I was deeply proud of CJ and Sophie. For all their squabbling and pettiness at other junctures, they jumped into an emotionally fraught situation and became the center of fun. The awkwardness of those early minutes at the residential facility gave way to hours of comfortable interaction. Sophie, CJ, and the other children bounced on the trampoline, and they laughed, and they played games, and they took selfies, and they shared a lovely afternoon.

◈ ◈ ◈

We were running out of empty pages in our passports. With no empty pages, we would not be able to get visas to enter the countries that lay ahead. In the "old days" of global travel—before 9/11—one could show up at any U.S. Embassy and have extra pages pasted into a passport: a twenty-minute fix. No longer. The only solution available to us was to get new passports—*while in Tanzania*. We made an appointment at the U.S. Embassy in Dar es Salaam, a sparkling new compound not far from our apartment. We were buzzed through the wall surrounding the embassy into a bulletproof security post. We passed through a metal detector and surrendered our phones and cameras. A security official escorted us to the consular building, which we entered through a heavy blast-proof door. Once inside, we were directed to a small room where we met with a consular official who was sitting behind bulletproof glass.

The shiny new embassy and the technology were impressive—and then I connected the sad dots. The U.S. Embassy in Dar es Salaam was one of the embassies bombed by al-Qaeda in 1998. There was a simultaneous attack on the embassy in Nairobi, Kenya. Hundreds were killed and thousands were hurt. The gleaming U.S. Embassy in Tanzania with its fortress-like security had been rebuilt after those attacks.

"How long will it take to get the new passports?" I asked the friendly consular official behind the bulletproof glass.

"They'll be ready in seven to ten business days," she told us. That was *almost* as much time as we had. We would be leaving Dar (as the locals called it) on a bus for Arusha in nine days. From there, we would depart on a safari, which we had booked back in India and was not flexible. We decided to take a gamble on the efficiency of the U.S. diplomatic corps.

❖ ❖ ❖

CJ was captivated by scuba diving after the Great Barrier Reef, especially once he realized that his penis would not explode. He persuaded us to take a side trip by ferry to Zanzibar, an island off the coast of Tanzania with excellent scuba diving. From the moment the island came into view, it was as interesting and exotic as "Zanzibar" would suggest. The water in the harbor was an arresting azure-blue. Wooden sailboats with large, billowing white sails skimmed across the picturesque sea. The architecture on shore suggested centuries of influence from different parts of the world.

Zanzibar was developed as a trade port, connecting the Arabian Peninsula to Africa. Ships ferried cargo back and forth across the Indian Ocean: spices, ivory—and humans. The Sultanate of Oman controlled the island for nearly two hundred years. The capital city of Stone Town, a World Heritage site, still has a Middle East feel: a labyrinth of narrow alleys winding between whitewashed stone buildings with elaborately carved wooden doors. The British took control of the island at the end of the nineteenth century. David Livingstone, the British explorer who disappeared while searching for the source of the Nile in Central Africa, filed his dispatches to London from the telegraph office in Stone Town. That post office is still open; I walked by it every morning on my way to write at an outdoor café. The place is still a cultural crossroads. Freddie Mercury, the lead singer of Queen (portrayed in the film *Bohemian Rhapsody*), was born in Zanzibar to an Indian family with ancestors from Persia.

Our hotel in Stone Town had a rooftop restaurant with lovely views in three directions. Early one evening I went up to the roof to have a beer. As the sun was setting in one direction, a full orange moon was rising in the other. The call to prayer rang out from a nearby mosque. Zanzibar would be a perfect setting for one of those big-budget adventure films in which the stars find themselves in an exotic locale racing through narrow alleys on motorcycles, overturning fruit stands, and surprising shoppers at open-air markets full of colorful foods and clothing. That was how we felt every day, except that we were wandering on foot rather than racing on motorcycles. We walked the alleys of Stone Town, enjoying fresh fruit, seafood, and local dishes born of the island's mélange of cultures.

We also confronted the reality of what had made Zanzibar this bustling cross-cultural outpost: slavery. There was a small museum documenting the island's role in centuries of trade in human chattel. Slaves were captured in the interior of Africa, brought to Zanzibar, and then exported to the rest of the world. There were maps and relics documenting this trade. The numbers were so large as to be numbing: at the height of the slave trade, sixty thousand humans were trafficked through Zanzibar every year. The exhibit that packed the most emotional punch was on the lawn outside: a full-scale sculpture of several women with chains around their necks looking up from a pit in the ground. I do not know what the rest of the family was thinking—it was a place where even CJ was silent—but as I looked into the pleading eyes of those enslaved humans, I could feel the weight of human cruelty in the depths of my soul.

◆ ◆ ◆

From Stone Town, we hired a taxi to take us about an hour up the coast to the tiny beach town of Nungwi, a destination CJ had picked for scuba diving. Sometime around noon we pulled up at a lovely resort overlooking a sandy beach and some of the clearest, most inviting blue water I have ever seen. The beach in Nungwi functioned like a road. The restaurants were on the beach, as were the hotels and even a little grocery store. We took off our shoes when we checked into the resort and did not put them back on for four days.

For all the loveliness of the ocean and the beach, the heat at midday was oppressive. We retreated to our small air-conditioned rooms, or to the big open-air restaurant with ceiling fans whirring away. At about five o'clock, as the heat began to dissipate, tourists and locals made their way to the beach. Women in bikinis walked past women in headscarves. There were spirited pickup soccer games up and down the beach. Groups of tall, thin Masai men wandered past in their bright red robes. They carried long sticks, which from a distance looked like spears. Sophie had the temerity to join some local guys playing volleyball. "How is it going?" I asked during a break.

"These guys are really good, and I'm out of practice," she said.

"Are you having fun?" I asked her.

"Are you kidding?" she said. "This is heaven."

"Come on, Sophie, we're starting up," one of the guys called to her. She held her own, despite being out of practice. These were the golden hours, both because of the vibrancy of the beach and because the setting sun bathed all the activity in a soft golden glow—a cinematographer's dream.

About a quarter mile down the beach from our hotel—a walk, like the others, that did not require shoes—was Spanish Dancer Divers, the dive shop that CJ had selected for our scuba adventures. The water and visibility were as impressive as the Barrier Reef, if not better. During the boat ride back from one of the dives, we encountered a pod of dolphins. CJ grabbed his mask and fins and jumped into the water with them. The dolphins swarmed around him for a brief stretch and then disappeared. "How long do you think I was swimming with them?" he asked when he climbed back into the boat.

"Ten seconds or so," I said.

"That's long enough," he declared.

"Long enough for what?" I asked.

"To cross 'swim with dolphins' off my diving bucket list," he explained.

After the dive trips, CJ remained behind in the Spanish Dancer office, a small open hut on the beach, where he paged through the reference books to identify the creatures he had seen. He befriended the staff, who answered his questions and loaned him equipment so he could snorkel off the beach. There was also a wild monkey that camped out in the Spanish Dancer hut. Each morning, the monkey came out of the trees and ensconced himself in one of the comfortable chairs. The first time I walked into the dive hut and saw the monkey, I was shocked that the staff had not noticed him. "There's a monkey over there sitting in one of your chairs," I told a dive instructor doing paperwork.

"He's here most days," the guy replied without looking up. Leah and I were amused by the image of CJ sitting in one chair for hours reading his diving books as the monkey sat opposite him—with the Spanish Dancer staff patiently indulging them both.

On our last day in Nungwi, which was also our final day in Zanzibar, CJ and I opted to do a night dive. Our dive instructor, Paul, gave us a briefing on the beach as we watched the sunset. He alerted us to something we had not encountered on the Great Barrier Reef: swarms of tiny fish. "If you begin to feel claustrophobic," he warned, "just press your flashlight against your chest to cover up the light." The tiny fish are attracted to the light and will dissipate if the light is extinguished, he explained. *Tiny fish?* I thought. We had seen sharks and barracudas and moray eels. *How scary can tiny fish be?*

The three of us waded into the dark water. The dive was shallow, which meant that we would see different things than we did on the Great Barrier Reef. Also, our air would last much longer. (The deeper one dives, the more compressed the air in the tank becomes, meaning that every breath consumes more of it.) We followed Paul along the bottom, observing an array of nocturnal creatures: eels; cuttlefish; an enormous flatworm; a spotted ray; an anemone that was delivering electric shocks to small fish.

And then the tiny fish came. To describe them as a "school" does not do justice to the blinding storm that enveloped me. I felt as if small stones were pelting every part of my body. All I could see were flashes of silver banging incessantly against my mask. Once my panic subsided, I put the flashlight against my chest and the swarm of fish disappeared. Only later, on the beach, did Paul tell us his most unnerving tiny fish story. On an earlier dive, one of the fish had swum straight into his ear canal, where it banged repeatedly against his eardrum. "It was like someone was using a power drill on my brain," he said. He had to abort the dive so he could return to shore and get the fish out of his ear.

CJ, Paul, and I stayed underwater for an amazing eighty-eight minutes. (Most dives are closer to half an hour.) We drifted slowly along the bottom as Paul pointed out fascinating night creatures. After the dive, we met Sophie and Leah for dinner on the beach. The restaurants stayed open late to take advantage of the cool evening temperature. Zanzibar was a place where everyone was happy: Sophie was playing volleyball; CJ was diving and hanging out at Spanish Dancer Divers; and Leah and I were feeling relieved by news from Katrina that she was taking her medicine without incident and enjoying her travels with Kati.

Thus, it was a rude awakening to put on our shoes and check out. When the ferry landed in Dar, we retraced our steps to the consular section at the embassy, where the woman who had helped us on our first visit slid three stiff new passports to us under the bulletproof glass.* She punched a hole in the old passports and returned them to us. In theory, the visas in those passports—including the Indian visas we had worked so hard to get—would still be valid.

With new passports in hand, we boarded a bus before sunrise the next morning for the twelve-hour ride from Dar es Salaam to Arusha. We were the only non-Africans on the bus; the other passengers were mostly families, including more than a few crying babies. The air-conditioning worked, the bathroom was not locked, and if I angled my legs properly, my knees did not hit the seat in front of me. There was a hostess on the bus in a crisp blue uniform. The best innovation in Tanzanian bus travel, however, was a law stipulating that drivers can

---

* Sophie still had enough pages left that she did not need a new passport.

be fined if they arrive at a destination too quickly. It is a clever way to enforce speed limits. "The bus used to do this route in six hours," one passenger complained to me. But I was delighted: the last thing I wanted was a lunatic driver racing along at eighty-five miles an hour.

The bus made its way at a languid pace through a landscape that was flatter, greener, and more open than what we had seen in South America and Asia. On occasion, the flat landscape was interrupted by towering acacia trees blooming with yellow flowers. We stopped for lunch at an open-air oasis that offered a buffet lunch: rice, cooked bananas, chicken, beans, and sautéed greens. I was responsible for buying the tickets for the lunch buffet, which cost seven thousand shillings, or about three dollars a person. "Why do you think it's so expensive?" I asked Leah.

"I think we've just been traveling for a long time," Leah pointed out. "Because that's really not very much money for a full buffet." The food turned out to be delicious—if overpriced by my distorted reckoning. The journey continued, and the hills gradually became bigger. Just before dark, we spotted Mount Kilimanjaro on the horizon.

The bus dropped us on the side of the road in the dark, roughly thirteen hours after we had departed from Dar es Salaam, also in the dark. We put on headlamps and walked along the side of the road until we came to a small guardhouse at the entrance to our hotel. This was a luxury establishment, included in our safari, and the attendant was puzzled to see guests with backpacks arriving on foot. We had vacillated over whether to include a safari in our travels. The expense was significant and would have to be "off-budget." On the other hand, a safari is much cheaper when one is already in Tanzania. A month earlier, my hand had been forced on this question, or at least nudged, when one of my Dartmouth colleagues sent me an e-mail asking if I would like to teach an extra class when I got back to Dartmouth. I accepted. The class felt like found money—much of which we promptly spent to book the safari. As we were checking into the hotel, Sophie used the bathroom in the lobby. "*That bathroom is bigger and nicer than most of the rooms we've been staying in,*" she exclaimed when she came out.

At breakfast (buffet included!), we met our guide, Stanford, who loaded us into a Land Cruiser decked out for safaris: tires with enormous treads; a roof that popped up so we could stand and look out in any direction; a metal "bull bar" on the front to protect the grille; and bench seats just uncomfortable enough to remind us that we were going on safari. Stanford drove us through rolling green hills, with the hue of the distinctive reddish soil changing subtly along the way. In describing the shades of "orangish red," I eventually turned to spices: paprika, cumin, cinnamon, chili powder. As we entered the Ngorongoro Crater, a hundred-square-mile indentation in the earth created by volcanic activity millions of years ago, I spotted two zebras in the distance. I stood up and began taking photos through the gap beneath the roof. Stanford did not slow down, which left me peeved. *Did he not see these zebras a mere three hundred yards away?*

"Zebras!" I yelled, snapping more photos of the tiny creatures on the horizon. Still no response from Stanford.

In fact, I was like a tourist who arrives in New York and begins snapping photos of five-story apartment buildings when the Empire State Building lies ahead. I was still annoyed that we had raced past the zebras when we drove into an open plain with wildlife in every direction: lions, elephants, zebras, wildebeests. The vista itself was impressive, the flat floor of the crater ringed by steep green hills. Every wildlife encounter seemed more amazing than the last: the baboon with a baby riding on its back; the zebras grazing lazily with an elephant behind them; the black rhinos—one of the most endangered species on the planet—trotting along in the distance. It was *The Lion King*, only for real.

Stanford stopped the Land Cruiser next to a male lion resting in the shade. We were close enough to smell him and see the flies buzzing around his mane. CJ was unable to resist leaning out the top of the Land Cruiser to take a selfie with the lion in the background. Thankfully, the open top of the vehicle was far enough off the ground that he did not earn himself a Darwin Award.[*]

---

[*] As one website notes, "The Darwin Awards commemorate those who improve our gene pool by removing themselves from it."

The next day we continued on to the Serengeti, which is Swahili for "where the grass meets the clouds." The land is vast, flat, and oddly entrancing for having no topography and few trees. The green and brown terrain stretches as far as one can see, creating an effect in which the ground does appear to meld with the sky. We drove through Masai villages, with their hallmark round thatched huts and wooden fences, just like the dioramas our kids had made in school. There were long stretches where we saw nothing, making it all the more interesting when we did: a pride of lions lounging in the shade; a small group of hyenas; a leopard resting in the V of a tree trunk.

The "tented camp" that night had electricity, comfortable beds, and an attached bathroom with a shower. Still, it was in the middle of the Serengeti; the animals were not the visitors, we were. We played cards as the sun set, with the noise of small birds as the soundtrack. Five or six storks—enormous birds up close—were roosting in a tree that towered over the camp. It was not hard to imagine Hemingway drinking heavily in a camp just like this, cleaning his guns for a morning hunt. Our sleeping tents were only fifty yards from the dining tent, but we were forbidden from walking that short distance at night without a staff member accompanying us. Stanford told us that he once saw three male lions walk right through the middle of camp. "Don't leave your shoes outside the tent," he warned. "The hyenas will take them."

The next day, we happened upon a lioness that had recently given birth and was resting in a patch of bushes at the base of a large rock. Some kind of deer-type animal was lying dead on the ground beside her. "She's resting before she shares the kill with her cubs," Stanford explained. "They're hidden in the bushes." As we were watching the lioness, Sophie tapped me on the shoulder. "Look," she said, pointing to a hyena approaching from the other side of the Land Cruiser. The hyena could smell, but not yet see, the freshly killed deer. We watched the hyena track the scent, pacing back and forth as it approached the lioness nestled in the bushes. When the hyena was within about twenty yards of the fresh kill, the lioness took notice, crawling out of the bushes and standing up on a rock to face down the approaching scavenger.

The hyena was not deterred. It moved steadily closer, locked onto the scent. I could see saliva dripping from its mouth. The lioness leapt off the rock and gave chase. Both animals moved shockingly fast. Early in the safari, I had been mildly annoyed that Stanford would not let me leave the vehicle to pee, even when there were clearly no predators in the area. I quickly came to realize that "clearly no predators in the area" is exactly what the gazelle is thinking two seconds before the lion lunges from the tall grass. On several occasions, I looked at the empty landscape only to have Stanford tap gently on my shoulder and point to a lion camouflaged less than twenty feet away.

The lioness chased the hyena at full speed for about fifty yards before slowing down and eventually returning to her perch. The hyena lingered in the distance and then slunk away. "It'll be back," Stanford said. "Probably with others." He was pessimistic that the lioness would be able to protect the kill from the hyenas during the night. Her cubs depended on that food; we were now emotionally vested in this family of lions (and not terribly impressed by what the father was contributing).

As our safari drew to a close, the one predator we had not seen was a cheetah, though not for want of trying. We had spent long stretches driving through relatively barren areas with no cheetah sightings. Now I was looking forward to returning to camp to have a beer, write in my journal, and enjoy the warmth of the afternoon sun. "We have two hours of daylight left," CJ pointed out.

"I plan to enjoy that time relaxing in camp," I said.

"Relax tomorrow," CJ replied.

"I'd like to use the bathroom," Sophie added.

"You can hold it," CJ told her.

"Cheetahs are very hard to spot," Stanford said.

"Let's just try," CJ implored.

"If I can't hold it, I'm peeing in your water bottle," Sophie told him.

"Fine," CJ agreed.

We drove on. We saw a lion give chase to a warthog, and then a leopard hidden in the grass slowly approaching an antelope drinking at a small stream. But no cheetahs. We drove some more. Sophie brandished CJ's water bottle. "I'm serious, you know," she said. He ignored her.

And then we heard a report on the radio of a cheetah sighting. Stanford drove us to a spot where a mother cheetah and a cub were relaxing in the grass. Cheetahs are the animal equivalent of a Ferrari: long, lithe bodies; tiny heads; engineered for speed. After observing for a while, we headed back toward camp. On the way, we spotted another cheetah sitting majestically on top of a termite mound, scoping out two antelope drinking from a stream about a quarter mile away. For the next half hour, we watched as the cheetah slunk through the grass, slowly and methodically making its way closer to the two antelope. One of them looked up suddenly and ran off. The other one was still drinking in the stream.

Having heard many lectures from Stanford on how difficult it is for predators to survive, I was pulling for the cheetah. As it got to about fifty yards from the stream, the second antelope took off. The cheetah gave chase but could not close the gap. On our way to camp, we drove by the site where the lioness had fended off the hyena the day before; the deer carcass was gone, presumably stolen in the night. We were left not only with an appreciation for the beauty of the Serengeti, but also the harshness of the struggle for survival. That felt less like *The Lion King*.

◈ ◈ ◈

The safari included a flight on a small bush plane back to Dar es Salaam. The airport consisted of one small building and a dirt airstrip plopped down in the middle of the Serengeti. A steady trickle of small planes landed and took off, none carrying more than eight or ten passengers. The place felt more like a bus station than an airport, and our flight operated the same way. We landed several times before arriving back in Dar. Each time, the pilot would ask, "Okay, who is getting off here?"

As we were waiting for the flight, I asked myself a policy question: Would the pilot be black or white? I was curious because it would tell me something about where the tourism money was going, which in turn would tell me something about East Africa. The pilot would be one of the better skilled, and therefore better paid, individuals in the safari business. Was Tanzania training local people to do these kinds of jobs? If so, that would be a great thing for the future of the country. Or would a white foreigner be flying the plane? In that case, money is leaking away from the local economy because locals are not equipped to do the top jobs.

We ducked our heads and climbed into the tiny plane. The pilot introduced himself: Gareth, a white guy from South Africa.

❖ ❖ ❖

From Dar, we did a Punjabi shortcut in the middle of our Punjabi shortcut: We flew fifteen hundred miles north to Ethiopia and then caught a flight in the other direction to Cape Town, at the southern tip of the continent. (The cheapest flight is rarely the most direct.) Cape Town is extraordinary on many levels. First, it is a stunningly beautiful city, with the ocean on one side—where the Indian Ocean meets the Atlantic—and Table Mountain looming above the city on the other. The climate is temperate. We took long walks and figured out the public bus system. When we got lazy, we ordered an Uber to take us back to our apartment, which was in a quiet residential area. We spent the better part of one day hiking atop Table Mountain with its interesting birds and flowers and postcard-worthy views of the city below. South Africa is more developed than any country we had been in since Hong Kong. We took great comfort in the shopping malls and other first world conveniences. Sophie bought some cheap new clothes in an H&M store; the rest of us sat outside the store and used the free Wi-Fi.

Second, Cape Town has become a great food and wine city. There was a café up the road from our apartment where I parked myself for hours every morning, drinking coffee, eating good food, and working to finish my novel. Sometimes I ate breakfast and lunch there. Our apartment was well equipped to cook and do laundry. While looking for pancake mix in the supermarket, we found real maple syrup. The combination of pancakes and clean underwear was a family-pleaser. We found a cheese shop in a mall near our apartment. We had eaten very little dairy while traveling, and almost no good cheese. We bought thirty dollars' worth of fancy cheeses and several baguettes with the intention of having a picnic in one of the city's parks. The cheese was so tempting that we never made it out of the mall. Instead we sat on a bench opposite the store and ate our picnic there.

But what is most striking about Cape Town, and South Africa more generally, is that it is an historical miracle in progress. As we walked the streets, I had to remind myself that Apartheid lasted into the 1990s. *Nelson Mandela was in prison when I graduated from college.* I traveled to South Africa in 1995 to visit a friend who was teaching there. Mandela had just become president, and it was not clear if he was going to be able to hold the country together. On my flight into the country, a white South African woman sitting next to me on the plane offered to exchange South African rand for my dollars. "How much do you need?" she asked. "I'll swap as much as you like, and I'll give you a better rate than the banks." Only later did I realize the motivation for her offer: She was trying to evade government restrictions on moving capital out of the country. She wanted my dollars in case things began to unravel in her country.

At the time of that visit, Robben Island, the prison off the coast of Cape Town where Mandela and other enemies of Apartheid had been held, was not yet a museum. Instead, it was a spectral presence on the horizon that prompted me to wonder how Nelson Mandela could spend twenty-seven years in prison and emerge willing to reconcile with the white South Africans who had put him there.

Twenty-five years later, South Africa survives as a multiracial state. There are struggles, to be sure. Every person we encountered, white or black, complained about government corruption, beginning at the top with President Jacob Zuma. We were listening to a news broadcast in an Uber when it was announced that President Zuma had fired his finance minister. "The finance minister was the only honest one. That's why he got fired," our driver lamented. Standard & Poor's apparently agreed;

they lowered South Africa's bond rating almost immediately. (Zuma resigned in 2018, after which he faced charges for fraud, corruption, money laundering, and racketeering.)

South Africa's crime and violence were indirectly visible in our upscale neighborhood, where the homes were hidden behind high walls with signs warning of "Armed Response" security systems. Metal bars protected every door and window. We needed three keys to get in and out of our apartment with its multiple gates and locks.

But still. One cannot spend time in South Africa without admiring the resiliency of the place. We saw an inspiring snapshot of South Africa's potential on a wine tour in of the Stellenbosch region just outside of Cape Town. Leah and I left Sophie and CJ behind. We gave them the keys to the apartment, bus passes, and cash, and told them to meet us at the end of the day at a mall near the waterfront. Yes, one could technically say that we turned our children loose and went drinking for the day.

Stellenbosch is arid and beautiful, similar to Napa. At the first stop—well before noon—we sampled two red wines and two whites. Each pour was nearly a half glass. As we enjoyed the wine, Leah turned to our guide. "How many glasses are we going to be tasting today?" she asked.

Our guide did a rough calculation in his head. "Probably another eighteen," he said. We moderated the size of our tastes after that. The guide (who was not tasting) drove nine of us around the vineyards in a van. Along with Leah and me, there was a couple from Brazil on their honeymoon and five nurses from Johannesburg who had come to Cape Town for a girls' weekend. Our group was chatty and friendly and grew more so with each pour. As we were walking through the manicured grounds at the last vineyard, one of the nurses said, "We should take a group photo." She gave her camera to a passerby and instructed us to pose. Leah and I had been talking with our guide and the Brazilian couple. The four of us stepped next to the nurses.

The nurses were black; the Brazilian couple, the guide, and Leah and I were white. We had arrayed ourselves with blacks on one side of the group photo and whites on the other.

"No, no, no," the nurse who had requested the photo said. "We have to be mixed." And then, after we moved around to create a photo more consistent with South Africa's aspirations, she added, "We have come too far for that."

Chapter 16

Home Is Where Your Friends Are

To recap: If everything went well, our journey would be rickshaw, bus, overnight train.

Everything did not go well.

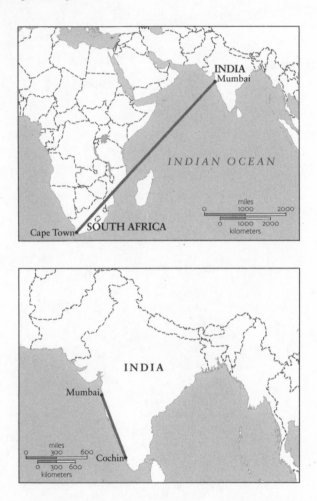

SUMER'S DRIVER PICKED US UP at the Mumbai airport after our overnight flight from South Africa—a dollop of convenience that presaged what lay ahead. An hour later, we were sitting on an outdoor terrace having breakfast and catching up. The Shankardass family apartment is lovely, but far smaller than most suburban American homes. What makes the apartment special is the warmness and functionality of it. There is a large living room with couches and an adjacent area with a dining table. This was where we hung out for many hours of the day, like the set of a TV sitcom: talking, reading, working on our computers. Periodically we were summoned to the table for a meal, and the cook would bring an array of wonderful dishes out of the kitchen. At one point, I described our typical day in my journal: "We eat, then we do some modest activity (e.g., visiting Sumer's office), and then we eat again."

Outside, Mumbai is huge, hot, crowded—and exhilarating. It is a place where irregular things happen on a regular basis. One evening, Sumer and I went for a walk to a local park. On the way back, we walked into a swarm of people gathered outside a large, elegant home. The women were in colorful burkas and white bonnets—a curious melding of the Middle East and the Amish. The men and boys were wearing long white collarless shirts (kurtas) and white caps. "What is going on?" I asked Sumer.

"They're Bohras," he explained. "A Muslim sect."

I had never heard of them. "Why are they here?" I asked.

"They're hoping to see their spiritual leader, the Syedma," Sumer said, pointing at the large house. "He lives there." The crowd continued to grow; young and old jostled eagerly. "Any contact with the spiritual leader is considered good luck," Sumer explained. "He can offer blessings and perform miracles." As we began pushing our way through the expectant crowd, the Syedma's limousine rolled into view. His followers rushed the car, trying to touch it and get a glimpse of the man in the backseat. The car passed right in front of Sumer and me. The crowd pushed us forward, and I ended up pressed against the rear door of the car, as if I had gone for a stroll in the Vatican and somehow

ended up face-to-face with the Pope. The curtains on the back windows were pulled open; the Syedma waved at me tepidly. Instinctively,
I waved back.

"Are we eligible for good luck from our encounter with the spiritual
leader?" I asked Sumer after the car had passed.

"I don't see why not," he said. So, to paraphrase Bill Murray in *Cad-
dyshack*, whose character claims to have been blessed by the Dalai Lama
after caddying for him, "I got that goin' for me, which is nice."

Everything that makes Mumbai exhilarating also makes it exhausting. At one point, I had coffee with an old friend from college who is
now a journalist. As I was leaving, I told her that I planned to walk about
four hundred yards to a shopping mall, where I would meet Leah. "Are
you sure you don't want to take a taxi?" my friend asked. We could see
the entrance to the mall from where we were standing. "It's just there,"
I said, pointing across a busy street toward the mall.

"Mmm," she acknowledged cryptically. I walked. Or, more accurately, I ran across the busy street, where the red, yellow, and green lights
had no more impact on driving behavior than if decorative Christmas
lights had been hung across the intersection. I narrowly missed two
open sewers. I detoured around a pack of wild dogs. I waved away the
taxis that swerved toward me on the sidewalk, honking incessantly in
the hope of getting my business. The hawkers yelled out to me from
their seats in the shade: "My friend, best price for you!"

At first I demurred politely: "I'm fine, thank you." This response
only encouraged them; they leapt from their seats brandishing samples
of their merchandise. I ignored the offers, which continued unabated.
Eventually I became annoyed, in part because I had just stepped in dog
poop: "Really?" I exclaimed in exasperation. "Do I look like a guy trying
to buy a cast-iron pot?" When I had set out on my four-hundred-yard
walk, I estimated the temperature at about ninety degrees; now I was
convinced it was at least a hundred and five.

"What happened to you?" Leah asked when I stumbled into the
lobby of the movie theater. "And what smells so bad?"

◆ ◆ ◆

Those who can afford it find places to escape from the chaos. During the British Raj, the Foreign Service officers who were "sent out" to India, built clubs where they drank and played cards and escaped the heat. There is some irony in the fact that India's elite now inhabit similar places where they do similar things. Sometimes they are literally the same clubs, inherited from the British after independence. One of those clubs is the Royal Willingdon Sports Club, founded in 1918 by then-governor of Mumbai Lord Willingdon.

The noise and chaos of Mumbai recede as one enters the gates of the Willingdon Club. There are tennis courts, squash courts, a golf course, a restaurant, a barbershop, a little grocery store, and a large manicured lawn on which members can drink and dine at small tables. Each table has a bell for summoning a waiter. Mumbai's wealthy and influential all seem to know each other; this is one place they assemble. I played golf with Sumer and two of his friends. We had six caddies for our group: one caddy for each of our bags, plus two forecaddies who stood out in the fairway to spot our balls as they came to rest.

For all the luxury of the Willingdon Club, there was one incongruity: a striking number of dogs wandering the grounds, many of whom were sleeping comfortably in the sand traps on the golf course. The dogs looked healthy but out of place roaming the manicured lawns of Mumbai's most prestigious club. Eventually I asked Sumer about this oddity. "Ah, Charlie," he said with a smile, clearly relishing an opportunity to tell a story, perhaps apocryphal. "When the club was British, there were signs posted on the grounds: No dogs or Indians. Now there are both." I am not going to try to justify the social order in India. I will say that a gin and tonic on the lawn of the Willingdon Club— following my haircut and head massage—felt very good after living out of a backpack for seven months.

We ate well. The apartment was cozy. But what made the visit

with the Shankardass family so joyful was that we felt like family. The
highlight of our stay was an engagement dinner for a nephew. Sumer's sister—the prospective groom's mother—had died of brain cancer
some years ago, leaving Sumer as a surrogate parent for her twin boys,
one of whom was engaged to be married. During our stay, there was
a party at which the bride's family and groom's family would meet for
the first time. The Wheelans were the only non-family invited. Sumer
loaned me some nice clothes and even a dab of cologne, making me feel
civilized in a way that I had not for a long time. We were invited for
eight o'clock; we showed up sometime after nine.

The ceremony began with the young couple exchanging rings. Next,
there was a prayer ceremony in front of a small temple in the corner
of the room. Sumer offered me running commentary as the ceremony
progressed. "Most Hindu families have a little temple like that in their
home," he explained. The future bride and groom covered their heads
with small cloths, a sign of respect, and asked for a blessing from God.
The families joined them in singing a prayer, after which the couple
bowed down and touched the feet of their parents and grandparents. "I
touched my granddad's feet every day," Sumer whispered. "It's a sign
of respect, like shaking hands." The prospective bride and groom gave
each other a sweet—"the sweetening of the mouth"—after which both
families offered them a champagne toast.

Over the course of the evening, we figured out who was who: siblings, cousins, in-laws. Sumer or Sonali would point out someone and
offer a tidbit of gossip. I was proud of CJ and Sophie for their social
adaptability. They spent much of the evening having fun with a flam-
boyant cousin of the groom. We arrived home after midnight and took
a group photo with all of us dressed up. Sumer poured us a nightcap and
deconstructed the evening, parsing the politics, the family history, and
other peculiarities surrounding the impending wedding.

Katrina had finished her leishmaniasis treatment in Germany. She
reported to us that everything had gone as well as possible. Once the
doctor cleared her to travel, she and Kati flew to Nepal. The two of

them planned to travel through India and Sri Lanka before eventually meeting up with us. We gave Katrina the choice of where that rendezvous would happen. She picked the Republic of Georgia, which meant that we now had an end point for our journey. We would meet Katrina and Kati in Tbilisi, travel together in Georgia, and then head home.

Meanwhile, Sophie's friend Isabel arrived in Mumbai for her spring break. She spent several days with us at the Shankardass home before flying with our family to the south of India for a beach vacation. India's southern region is more tropical and slow-paced than the north. We stayed in the city of Kochi at a little resort on a beach at the end of a long dirt road. We rented several little guest cottages, which were arrayed around a green lawn with a big open-aired dining room in the middle. We walked on the beach and swam and rented bicycles to explore the meandering lanes around the resort. Mostly, though, we relaxed. At one point Leah and I looked up from the dining area and spotted CJ on the lawn trying to break open a coconut. He was throwing it against the ground over and over, like some kind of semi-intelligent animal with a toy. "That boy needs some other kids to play with," Leah said.

Such an opportunity soon presented itself. On one of our walks, we came upon a group of boys and girls roughly CJ's age, playing cricket. We stopped to watch and the cricket players urged CJ to join them. He batted for a while, and not terribly. And then he bowled (the equivalent of pitching in baseball). This was more unpredictable, though the other kids cheered his modest successes. Leah and I left CJ there: playing pick-up cricket on a small lane in a remote area outside Kochi.

As we relaxed in South India, two very different writing projects were coming to fruition. The first was CJ's paper on deforestation. Our homeschooling efforts were not always exemplary, but I felt strongly that CJ needed to be able to write decently before he started high school. His outline for the paper was excellent. He and I agreed on a deadline for a rough draft. The second writing project was my novel, for which an end was also in sight. (I came up with the ending while sitting on the sofa in Sumer and Sonali's Mumbai apartment.) My goal was to have a complete draft before we touched down in Boston, and we now we knew exactly when that would be. Sophie needed to be home to take the SATs on June 3. We booked a flight for all of us from Tbilisi to Boston.

❖ ❖ ❖

Our one adventure in Kochi featured renting a houseboat to cruise the waterways of the region, which are famously picturesque. The house-boats are essentially floating guesthouses with a small crew, including a chef. Each houseboat has TripAdvisor reviews, just like a hotel or restaurant. Leah studied the reviews and booked a boat for the five of us. Remarkably, chartering our own houseboat fit comfortably in the budget, which was now back on track thanks to low prices in Asia and the Shankardass hospitality. We went to the dock at the appointed time and met the proprietor of our houseboat, who reminded me of the Dev Patel character in *The Best Exotic Marigold Hotel*. He proudly showed us around: three staterooms with air-conditioning and a shaded deck with couches and a dining table at the front of the boat. We cast off and began motoring slowly through the channels, listening to Hindi music and watching life on shore go by.

The waterways are narrow, which meant we were near to land but could observe the places we were passing relatively unobtrusively. I sat on the deck shooting photos: men fishing; students walking to school; women washing pans; bicyclists riding on paths parallel to the water— all with the colors of southern India behind them. We ate delicious South Indian meals at the outdoor table, enjoying the cool breeze gen-erated by the steady puttering of our houseboat.

❖ ❖ ❖

The long trip from Kochi back to Mumbai was less peaceful. It began with a short auto-rickshaw ride to the bus station. From there, we planned to catch an express bus to the train station, where we would board an overnight train to Mumbai. We had spent a relaxing beach holiday together in South India. Now it was time to make the deliberately less relaxing train journey to Mumbai. These were the tickets we had booked a month earlier in Calcutta when the travel agent had advised us repeatedly to fly.

To recap: If everything went well, our journey would be rickshaw, bus, overnight train.

Everything did not go well.

The rickshaw dropped us at the bus station, which was a small open-air building on a busy road. None of the signs were in English, including the lettering on the buses. The temperature was unpleasantly hot, even in the shade. Leah had purchased tickets online for the "super-fast" bus, as opposed to the less direct "fast" bus. Buses were pulling into the station every few minutes. It was not clear how we were going to figure out which one would get us to the rail station. Leah asked an attendant at the information desk for guidance. He told her that our bus would be red and would depart at ten o'clock.

Not long after that, a red bus rolled into the departure area. We rushed to the door of the bus and asked the driver, "Train station?" He nodded yes, and we climbed aboard. There was air-conditioning and space for our luggage, both of which felt like luxuries. The bus left the station on time. Mission accomplished.

As our bus navigated the congested road, a ticket taker slowly made his way down the aisle. Leah showed him our tickets, which we had purchased online and printed at our beach hotel. He shook his head in disapproval. At first we thought he was rejecting the e-tickets. Leah explained that we had purchased them on the official transit site. All the while, our "super-fast" bus was plodding along, block after block. This is relevant because the ticket taker eventually made clear to us that we were going "super-fast" on the wrong bus.

We had now traveled seven or eight blocks from the station, and it was past ten o'clock. The ticket taker communicated our problem to the driver, who stopped the bus. The five of us filed out into the street with our packs. It was still oppressively hot, and now we were standing in the sun in the middle of a dusty street. CJ let loose a string of profanity.

Once the swearing stopped, he made several suggestions, all of which involved things that we should have done differently in the past. "Let me get a time machine out of my pack," I said angrily.

Sophie insisted that we take a rickshaw back to the bus station. This was a defensible suggestion given the heat and the distance we needed to travel quickly. But it also presented a problem: The bus to the Kochi rail station had most likely departed and we would need to flag it down in the road. This would be more difficult if we were traveling in the opposite direction in a rickshaw. Instead, we walked fast. With our packs. In the hot sun.

Isabel was a total trooper. She was wheeling a large suitcase but contributed almost nothing to the string of profanity and criticism that was unleashed as we walked briskly toward the station. "We should have gotten on the right bus!" CJ said.

"This sucks," Sophie added helpfully. After a few blocks, I spotted a red bus coming at us. I stood in the middle of the street and flagged it down. Not to be overly self-congratulatory, but standing in the middle of a busy Indian road to flag down a "super-fast" bus requires a modest amount of courage, or perhaps a touch of heatstroke. I had one, if not both.

The bus stopped. I jumped aboard to confer with the driver, who informed me that this was not the bus to the Kochi rail station. I scurried back into the street and delivered the bad news. "Why isn't that the right bus?" CJ asked, a question that was simultaneously deep and ridiculous. We walked on and soon arrived back at the station bathed in sweat and frustration. Leah returned to the information desk and demanded more detailed information from the attendant. He made a phone call and reported back that our bus was running ten minutes late. He also gave us a bus number—an identifying characteristic that would have been helpful the first time, since the numbers were the only things printed on the buses that we could understand.

Our "super-fast" bus pulled into the station and we climbed aboard. The ticket taker confirmed that we were headed to the rail terminal. He even moved some passengers around so the five of us could sit together.

The bus windows were open, generating a cool breeze. South India is remarkably green and lush. The views out the window were beautiful, especially the red flowers of the Indian coral trees lining the sides of the road. As our pulses returned to normal and the perspiration dried in the breeze, Leah leaned across the aisle. "That was more fun than the beach resort," she said. I knew exactly what she meant. There is a rush that comes from plunging into chaos and emerging successful.

I turned to CJ and said, "Tell Isabel that we wanted to give her the real India experience."

"I think she figured that out on her own," he replied tartly.

❖ ❖ ❖

We boarded the train at midday for the eighteen-hour overnight trip to Mumbai. We found our way to our reserved seats in the second-class cabin, which smelled of urine. The only evidence of the air-conditioning was that the windows were sealed shut. Leah and I shared our compartment with a middle-age man who was traveling another thousand miles beyond Mumbai—three days on the train—to visit his family. Sophie, Isabel, and CJ were in a compartment at the end of the car. Each cabin had two bench seats facing each other. There were two more bunks strapped against the wall above our heads. At night, the porter lowered the bunks, creating four beds for sleeping.

The wonder of rail travel anywhere, but especially in India, is that one glides through the countryside, watching whatever is happening in the cities and villages along the way. We stopped at numerous stations, big and small. At each station, some passengers got off, some got on. Vendors rushed on to the train peddling snacks, drinks, tea. They moved quickly through the cars, filling orders, making change, and then getting off before the train departed, or sometimes riding to the next station before getting off and catching a train the other direction.

I like sleeping on trains. As the temperature outside dropped and the cabin cooled down, I drifted off to sleep, enjoying the gentle rocking of the car. This was exactly the overnight train experience I had been hoping for . . . until I was awakened from a deep sleep because of yelling outside our compartment. When I opened the curtain, Sophie was standing in the corridor. "I just threw up, and I don't know what to do!" she announced loudly. Sophie does hysteria well. By that, I do not mean that she handles hysteria well. I mean that she is really good at being hysterical. She also has a history of vomiting from high places. When she was younger, she and Katrina shared bunk beds; Sophie was on the top. I won't dwell on the physics, but suffice it to say that getting sick five feet off the floor amplifies the problem.

I walked to the end of the train car to survey the blast site. Sophie had managed to hit just about everything: her bed, the lower bunk, her pack, the floor. Across the hallway, an entire Indian family, including Grandma, had opened their curtain slightly and were peering out. There was no obvious way to clean up the mess. The best idea I could come up with was to use the sheet from my bed. I rushed back to my cabin, pulled the sheet off my bunk, and returned to the accident site, where I began cleaning while Sophie looked on in shock. I did not enlist her in the cleanup for fear that she might get sick again. Soon several railway officials appeared. They had little to offer other than a cardboard box in which I could dispose of the sheet once I was done.

"The smell will come!" one of the railway guys began exclaiming over and over. He had a valid point. On the other hand, it was not clear what I was supposed to do about it. The other railway official asked me for a hundred and fifty rupees, about two dollars, to cover the cost of the sheet that I was now using to mop up. He was an earnest guy who I assume was responsible for ensuring that all sheets were accounted for at the end of the journey. Still, his timing could have been better. I was on my hands and knees cleaning up vomit. Also, we were on a moving train, so it was unlikely that I would escape without paying for the despoiled sheet. He was insistent, so I paused the cleanup effort and offered him a five-hundred-rupee note. He did not have change. "Smaller bills?" he asked.

"That's the smallest I have," I said. "I *promise* I will pay later."

I cleaned up the mess more successfully than I had thought possible at the outset. Sophie was grateful for the effort. I was wise enough to ask only three more times why she did not make it to the bathroom. Remarkably, the cabin did not smell bad—or at least no worse than before the incident. In the morning, the railroad official appeared in my cabin, once again looking for his one hundred and fifty rupees. The fundamental barrier to payment had not changed: I still did not have anything smaller than a five-hundred-rupee note, and he still could not break it. We found a food vendor in the corridor who produced an impressive wad of cash and made change for my five hundred. I paid the railway official, who gave me a receipt, making me the official owner of a vomit-covered Indian Railways sheet—now wedged in a box in a trash bin at the end of the corridor.

◈ ◈ ◈

The next day Isabel would fly back to the U.S.; the rest of us would head to Dubai. Isabel's large suitcase presented an opportunity to send some things back with her that we would not need for the balance of the trip. Isabel was amenable to packing whatever would fit. However, I once again found myself facing an intransigent gatekeeper: Sophie, who had positioned herself as the arbiter of what Isabel would or would not carry. Nothing would go in Isabel's (large, not full) suitcase without Sophie's approval.

I had learned a few things about my children over the last eight months. *Sophie was going to reject about half of what I proposed to send with Isabel, regardless of whether that was two tiny handkerchiefs or a volume of encyclopedias.* She did not care what was going in Isabel's suitcase. She cared about exercising power by screening some things out. Thus, I would have to use strategery: ask Isabel to pack twice as much stuff as I wanted her to take.

I went into our bedroom and gathered up the things I wanted to send home—plus some bulky items for Sophie to reject during the inevitable negotiation: a brick-sized book on the history of Africa, my rain jacket, a large water bottle. As predicted, Sophie said no to the Africa book and the water bottle. Now I just needed her to reject my rain jacket, which I would need in Europe, and the parenting experts would be teaching this maneuver as a case study for years to come.

"Okay, the rest is fine," Sophie said.

"All of it?" I said in surprise.

"There's plenty of room," Isabel offered.

"What about the rain jacket?" I asked solicitously. "Isn't that too much?"

"It's fine," Sophie said. "We can just wad it up."

Somehow I needed to claw my raincoat back from the suitcase without exposing my grand strategy. It was like one of those heist movies—the elaborate plan had gone off-track, and now my next move, an improvisation, would determine the success or failure of the mission. "Does it rain a lot in Europe in the spring?" I asked.

Isabel and Sophie looked at each other. "Probably, if it's like home," Sophie said. "Maybe you should take the jacket."

"Do you think?" I said skeptically. If I was going to get that jacket back, it had to be Sophie's idea.

"Definitely," Sophie said, pulling the jacket from the suitcase and handing it to me. Isabel nodded in agreement. "How could you think you wouldn't need a rain jacket in Europe?" Sophie asked, exchanging a glance with Isabel that suggested I was a complete moron.

Sophie was pleased with her gatekeeper role. Isabel was heading home healthy after a great India experience. And, for a brief but glorious moment, I had figured out the teenage brain.

Chapter 17

Heading to Hanover

I had not shaved in some time; my Indian haircut was not growing out well. Then I spilled coffee down the front of my shirt. CJ walked out of his bedroom, took one look at me, and said, "Dad, you look like a homeless guy."

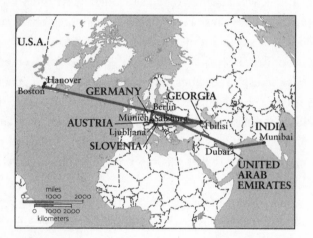

THE INCIDENT BEGAN INNOCUOUSLY at a train station on Dubai's shimmering metro system. CJ noticed that when he rubbed his shoes on the surface of the floor in the station he could gather static electricity. After he shuffled around for a while, he could give someone a small shock. As we waited for the train, CJ repeatedly shocked me. After I became bored with his antics, he shocked Sophie, who warned him angrily that he needed her consent to shock her. CJ argued that he did not. We boarded a train, at which point Sophie declared, "It's always crucial to get someone's consent."

CJ missed this subtle turn in the conversation. "Not if it's someone I know," he answered.

Sophie pounced. "*That's rape!*" she declared.

"Huh?" CJ replied.

"What are you talking about?" Leah asked anxiously. I explained the static electricity situation in the station. Sophie then connected the dots of the conversation more explicitly for CJ. Unfortunately, he just dug deeper, mostly because he had no exposure to the topic. "If my girlfriend has given consent, I don't need to ask one minute later," he said, prompting Sophie to launch into another lecture about the nature of consent. I, too, was alarmed by CJ's insouciant attitude. I work on a college campus, where these kinds of situations routinely derail young lives. CJ added, "I assume someone would tell me to stop."

"That is not how it works!" I said. The conversation wandered back and forth between sex and shocking people with static electricity, leaving CJ confused. He began to cry. "Would someone please tell me if we are talking about sex or shocking people?" he said with tears running down his face. It was at about this time that I noticed a sign in our train car declaring that it was reserved for women traveling with young children.

Leah, who is nonconfrontational and generally protective of CJ, urged us not to have this discussion in public, especially on a train car that I was not supposed to be on. We got off the train and walked to a quiet place in the station. I told CJ to forget about shocking people with static electricity and focus on what we were trying to teach him about sexual consent. Sophie presented him with a series of scenarios, asking in each case whether it would be acceptable to proceed with sex or not (e.g., "You are really drunk, and she's really drunk . . ."). CJ figured out the pattern and, in good humor, began saying, "No," as soon as Sophie started speaking. "You've been dating—"

"No!"

"Very good," Sophie said. "Now suppose there is—"

"No!"

"What if—"

"No!"

Once there was more levity in the conversation, I offered my own scenario: "A supermodel comes up to you on the beach and says, 'CJ, I think you're really hot and I want to have sex with you but only if my supermodel friends can join in.'"

CJ thought for a while and looked around cautiously. "Yes?" he answered. Right answer, we assured him.

"I wouldn't get too excited about that possibility," Sophie offered.

"Okay, next scenario," I said. "You are in Emirates first class with your own cabin." CJ has a fascination with the first-class cabins on Emirates, so I knew this hypothetical situation would grab his attention. "A hot woman comes up from the back of the plane and says, 'I'd really like to have sex with you in your private cabin.'"

"Yes!" CJ yelled with great enthusiasm.

"Wrong!" I admonished. *"Passengers from coach are not allowed in first class!"*

With that, we went to the mall.

◈ ◈ ◈

Dubai is like the love child of Saudi Arabia and Las Vegas: a gleaming city-state in the desert where many things are new, shiny, and bizarrely large; but also an absolute monarchy in which Islam is the official state religion and one can be deported for kissing in public. Dubai is home to the tallest building in the world, the architecturally impressive Burj Khalifa, and also some of the world's largest shopping malls. The Dubai Mall, for example, is so big that we walked five miles without finding one end or the other. The Mall of the Emirates has an indoor ski hill. The phrase "shopping mecca" takes on a more literal meaning in these places; many of the female shoppers are in full burkas.

We explored by walking and eating—our preferred mode of travel— only now it was indoors. In one of the megamalls, I wandered into an enormous bookstore and encountered two noteworthy things. First, there was a large poster advertising a new book of poetry by Dubai's Crown Prince Hamdan bin Mohammed Al Maktoum. I am no judge of poetry, nor can I read Arabic. The crown prince may write some lovely verses. On the other hand, I found it amusing that the leader of an autocratic monarchy had become a poet. It would be like Kim Jong Un deciding to write short stories. Of course the bookstores will display his work prominently. How do the critics describe the writing of an autocrat with unfettered power to imprison or expel them? *"The Crown Prince has done it yet again, another work with which I can find no fault . . ."*

Second, I found a different title in a far corner: *Naked Economics: Undressing the Dismal Science.* This was my first book (now available in a third edition!), and I was pleasantly surprised to find it in Dubai, even if it was less prominently displayed than the crown prince's poetry. When Leah and I traveled the world after college, I desperately wanted to be a writer. A quarter century later, I took a moment to appreciate that my 1988–89 self would have been thrilled to know that I would one day have a book for sale at the Dubai Mall.

CJ loved Dubai's clean efficiency, especially having just come from India. I saw things differently. India is a huge, fractious, relatively poor country with no extraordinary mineral wealth. Dubai is a tiny autocracy that has grown rich on oil, grants citizenship to a select few, and hires immigrant labor for whatever else is needed. Dubai is richer and more orderly, but India is arguably the more impressive society for having built the world's biggest democracy from a remarkably diverse population—*twenty-two official languages.* Still, we were happy to be in "malaria pill countdown." (We had to take the pills for seven days after leaving the last malarial country.) I found myself fantasizing about wearing nice clothes. Perhaps it was all the designer stores, or maybe it was eight months with the same two pairs of pants. In any event, I was growing excited about putting on nice wool trousers and a sweater.

Leah had booked the cheapest tickets from Mumbai to Tbilisi, Georgia. Dubai was a free stop along the way. After a few days there, we continued on to Berlin. Our flight left from the old Dubai airport, not the shiny new one. To clarify, Dubai has one of the largest and most impressive airports in the world—a gigantic shopping mall with airline gates. Dubai also has an older airport, which is the infrastructure equivalent of a crappy car that you keep for the kids after you buy a new one. We learned this only after we arrived at the new airport and could not find our flight on the departure board. Leah showed our tickets to a man at the information booth. "I've never heard of that airline," he said. "It must leave from the other airport." We hired a taxi to take us to the old airport, which looks more like a government warehouse for surplus crops than it does a shopping mall, though I did see one kiosk with a guy selling nuts. Our flight departed at 4:20 a.m. The plane boarding at the gate next to ours was headed to Kabul, Afghanistan. To circle back to the beginning of this paragraph, the flight was cheap.

Later that morning, we were in Berlin, a beautiful city made more so by spring flowers and blooming trees. We were delighted to be able to walk around comfortably in fleeces and jackets. Sophie, who is five-foot-ten, was pleased to be back in a place with other tall people. "I don't feel like a freak show anymore," she explained. We enjoyed sausages and beer and kebabs. The German drinking age is sixteen, so even Sophie could order a beer.

CJ and I bought tickets to see a professional soccer game: Union Berlin versus SV Sandhausen. The stadium where the Union team plays is in a part of the country that was formerly East Germany. There are still significant economic and cultural differences between the old East and West, and we were headed into the heart of the old East. By coincidence, one of my Dartmouth faculty colleagues was in Berlin for the year. When we explained our soccer plans to him, he said, "There are some people who wouldn't go there because of the nationalism on display." And then he added with almost comic understatement, "Germany has a complicated relationship with nationalism."

CJ and I took the subway out of Berlin and transferred to a commuter train that dropped us within walking distance of the stadium. The football (soccer) crowd was distinctly different from the German population at large. For example, the German population has women; the football crowd did not, or at least none that I saw. Our train was full of groups of young men smoking and drinking large bottles of beer. If there are open container laws on the German trains, they were not enforced on this route. We got off the train in a leafy neighborhood and followed the crowd. As the stadium came into view, we encountered a large group of men peeing in the bushes at the edge of an open field. This was not four guys bashfully relieving themselves. There were thirty men lined up in a row urinating in the bushes—a combination of German organization and third world sanitation.

Security officials searched us on the way into the stadium—not the cursory pat-down one gets at a U.S. sporting event, but a full-blown body frisk *after we went through the metal detectors.* I grew up going to Chicago sporting events, including the Bears-Packers games. Those events seemed like dance recitals compared to the vibe we were getting. There were no assigned seats on our side of the stadium. *Because there were no seats.* Our entire section was for standing; every inch was packed. Just before game time, CJ and I sidled up to a spot at the back of the viewing area. The crowd was similar to what we had seen on the train: mostly young, white men who were, as my dad might say, "a little rough-looking." I still had not seen any women. The spectators were decked out in Union paraphernalia. If there were any fans for the opposing team, they were wisely keeping a low profile.

As the game began, the stadium erupted in song: nearly the entire crowd chanting in a language we could not understand and raising their arms in unison. CJ would later say, "I felt a Hitler vibe. I have to admit." We were not able to see much of the football because of the tall men standing in front of us. As we strained to see, several young guys invited CJ to stand in front of them, giving him a nice view. CJ looks German enough, but once he opened his mouth it was clear we were not local. The guys around him began eagerly explaining the finer points of Union football.

A new cheer reverberated throughout the stadium: "Onion, Onion, Onion . . ." CJ and I exchanged a puzzled glance. "Cheer for Onion," one of the men encouraged us—at which point CJ and I realized that Union is pronounced with a soft *U* in German. The Union fans offered an interesting lesson into sports psychology, and perhaps life more generally. When the opposing team scored a goal, they did nothing. *No reaction from anywhere in the stadium.* No jeering, no cries of disappointment. At first this left CJ and me confused. "Didn't the other team score?" I asked.

"I think so," CJ said. "The referee just pulled the ball out of the net."

"Why is there no reaction?" I wondered, looking around at the fans as they universally refused to acknowledge the goal, the sports equivalent of shunning. It was devastatingly effective: *Do not give your opponent the satisfaction of seeing you react.*

When our new football friends were not busy doing scary chants with the crowd, they were remarkably kind to us. One of them bought CJ a mineral water in a Union collectors cup and also a Union pin that he proudly affixed to CJ's Patagonia pullover. I tried to reciprocate by buying beers for the two men nearest to us (along with one for myself). When I returned from the concession stand with three beers, one of the guys told me that he did not drink. I was left with an extra beer, my third of the night. All told, CJ and I returned home with six Union collectors cups. The game ended around eight-thirty and it was still light out—part of the joy of being in the northern hemisphere in spring. We bade farewell to our fellow fans. "Did you have fun?" one of them asked eagerly.

"It was wonderful," I said honestly.

"Thank you so much," CJ added.

❖ ❖ ❖

We took our last malaria pills on May Day, which we spent exploring an area of the city where East and West Berlin had formerly been divided. Part of the Berlin Wall remains intact, along with a guard post and a stretch of "no-man's-land" where some of those trying to escape from the East had been gunned down. The last time I had been in Berlin was in 1986, when the Berlin Wall was still standing. On that visit, I crossed from West Berlin to East Berlin through Checkpoint Charlie. Now, barely a generation later, what's left standing of the wall is testimony to that period of Orwellian repression—but also a reminder that the people ultimately rose up and tore it down.

My Dartmouth colleague Michael adores Berlin: the music, the parks, the food, the public transit. He eagerly sought out an opportunity to spend a year there on sabbatical. The fact that he is Jewish adds a layer of complexity to his relationship with the nation. He remarked to me at one point that the math on "good Germans" does not work. What he meant was that many German families have been told that their grandparents were not supportive of the Nazis. Michael's point is that there could not have been that many good Germans, or the bad ones would not have prevailed. The Jewish Museum in Berlin is a reminder of this. The Holocaust is only one piece of the museum's much larger story. The most powerful exhibit is on the history of anti-Semitism, which has ebbed and flowed for centuries. There were waves of persecutions and massacres during the Black Death in Europe, for example, as Jews were blamed for the plague. The lesson is clear: when the going gets tough, humans find scapegoats.

For East Germany, the horrors of World War II were followed by the tyranny of the Communist regime. Berlin's Stasi Museum documents how the East German secret police propped up the government through intimidation, arrests, blackmail, and legions of informers. The museum is located in the old Stasi headquarters in East Berlin, where there are rooms documenting the Stasi's nefarious tools and techniques—everything from steaming open envelopes to recruiting informers. The most foreboding exhibit is the building itself: a squat, nondescript warren of offices in which people went to work every day doing the tasks necessary to hold a totalitarian state together. I assume George Orwell had not seen the Stasi headquarters when he wrote *1984*, but the bureaucratic apparatus he describes is eerily similar to what the East Germans managed to assemble in this ominously ugly gray building.

Our time in Berlin inspired us to rent several films that put a finer point on the history lurking around us. *Bridge of Spies*, the Tom Hanks film about the prisoner swap for U2 pilot Gary Powers, offered a snapshot of East and West Berlin at the height of the Cold War. *The Lives of Others*, a haunting German film about Stasi surveillance, reinforced what we had seen at the Stasi Museum. Meanwhile, the formal home-schooling requirements—the stuff the state of New Hampshire was keen on—were not going as well. At one point, Leah gave CJ a tough geometry problem in our Berlin hotel room. He collapsed to the floor, where he began crying and saying repeatedly that he wanted to be a taco.

This was a moment for Sophie to shine by comparison, but she whiffed it. She had a discussion-based assessment (DBA) scheduled with one of her instructors for eleven o'clock that night (a saner hour for the teacher back in New Hampshire). The DBAs use special software that requires fast Internet. As eleven o'clock approached, the Wi-Fi in our hotel room was too weak to launch the software. Sophie panicked. "I have to cancel," she said.

"You are not canceling," I told her.

"There's nothing we can do!" she insisted. "The software won't work."

"Get your laptop and follow me," I ordered. With Sophie clutching her computer, we ran out of the room, down the stairs, out of the hotel, and into the underground train station on the corner. Berlin's underground train stations have excellent public Wi-Fi. Sophie opened up her computer. The Internet in the Adenauerplatz underground station was better than in our hotel, but still not good enough to launch the DBA software. "It's not going to work," Sophie proclaimed.

"Send your teacher an e-mail and ask if you can do it by phone," I instructed.

"It has to be by video," she protested.

"Just do it," I said. The teacher responded to the e-mail immediately and agreed to do the assessment by phone. I handed Sophie my iPhone and sat on a nearby bench as she and her teacher had the requisite discussion. They paused periodically as the noise from an arriving train made it impossible to carry on a conversation.

When we got back to the room, both Sophie and I were in lousy moods. This led to a massive VLACS argument—the first in a long time. Sophie began angling to finish her VLACS work at home over the summer. That was a nonstarter. The last thing I wanted was the VLACS nightmare bleeding into our return. Also, it seemed reasonable to expect Sophie to finish her academic work during the academic year. The argument devolved into the same discussion we had been having for eight months: Should we set deadlines for Sophie or let her manage the process on her own? After going around and around, we came to a compromise. The VLACS work had to be done by the day we returned to Hanover. In exchange, we would scrap the interim deadlines. "No lame-ass excuses," I pronounced. *"Done means done: all work submitted in a readable format in all classes."*

On a more positive homeschooling note, Leah asked CJ to explain the arc of U.S. history from World War I to Vietnam. I was impressed by his understanding of the interconnections—how World War I made Americans wary of another European war, for example, and how the Cold War created the fear of communism that motivated U.S. involvement in Vietnam. He was clearly learning things—when he was not crying in the fetal position.

◈ ◈ ◈

We traveled by bus to Munich, where we stayed in a cheap hotel in a neighborhood that had a large concentration of Arab immigrants. Many of the signs up and down the street were in Arabic. There were excellent Middle Eastern restaurants, which made for good, cheap food. We soon encountered the immigration backlash, too. As we walked along the main pedestrian thoroughfare on our first day, we came upon an anti-Muslim demonstration. The speeches and signs were in German; it was hard to discern the specifics of the protest, yet easy to get the gist of it. The speakers appeared unhinged as they yelled into microphones. In an odd way, the demonstration was positive testimony to the country Germany has become. The crowd was small; most pedestrians passed without taking notice. The police were dutifully protecting the demonstrators, who seemed more pathetic than anything else.

I found a small museum with an exhibit on the work of Peter Lindbergh, a German photographer who took many of the iconic fashion photos of the 1980s and 1990s. These are striking black-and-white images of Naomi Campbell, Cindy Crawford, Christy Turlington, and

others who became the first "supermodels," in part because of Lindbergh's work. (If you grew up during that era, you know the photos
I'm describing.) I appreciated the artistry of Lindbergh's photography.
Remember, I was nurturing my inner artist at this point. My novel
was at 350 pages. I gave it to Leah that night and asked her to read the
first 200 pages. "Ignore everything after that," I said. "It's still a work
in progress."

The next morning I asked anxiously: "What do you think?"

"It's good," she said before rattling off a handful of plot points that
did not make sense.

"That's all in the last hundred pages!" I protested. "You weren't
supposed to read that far."

"I couldn't stop," she said.

CJ persuaded me to take him to BMW World, a sprawling complex with a production facility, a museum, and a multilevel showroom.
After CJ ogled every new model of BMW car and motorcycle on display, we walked across the street to the Olympic Village from the 1972
Munich summer games. These were the first Olympics held in Germany since Hitler had presided over the 1936 summer games in Berlin.
The Munich Olympics were supposed to be part of West Germany's
post–World War II rebirth—a powerful statement of global reconciliation. Instead, they devolved into tragedy when Black September, a Pal-
estinian terrorist organization, kidnapped and murdered eleven Israeli
athletes and coaches. CJ set out to see fancy cars but ended up getting
another dose of history.

After we walked through the Olympic Village, CJ wanted to go back
to the BMW museum. I had had my fill of cars. "Do know where our
hotel is?" I asked. He assured me that he did.

"Here," I said, handing him a ten-euro note. "Take the subway home
when you're done at the museum." CJ arrived at our hotel that evening
with Mexican food that he bought in the train station with his change
from the subway ticket.

❖ ❖ ❖

We watched *The Sound of Music* on the train to Salzburg while passing through small Bavarian towns: green meadows, charming chalets, and steep snow-covered peaks. CJ kept remarking on the views, describing everything as "crisp and clean." Salzburg is a lovely city, but we arrived during a long stretch of spring rain. We used the rain delay and the solid Wi-Fi to begin coordinating our "reentry." We sent e-mails to the families who had been taking care of our two dogs, both of which were doing well. Sophie registered to take the SAT. I suggested to Leah that we use some of my fun money to go out for a proper Austrian meal. "You don't have any fun money left," Leah said.

"That's your view," I said, drawing approving laughter from CJ and Sophie.

"I have the spreadsheet," Leah replied.

"Katrina has fun money left!" I said. "Maybe she'll give me some of hers." Katrina, who is a notorious penny pincher, still had more than half of her fun money left with only weeks remaining in the trip. The fun money policy was, "Use it or lose it." I texted her in Sri Lanka: "Will you transfer $50 of your fun money to me so I can go out to dinner with Mom?"

The reply came back immediately: "No."

I pressed: "Why not?"

"No."

"You're not going to use it."

"No. Stop asking."

"How is Sri Lanka?"

"No."

Leah and I went out to dinner anyway. We were getting looser with the budget now that we had so little time left. One dinner out in Austria was not going to make much difference in the overall spending. Also, asparagus was in season: asparagus soup, sautéed asparagus, asparagus baked with cheese. The true joy of the meal, however, came when we returned to the apartment. *Sophie had finished her criminal justice VLACS course.* One down, two to go.

The train rides between European cities are short, easy, and beautiful. After a few hours, we were in Ljubljana, Slovenia, a city that looks like it was designed by a model train enthusiast: pastel buildings arrayed along a canal; stone bridges; cobblestone paths; outdoor cafés; and, of course, a castle perched on a bluff. We could feel the transition from Northern Europe to Southern Europe: less beer and sausage, more wine and gelato. I wandered off with my camera, both to enjoy some alone time and to capture the charm of the city. As I was shooting across the canal, three people walked in front of a vibrant mural covering the entire side of a building. The walkers, evenly spaced and striding with purpose, gave the picture a sense of motion. The mural behind them offered a burst of color. The canal in the foreground was the essence of Ljubljana.

I snapped away until the three people had passed out of the frame. I looked at the small display on the back of my camera and was pleased to see that I had captured the image I wanted: the beauty of the canal, the jarring colors of the mural, and the three people, evenly spaced, walking with purpose. Then I looked more closely. Was I imagining it? I enlarged the photo: The "walkers" in the picture were Leah, Sophie, and CJ.

I worked in the mornings at a café that offered free fresh bread with butter, jam, and honey to anyone who ordered coffee. The honey was a local delicacy. I worked outside, where tables had been set up along the pedestrian walkway. One morning Leah arrived after I had been working for an hour. She was eager to sample the bread and honey that I had been raving about. "Before you sit down, take a picture," I implored. She took an "action shot" of me writing at a European café. Maybe it wasn't Hemingway in Paris, but I was on the continuum.

Even in Europe, our wandering offered up quirky experiences—*because there are always quirky experiences.* Leah guided us on a hike through a large public park. We became terribly lost and ended up at an art house cinema that was showing the film *Liberation Day.* This is a documentary—I'm not making this up—about a Slovenian cult band called Laibach that was invited to North Korea to perform songs from *The Sound of Music*. A camera crew accompanied them on the trip, which, needless to say, did not go exactly as planned.

❖ ❖ ❖

In Vienna, we rented an Airbnb apartment in an old building with plaster walls and stone steps. There was a small bronze plaque on the sidewalk in front of our building commemorating a family who had been sent to Auschwitz. These small markers are called Stolpersteine, or "stumbling stones." We had seen them in German cities as well. The specificity of the plaques—names, places, and dates—forces one to confront the Nazi horror in all the places it touched. Every time we went through the large wooden front door to our apartment building, we were reminded that the Nazis had hauled away the Hofling family—Kurt, Genendia, and Renée—from this lovely building on June 15, 1942.

I was writing frantically in the hope of finishing the novel before the end of the trip. One morning I was working in the Vienna apartment in my pajamas, which consisted of a pair of blue shorts I had bought in Bolivia and a bright yellow T-shirt. I had not shaved in some time; my Indian haircut was not growing out well. Then I spilled coffee down the front of my shirt. CJ walked out of his bedroom, took one look at me, and said, "Dad, you look like a homeless guy." I took his observation as a badge of honor. I felt like a novelist. Also, we were close enough to the end of the trip that I had already booked a haircut *in Hanover, New Hampshire.*

I changed out of my pajamas and moved to a café across the street from our apartment, where I was within hours of finishing the novel when my computer's battery gave out. The rest of the family joined me for a walk on the pedestrian mall, but my mind was on the book. After lunch, with the computer recharged, I returned to the café, ordered a cupcake and a double Americano, and set to finishing it. Which I did: 441 pages, including the epilogue. Whether it was terrible or not, I had a finished novel.

Our most significant family adventure in Vienna took place without leaving our apartment: the Myers-Briggs moment. Sophie was theoretically studying for the SATs, but somehow during her intense preparation she came across several websites related to the Myers-Briggs personality assessment. Myers-Briggs uses a series of questions to sort people into one of sixteen personality types. For example, each of us is an introvert or an extrovert. As the makers of the tool describe it: "Do you prefer to focus on the outer world or on your own inner world?" Other questions probe how individuals make decisions, what kind of structure they prefer, and so on.

Leah and I had taken the assessment years earlier. I am an INTP: Introverted, Intuitive, Thinking, Perceiving. Leah is the opposite of me on every dimension, ESFJ: Extroverted, Sensing, Feeling, Judging.* We had learned long ago to manage this difference. She loves planning; I like going to the café alone in the morning to write. Katrina had done Myers-Briggs in school, and we knew her personality type, too. CJ and Sophie did the assessment online in the Vienna apartment.

The results brought our family into sharper relief. When Meyers-Briggs arrays the sixteen personality types in a matrix with similar types clustered near each other, Katrina and CJ and are at opposite ends of the diagram. Leah is adjacent to CJ, and I'm adjacent to Katrina— which is pretty much how that first Complete Family Meltdown felt on the banks of Lake Titicaca in Peru.

We read aloud our personality descriptions, including strengths and weaknesses. Sophie's profile describes her type as "not good with deadlines or long-term planning."

"Now, there's a shocker!" CJ yelled when he heard the description— which is exactly the kind of thing his personality type would do. It turns out that CJ the Eco Warrior is an ESTJ, a type who tend to be "great believers in doing what they believe is right and socially acceptable."

"You're Saddam Hussein!" Sophie gleefully told CJ. She was now

---

* Myers-Briggs has four personality dimensions: Introvert or Extrovert; Intuitive or Sensing; Thinking or Feeling; and Perceiving or Judging. This creates sixteen personality types.

on a different website, admittedly less scientific, that maps one's Myers-Briggs personality type to famous people who supposedly share the type. CJ's personality type also matched George W. Bush and Lyndon Johnson. Leah is Dwight Eisenhower, the guy who managed to pull off D-Day. Their type is described as typically "warm-hearted, talkative, popular, conscientious, born cooperators." They are people who "need harmony and may be good at creating it."

I am Albert Einstein. My type, "the thinker," is described as "not interested in practical, day-to-day activities."

"Remember Robben Island?" Sophie shrieked. One of my few logistical responsibilities during the trip had been to buy tickets for the museum on Robben Island in Cape Town. This was where Nelson Mandela was imprisoned for nearly thirty years. When we arrived at the front of the ferry line and presented our tickets, the friendly gentleman said, "These tickets are for tomorrow, sir."

Might it have been helpful if we had done this assessment *before* we left on the trip? Perhaps, though I am not sure the results would have resonated as strongly.

❖ ❖ ❖

We flew to Tbilisi, Georgia, and awaited the return of the prodigal daughter. Tbilisi is a place where cultures have intersected for centuries: Ottoman, European, Russian. The architecture, food, and dress reflect this melding. A person plopped on a main street in Tbilisi for the first time would recognize much while still struggling to identify the country: Ottoman architecture, but it's not Turkey; bustling and developed, but it's not Western Europe; vestiges of the USSR, including massively wide streets, but it's not Russia. It is the Republic of Georgia.

We rented an Airbnb apartment one might describe as "post-Communist chic." The outside of the building was so dilapidated that it looked condemned. There was a large crack running the length of the brick exterior. The inside was reasonably nice, with a big common room, a functional kitchen, and four bedrooms. The father of the unit's owner gave us a tour of the apartment. He was about eighty years old and took great pride in his Airbnb greeting responsibilities. In the kitchen, he turned on the faucet to show us how it worked (which was pretty much like every other faucet I had ever used). "Water," he said.

"Yes," we agreed.

He pointed out a shoehorn hanging on the back of the front door. "You can use that," he said.

"Excellent," I said, making an effort to admire the shoehorn. He pointed to a patio outside the kitchen and told us we could smoke there. "We don't smoke," I said.

"Okay, okay," he acknowledged.

The man was so sweet and proud that we did not dare cut his tour short. He turned on the faucet in each bathroom. They all worked just like the one in the kitchen. He took us through all four bedrooms and then pointed to another outdoor space. "You can smoke there, too," he said.

"We still don't smoke," I said.

"You will be okay?" he asked solicitously at the end of the tour.

"We feel very prepared now," Leah answered earnestly. "Thank you."

The next day, Katrina and Kati arrived at the apartment by taxi. Katrina looked healthy. Her ulcers had healed, leaving only two round scars. She and Kati proudly described their travels in Nepal and India and Sri Lanka: "We needed to take three buses to get from Kathmandu to Gorakhpur, but then the bus broke down . . . We crossed the border on foot into India . . . All the rail tickets were sold out and we didn't have any Indian rupees . . . The power went out, so none of the ATMs would work . . . This guy who worked at the rail station took us to a shopping mall that had a generator so that we could get money . . . And then it was a seventeen-hour train ride to Delhi." They took turns exuberantly describing their adventures and travails.

"You're lucky that you didn't have any side effects from the treatment," Leah said.

Kati gave Leah a puzzled look. "What?" she said. "Katrina was sick all the time." Apparently Katrina's leishmaniasis treatment had not been as uneventful as she had been reporting to us. The medicine was highly caustic, and Katrina had spent a lot of time in Europe throwing up.

"It was fine," Katrina said.

We explored Tbilisi, enjoying wonderful food and cheap wine. (Georgia is the region where wine was first produced.) Nearly every street had a small bakery selling fresh bread, often still warm from the oven. We would stop, buy several of the flat loaves, and then walk and eat. One of my favorite photos of the trip captured CJ, Sophie, Leah, Katrina, and Kati all walking, smiling, and eating handfuls of bread.

Kati, the architect of the plan to have Katrina treated in Munich, was a hero to our family. Over a dinner of eggplant, kebabs, trout, and a pot of beans, we proposed inducting her into the family as an honorary member. We decided that this would require a test on Wheelan family history—a subject Katrina had prepped her well on during their long train, plane, and bus rides.

I began the questions. "What was the Wheelan family business for four generations?" I asked.

Kati thought for a moment and then exclaimed, "Funeral directors!"

"That is correct," I said. "Leah's grandfather's brothers were all killed in what conflict?"

"The Armenian genocide," Kati answered. "But he was okay because he was studying in Ohio. No, Iowa! Iowa!"

"Yes, that is correct. When CJ was born, he weighed—"

"Really?" CJ interjected. "Does everyone need to know this?"

"It's multiple choice," I said. "He was just over eight pounds, nine pounds, ten pounds, or eleven pounds."

"I know he was huge," Kati said. "I'm going to go with eleven pounds."

"That's right!" I said. Seven questions later, Kati was pronounced an official member of the Wheelan family.

❖ ❖ ❖

As our final adventure of the trip, Katrina suggested a trip to the town of Kazbegi in the heart of the Caucasus Mountains. We hired a taxi for the three-hour drive over a mountain pass. The surrounding mountains were still capped with snow. Herds of goats and cows periodically clogged the road. Our driver raced along, livestock and a light rain notwithstanding. He crossed himself every time we passed a church and then touched an idol hanging from the rearview mirror. The rain turned to hail, which did not bring any reduction in speed. We rounded a corner while the driver was looking at his phone and suddenly came upon a herd of cows crossing the road. I screamed, "Cows! Cows! Cows!" The accident was averted.

Kazbegi is a beautiful town surrounded on all sides by mountains. The Gergeti Monastery is perched atop one of those mountains; that was our goal for a hike, if the weather cleared. The first morning brought more rain, which was not altogether unpleasant, as we used the indoor time to work and relax. We were staying in a small hostel with a cramped but cozy kitchen that doubled as a common area. Sophie worked on VLACS—I think. I wasn't allowed to ask. CJ was finishing his research paper, which was due to me in less than a week. "Writing is hard," he whined. "*It's so hard.*"

"Really?" I replied facetiously.

Leah and I took a walk to escape CJ's histrionics. We strolled along a dirt path with forest on either side. The spring flowers were popping through the green forest floor; the snowmelt created small, glistening creeks. If I were a watercolor painter, I would have set up my easel and spent the day trying to capture the colors and textures of spring. Mist and fog obscured the mountains but gave everything else we encountered an otherworldly feel. We turned up a lane with rolling fields on either side demarcated by rickety barbed wire. Near the end of the walk, we stopped outside a small grassy field to watch a foal nursing from its mother. I would have tried to paint that, too.

The weather cleared the next morning, giving us a perfect day for a hike up to the monastery. The walk was relatively short; much of it was on a road that led from town into the mountains. The view was beautiful in both directions: looking up at the monastery with snow-covered peaks beyond, and also looking down at the town in the valley below. When we arrived at the monastery, Katrina, Sophie, Leah, and Kati donned headscarves so they could explore inside. (Women visiting Christian Orthodox churches in Georgia are expected to cover their hair.) I rested outside, basking in the sun and the satisfaction of our final mountain climb.

If anything, our driver was more insane on the way back to Tbilisi. *The police stopped our car twice.* I was delighted to see the flashing lights. I assumed any intervention by law enforcement would moderate our driver's speed. I was wrong: Both times he got out of the car, walked back to the officer, kissed him on both cheeks, and exchanged friendly words. When our driver returned to the car, we drove off at the same ridiculous speed. Any lessons he learned were the wrong ones.

Small things made us realize that the trip was effectively over. I checked the weather forecast for Hanover because we would be back soon enough that it was likely to be accurate. We desisted from asking Sophie about VLACS; her deadline was days away. CJ had one final meltdown in our Tbilisi hotel room. He had given me a rough draft of his research paper, and I offered constructive feedback. CJ felt I was overcritical. He began blubbering, "You're treating me like your Dartmouth students, even though I'm only an eighth-grader!"

"That's a good point," I said. "I will try to take your limited ability into account."

"You can't say that!" Katrina yelled. "If you were a middle school teacher, you would be fired on your first day!"

"I hope so," I replied. "Or I would have to quit on the second day."

❖ ❖ ❖

The flight home was long. We transferred in Doha, where I managed to take a two-hour nap on the floor using my camera bag as a pillow. The floor of the insect-free, air-conditioned Doha airport was more comfortable than many of the places we had slept. We landed in Boston and caught the Dartmouth Coach up to Hanover—the same bus we had taken the other direction nine months earlier. The day was gray and rainy, so we did not have a beautiful ride for that final leg. Mostly we slept. When the bus pulled to a stop in front of the Hanover Inn, Sophie's and Katrina's friends were waiting to meet them. I got off first so I could snap a picture of Sophie coming down the steps of the bus, utterly delighted to see her friends. The kids disappeared almost immediately, but not before I corralled them for one final family photo.

We were home.

Chapter 18

The Things We Learned

But let me be clear: I was in no mood to chuck my worldly possessions upon our return.
I really like fountain pens and cashmere sweaters. And I prefer to shave.

FOR MANY MONTHS AFTER WE GOT BACK, I could not read the travel
section of the Sunday *New York Times*. I had no interest in exotic places.
Instead, I relished wearing regular clothes, sleeping in the same bed
every night, and having hot water with good pressure every time I
stepped into the shower. Reentry was so easy that it felt almost bizarre.
One day I was sleeping on the floor in the Doha airport, the next I was
back shopping in our local grocery store. We returned to the same home.
I went back to the same office. We picked up the dogs and brought them
back to the house. They were excited for forty-five seconds and then
went to sleep in their favorite spots. We felt fortunate to return to lives
that were comfortable in every sense.

Nine months felt like a long time for us, but it was a relatively quick
stretch for our friends and acquaintances. We became good at suc-
cinctly answering the question: "How was it?" (This book is my long
answer to that question.) We had stepped away from our lives for a
while and then we stepped right back in. CJ finished the final draft of
his research paper before our bus arrived in Hanover. It turned out to
be really good. He came away with a more nuanced understanding of
deforestation, particularly the economic causes, which was what I had
been hoping for months earlier.

Miraculously, Sophie finished all of her VLACS classes on time,
more or less. She finagled a one-day extension from the "final deadline"
so she could spend her first day back at Hanover High School with her

friends. Leah and I appreciated the irony: The child who fought us on her schoolwork all the way around the world pleaded for an extension so she could go to school. We felt like bankers who had arranged repayment of a hundred-million-dollar loan: even if it came in a day late, we were happy to have it. The state of New Hampshire allowed both Sophie and CJ to advance to the next grade—and I hope I will never have to homeschool another child.*

One of our cars would not start. I jumped the battery and put air in the tires; after that it ran fine. Everything else was pretty much as we'd left it. I began preparing for summer classes. Leah started a training program to become a school principal. The kids went to work at summer jobs. Sophie put in long hours at a local pizza restaurant, which I'm convinced made her more serious about school.

During the trip, I often spent hours downloading photos and posting them on our blog. Once we were home, I had thousands of pictures from the trip and no time to organize any of them. My plan was to curate the photos and make a photo book for each member of Team Wheelan. That photo book still has not happened. I did buy an electronic picture frame into which I downloaded all the photos. I put the frame on the kitchen counter. It has a motion sensor, so whenever one of us steps into the kitchen, the frame turns itself on and begins displaying photos from the trip in random order.

Life went back to normal, as if we had never left. Yet the five of us were different people for having made the trip, both individually and as a family. What did we learn? Having had some time to reflect on that, here are some answers to that question:

The world is still an interesting place. One fear we had when we set out was that even distant places would feel homogenized—indistinguishable cities with the same chain restaurants and everyone speaking English. Would Ho Chi Minh City feel like La Paz? Would Tasmania be just

---

* Of course, when the coronavirus arrived, the entire world became more familiar with the joys of homeschooling. Our children were old enough by then that we no longer had to offer much guidance.

like the United States, only with an Australian accent? No, thankfully. South America feels radically different from Southeast Asia, which feels different from East Africa. Within those regions, each country has its own feel and personality. So does each city and each neighborhood. The world is alive with fascinating and quirky cultures. Yes, there are emerging similarities around the world. You will see people walking around checking their phones wherever you are, including remote villages without running water. Yes, the Internet has connected us to one another in ways that cannot be undone. The anonymity that we had on our first global trip is gone forever. Still, there was no stop along the way that did not have its own unique sense of place. I am now guardedly optimistic that that trend can continue indefinitely—that a richer Ho Chi Minh City will always be distinct from a richer La Paz, just as New England feels different from Texas or Northern California.

We pulled it off. We made it around the world: nine months, six continents, three teenagers, and one flesh-eating parasite. For years, the trip was a vague family aspiration. Then it was a goal, and finally it became a plan. Along the way, lots of people dismissed the idea as crazy talk, either explicitly or with some patronizing acknowledgment: "Well, now, that would be interesting." People don't usually take off with their family and go around the world, and that pitted us against some powerful social forces. I worry that some of the most talented people I know, including the students I teach, have been suffocated by conformity—an American culture in which we "live to work" and mindlessly accumulate. This adventure was, in part, an effort to push back on that. I've tried to make the case that the barriers to doing something like this are lower than one might think. A big reason many people don't do it is because many people don't do it.

Leah is a great teammate. At our wedding in 1992, I gave a toast in which I declared that my future bride, among her many other wonderful attributes, would be a great teammate. I was right. Marriage is about picking a person you want at your side to help navigate whatever might come along. Traveling on a low budget to bizarre places is a good example of that. Would I have preferred that she allowed me a cup of coffee on days when I had bumped up against my food budget? Yes and no. Yes, I wanted that coffee, but no, if we had blown the budget early in our travel, the whole adventure would have unraveled. The trip worked because Leah and I shared a vision of what we wanted to do, and then we shared responsibilities along the way. If I had tried to do this trip alone, I would still be wandering somewhere in Africa, lost and broke.

The teenage brain is a bizarre thing. Plenty of research supports this claim. Don't get me wrong: Katrina, Sophie, and CJ were great travelers (as were Tess and Isabel and Kati). They shared our sense of adventure and managed the roughest of circumstances with aplomb. We asked a lot of them and they stepped up. But it is also true that being with teenagers 24/7 gives one a special appreciation of their unique worldview. One of my most common refrains in trying moments was, "You can't make this shit up."

A particular incident near the end of the trip stands out. Leah, Katrina, and I had spent the morning in the Museum of Soviet Occupation in Georgia. After hours in the museum, Katrina tried to persuade us to visit a particular Orthodox church. Leah and I had no interest; we declined, which caused Katrina to declare that we were "unintellectual and uninteresting." That is a curious charge to make against two people who have just taken their family around the world. At any rate, Leah and I did not quibble over the substance of the charge. Rather, we decided it was time for Katrina to have some time to herself. As we walked away, Katrina yelled, "Wait, how do I get back to the apartment?" We just kept walking.

For all those moments—some of which I have documented in the book and many of which I have not—I will be eternally grateful that we had this uninterrupted time with our teenage kids. It was parenting on steroids: the good, the bad, and everything in between. One thing about raising children—the research is clear on this—is that there is no substitute for spending time with them. Even when they tell you they don't want you around, the truth is that they do. This trip was the ultimate family dinner. When Sophie locked herself in her room in Peru, and when CJ curled up in a ball and said he wanted to be a taco, we worked through it.

And when the mood generators all fired in the right direction at the same time, as they did in many places, it was pure bliss. I want to thank each of my children for having the stamina and curiosity and resilience and sense of adventure and good humor necessary to do what we did.

Life goes on without you. We came back to a place that was—the presidential election excepted—pretty much the same as we had left it. I mentioned earlier that our dogs wagged their tails excitedly for less than a minute and then went to sleep in their usual corners. Our friends did the human equivalent. The great news is that we appreciated the lives we were returning to: our friends, our jobs, our community. One way to take stock of your day-to-day existence is to step away from it for a while. By living out of a single backpack for nine months, we learned what we could do without. There was a simple elegance to getting dressed every morning when I had a choice between two pairs of travel pants and three shirts. (Since most of those clothes were likely to be dirty at any given point, I have overstated the degree of choice involved.) But let me be clear: I was in no mood to chuck my worldly possessions upon our return. I really like fountain pens and cashmere sweaters. And I prefer to shave.

The greatest luxury is time. We slept until we woke up refreshed. We read for long stretches at any time of the day. We wandered aimlessly or sat on a park bench for no particular reason. Our meals were not rushed. For most of the trip, if we missed a train or a bus or a plane, we took the next one. (The irony is that we had so much time on our hands that we typically arrived early.) I had accumulated a long list of books that I hoped to read on the trip; I made it through most of them. I will offer up one personal confession: I tried to finish *Infinite Jest*, David Foster Wallace's 1,079-page "uniquely American exploration of the passions that make us human." I gave up somewhere around Zanzibar.

The world is significantly less poor than it was in 1988. If you are looking for good news in the world at the moment, this is it. I study public policy, so the trip was fieldwork in a way. There is no doubt that the poorest places in the world are significantly better off than they were when Leah and I traveled in the late 1980s. Some of this is apples and oranges; we were in China in 1989 but did not return on this trip. We went to Africa this time but not on the first trip. Still, there were some straight-up "then" and "now" comparisons in places like Calcutta, which feels remarkably less impoverished (though still like Calcutta).

The data support what we observed. The number of people living in poverty around the world has fallen sharply in recent decades, both as a percentage of the global population and in absolute terms. One of the United Nations Millennium Development Goals was to cut the number of people living in extreme poverty around the world in half; that goal was achieved five years ahead of its 2015 deadline. The fraction of the world's population living in absolute poverty has fallen from around forty percent in 1990 to below ten percent today.[*]

Now the bad news: We saw evidence of serious environmental damage along the way, particularly air pollution in big cities and deforestation in less developed areas. We were not imagining this, either. The World Health Organization warned recently: "Global air pollution is worsening, and poor countries are being hit the hardest."[†]

The past decade has also been one of the worst on record for deforestation.[‡] A specific moment from the trip stands out in this regard. Katrina and I were on a short trek in Laos. Deforestation had left scars on the hills in every direction—huge swaths in which all the tree cover had been cleared away. On the second day of our trek, we were walking along a narrow trail when we heard the pounding of an ax somewhere

[*] I will point out, perhaps gratuitously, that much of this success is due to globalization, particularly the integration of India and China into the global economy. Trade turns out to be one of the most powerful anti-poverty tools in our arsenal, so if you care about global poverty, globalization is a good thing.

[†] Chris Mooney and Brady Dennis, "WHO: Global Air Pollution Is Worsening, and Poor Countries Are Being Hit the Hardest," *Washington Post*, May 12, 2016.

[‡] Brad Plumer, "Tropical Forests Suffered Near-Record Tree Losses in 2017," *New York Times*, June 27, 2018.

ahead of us. Seconds later, there was a cracking noise and a large tree fell across our path. As the tree hit the ground, two bats flew out of the canopy. There was something particularly depressing about that one tree and those two bats. Stalin supposedly said that when a million people die, it's a statistic, but when one person dies, it's a tragedy. What we saw on that path felt like the deforestation equivalent of Stalin's tragedy.

Nor did Leah and I imagine the changes we discerned on the Great Barrier Reef. In the thirty years between our two visits, the largest reef on earth has lost half its coral cover. Rising prosperity and increased environmental degradation are related, particularly in the developing world, as CJ learned in writing his research paper. That said, there are policies, in rich countries and poor countries alike, that would promote more sustainable kinds of growth. That is the subject for another book. Maybe CJ will write it someday.

It was really fun. Okay, back to us. We had a great time. Not every moment, but most of the time. Many of the adventures we had been looking forward to—exploring the Amazon, visiting the Galapagos, going on safari—turned out to be worthy of that anticipation. But there were many more great moments that were entirely circumstantial: making chocolate; eating street food; happening upon a concert or an amusement park; eating fresh bread and cheese while walking the streets of Tbilisi.

It was like a family vacation that worked out well. And it turns out that experiences, rather than things, are what make us happiest in the long run. This is a paradox, admittedly, because spending money on objects gives you things that last while experiences are ephemeral. But here is the weird thing: research has shown over and over again that experiences have the most positive long-term impact on our well-being.

How could that be? Because experiences "become an ingrained part of our identity," says Cornell psychologist Thomas Gilovich, who has synthesized a number of studies on this subject. Here is his explanation. First, experiences connect us to the people with whom we share them. Second, experiences make us into the people we are. And last, even bad experiences morph into positives over time. Gilovich writes,

"Something that might have been stressful or scary in the past can become a funny story to tell at a party or be looked back on as an invaluable character-building experience." Like getting lost on the metro in Medellín, or contracting a flesh-eating parasite in the Amazon. To be clear, the latter took longer to become a good story than the former.

Carpe Diem: That means "seize the day," for those who never saw Robin Williams in *Dead Poets Society*. In planning our trip, we knew that family circumstances gave us a small window during which we could make the trip work. We did not anticipate, of course, that global events would later slam the window closed on all travel. Not long after we returned from our trip, Hong Kong was engulfed by protests. In Chile, too, protests broke out on a scale that disrupted the country. I remember feeling fortunate that we had made it to those places when we did. And then covid-19 came on the scene—first in China and eventually the rest of the world. Before long, we could not leave our home, let alone the country.

As with so many other things, we got lucky. But it's also true that while the window was open, we went through it. Coronavirus will eventually recede, making travel safe again. International events will continue to affect the travel map. Some countries will become harder to visit, or less safe; others will become more accessible. One thing will never change: fortune favors those who get their passports and go.

Where Are They Now?

KATRINA HEADED OFF TO Williams College not long after we got home. There has been no recurrence of the leishmaniasis. The FDA has now approved the treatment she received in Germany for use in the United States. Her absence felt familiar, even as we missed her. For her, the trip offered the independence she was craving. I would like to think—though I'm sure she would deny it—that we imbued her with some of her sense of adventure. She opted to ride her bicycle to college: a two-day, one-hundred-and-twenty-mile journey. We drove separately with her belongings.

Sophie put VLACS behind her (forever, I hope) and returned to Hanover High School for her senior year. She was a much, much more serious student. It is hard to know if that had anything to do with the trip, or if it was just maturity taking its course. She became a teaching assistant for a calculus class, which, given our battles over pre-calculus, was like a longtime prison inmate becoming a warden. She was accepted at John Jay College of Criminal Justice in New York, where she is captain of the varsity volleyball team. This was the college that she discovered while hanging out in our hotel room in Hobart, Tasmania. She is working so hard that she is on pace to graduate in three years—in large part because of extra online courses she has taken.

CJ is in high school. The last time we were in New York City, he set out alone in the morning with twenty dollars in search of good Mexican food and came back five hours later. He talks about taking a gap year to go to Zanzibar to become a dive instructor with Spanish Dancer Divers. He does not eat red meat unless it was grass-fed and raised locally. He persuaded us to begin composting. He still ogles fancy cars, but of late Teslas get him most excited.

Leah went back to teaching for a year and then became an elementary school principal, a job in which she spends her days making the buses run on time, literally and figuratively. She envelops small children with love while dealing with one crisis after another, from the predawn hour when teachers begin calling in sick until late afternoon when the last child has been delivered safely home. Her school is in a rural area profoundly affected by the opioid epidemic. Many of the challenges facing even elementary school students are sad and serious, but many are fun and/or funny, like the spelling test a third-grade teacher brought worriedly to the principal. One of the spelling words was "trace." A third-grader used it in the following sentence: "My dad left traces of pot on the table." Principal Wheelan decided: (1) full credit for the spelling test; (2) keep an eye on the situation.

Leah loves the challenge, just as her Myers-Briggs profile would predict: "Main interest is in things that directly and visibly affect people's lives." Dwight Eisenhower would be proud.

I went back to teaching at Dartmouth. My first term began almost immediately. As the summer unfolded, I revisited my novel and shared it with a few people. My mother passed it along to a friend of hers who owns an independent bookstore—because that is what mothers do. The feedback was positive. To make a long story short, I really have become "an artist." *The Rationing* was published by W. W. Norton in May 2019.

And then there is my niece Claire. Have I not mentioned Claire? She is the daughter of Jeff and Noel, who lived in our house while we were traveling. Claire decided that she really liked living in Hanover—so much so that she did not want to return home to Colorado to finish high school. After extensive discussions and negotiations, Claire ended up living with us in Hanover for two years so she could finish high school here. Yes, it is ironic: after all my kvetching around the world about the teenage brain, we ended up with another teenager. One thing that influenced Leah and me in making this decision is something we observed while traveling: Extended family tends to play a more important role in many of the countries we visited than it does in America. In India or Tanzania, there would be nothing unusual about raising a niece or nephew for a couple of years. So that is what we did. I bet you did not see that coming back in Chapter Three. Neither did we.

As for the other characters who joined us along the way, Kati, hero of the leishmaniasis challenge, is finishing her degree in biology in Munich. She is considering a graduate program that would combine a medical degree and a Ph.D. in molecular and cellular biology. My niece Tess, CJ's chatter buddy, returned to her family in Boulder and has been urging them to visit exotic places ever since. Isabel attends Fordham University in New York City and has plans to travel after graduation. She is just one borough away from where Sophie is in school, and they often meet for brunch on the weekends.

◈ ◈ ◈

At some point, I started to read the *New York Times* travel section again. *There are so many cool places in the world that we still have not visited.* How is it that we have never been to Morocco? Or to the Dalmatian coast? Or to North Korea? The wanderlust never goes away. Sometimes when several of us are in the kitchen, we stop what we are doing and watch the electronic picture frame as it cycles randomly through the photos. I took most of the photos, so I often have an emotional reaction. I can remember seeing the image through the viewfinder of the camera. One of us will usually identify the picture: "That was the amusement park in Vienna," or "That was at lunch after Katrina and I went to the medical clinic in Hanoi."

Often I think to myself, *Wow, we did that.*

We came, we saw, we left.

ACKNOWLEDGMENTS

THIS WAS A HARDER BOOK to write than I had expected, in part because of the challenge of distilling nine months of experiences into a few hundred pages. It feels almost unfair that I have such good editors, Drake McFeely and Bee Holekamp. They were the miracle workers who helped me sort through the raw material to focus on the events and moments and stories that brought the whole adventure to life. The readers should thank you, and I do, too.

Of course, there would have been no book without Team Wheelan. Thanks to each of you for making this journey, and then thanks again for having the self-confidence and forbearance to allow me to tell our story.

Tina Bennett enabled me to do what I love to do, which is write about interesting things. She made this book possible, and then when I returned and announced that I had written a novel during our travels, she brought that book to life, too.

Thanks to so many people around the world who helped to make our experience what it was. Some of those wonderful people appear in the book, such as Kevin and Maria and the Shankardass family, but many do not. I mention in the text that the world is still an interesting place. I would add here that the world is also a kind place (with some notably sad exceptions). The trip was delightful in large part because so many of the people we encountered were interesting, friendly, welcoming, curious, and humane.

I owe a debt to Dartmouth College, and the Rockefeller Center in particular, for giving me the time to make the trip while still having a job—a home, really—to return to.

And although I have already thanked Leah as a member of Team Wheelan, I would like to thank her separately for being the greatest life partner one could imagine.

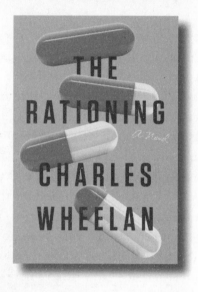